Media, Masculinities, and the Machine

Media, Masculinities, and the Machine

F1, Transformers, and Fantasizing
Technology at its Limits

Dan Fleming
and
Damion Sturm

BLOOMSBURY

LONDON · NEW DELHI · NEW YORK · SYDNEY

Bloomsbury Academic
An imprint of Bloomsbury Publishing Plc

175 Fifth Avenue
New York
NY 10010
USA

50 Bedford Square
London
WC1B 3DP
UK

www.bloomsbury.com

First published by Continuum International Publishing Group 2011
Paperback edition first published 2013

© 2011 by Dan Fleming and Damion Sturm

Library of Congress Cataloging-in-Publication Data
Fleming, Dan.
Media, masculinities and the machine: F1, Transformers and fantasizing
technology at its limits/Dan Fleming and Damion Sturm.
p. cm.
Includes bibliographical references and index.
ISBN-13: 978-1-4411-1554-6 (hardcover: alk. paper)
ISBN-10: 1-4411-1554-4 (hardcover: alk. paper)
1. Mass media—Technological innovations. 2. Masculinity. 3. Technology—
Social aspects. 4. Automobiles—Social aspects. 5. Toys—Social aspects.
6. Affect (Psychology) I. Sturm, Damion. II. Title.
P96.T42F57 2011
302.23—dc22 2010043691

ISBN: HB: 978-1-4411-1554-6
PB: 978-1-6235-6511-4

Typeset by Newgen Imaging Systems Pvt Ltd, Chennai, India.

To love what aids fantasy, and so to gradually break down imaginative resistance . . .

—Nigel Thrift

Contents

Acknowledgments

Our epigraph is from Nigel Thrift's *Non-Representational Theory* (2008, vii). Chapter 4 is based on Damion Sturm's doctoral thesis. We are grateful to the School of Arts, Faculty of Arts and Social Sciences, University of Waikato, Aotearoa New Zealand, for permission to use portions of it here. Damion Sturm is grateful to Toni Bruce, Richard Pringle, and Sean Cubitt for their guidance and support throughout his doctoral research. Earlier versions of portions of Chapter 5 were given by Dan Fleming as papers at the Game and Entertainment Technologies conference, Algarve, Portugal, June 2009, and the 2008 International Forum on Media and Children's Culture, Children's Culture Institute, Zhejiang Normal University, Jinhua, China, October 2008. We are grateful to conference participants for the feedback received. Earlier versions of portions of Chapter 6 were given as presentations or seminar papers at the University of Strasbourg in France, Halmstad University in Sweden, and at Aichi Shukutoku University in Nagoya, Japan, and have benefited from the constructive criticism received. Waikato graduate student Steven Hitchcock allowed us to use portions of his directed study project (Autoethnographies of Transformers) for which we are most grateful. Both authors wish to express a particular debt of gratitude to our students. Dan Fleming is grateful to the University of Waikato for the period of study leave during which the writing of this book was completed.

We would like to thank our editor Katie Gallof and copy-editor Molly Morrison for turning manuscript into book with such expedition and charm. This book is a project of *Mediarena*, a teaching and research facility at the University of Waikato that supports innovative approaches to studying and imagining the cultural impact of media and technologies.

List of Illustrations

Foreword

"Masculinity is shaped in relation to an overall structure of power (the subordination of women to men), and in relation to a general symbolism of difference (the opposition of femininity and masculinity)" (Connell 1995, 223). This book begins with a different but not unrelated premise: that today masculinity is also shaped in relation to another overall structure of power—the subordination of technology to men—and in relation to another general symbolism of difference—the opposition of human and machine. The interrelation of these structures and symbolisms constructs a complex matrix for contemporary masculinities to negotiate their way through. Indeed, it becomes more complex still with potential reversals of the power relations and interpenetration of the symbolisms. So just as *The Atlantic* magazine can run a cover story (July/August 2010) on "The End of Men: How Women are Taking Control of Everything" so too it becomes very easy to recognize everywhere the apparent subordination of men to technology (How Technology is Taking Control of Everything). And just as various types of new man celebrated by popular culture, such as the urban "metrosexual" with his groomed body image, suggest some feminizing of masculinity but more importantly a destabilization of the underpinning symbolic opposition, so the many cyborgs walking the popular media landscape suggest a symbolism of renegotiated or even collapsing difference between human and machine. What *is* a man to do?

In 2009 an English television presenter—James May—made a six-part television series called *Toy Stories* that seems like one response to that question. The DVD cover calls it "Ludicrously ambitious adventures and extraordinary feats of engineering using the world's best-loved toys." James May was better known as copresenter of *Top Gear*, the astonishingly successful—slick and yet quirkily engaging—British television show about cars that screens all over the world to huge viewing figures, with localized spin-off series on three continents. May is also a recognizable category of television presenter. To call this a type would be unfair, but he has discernible similarities with, for example, Jamie Hyneman and Adam Savage who present *Mythbusters*, originally a highly successful Discovery Channel asset and now also screened by numerous other television channels internationally (they use technology to test popular myths, such as bulletproofing a car with telephone directories). Although especially comfortable in these incarnations when "playing" with technology, this figure also occurs doing other practical things on television, as for instance British television's Hugh Fearnley-Whittingstall whose long-running *River Cottage* series documents his operation of a largely self-sufficient smallholding in rural England, or even somewhere in the background the fictional character Tim Taylor as played by Tim Allen in the 1990s American sitcom *Home Improvement*, although there it descended quickly into a reversible-screwdriver-celebrating, power-tool-wielding stereotype. More importantly, a Tim Taylor bespoke a moment when the mundane subordination of technology to men (and traditional family values as context) still seemed like a truth to many, whereas a James May inhabits a much more complicated world of reversible power relations and his response to it is considerably more knowing and ironic. Nonetheless, what all these manifestations share is that they are versions of an answer to Donna Haraway's oft-ignored question in her seminal essay on the cyborg, "What about men's access to daily competence, to knowing how to build things, to take them apart, to play?" (1991, 181). Haraway was querying a credible feminist argument, making visible undervalued aspects of women's lives, that women have had a privileged claim over "dailiness," the ordinary in everyday life. James May, however, makes the ordinary the very basis of his "ludicrously ambitious adventures," which is quite possibly a very masculine talent to have.

The second episode of his *Toy Stories* series staged the world's longest slot-car race at England's old Brooklands racing circuit, the world's first purpose-built motorsport track, not raced on since 1939 and now encroached upon by suburban sprawl. With the help of an enthusiastic local community of several hundred people, James May oversaw the construction of nearly 3 miles of "Scalextric" slot-car track (a nostalgia-inducing plaything dating back to the 1950s), over a river, through office buildings, around the overgrown remains of Brooklands' banked section. Two little slot-car vehicles, chased by mobs of excited children, raced each other around the track, operated by local people in relays and given television coverage not unlike the real thing, with expert track-side commentary, onboard miniature cameras providing track-level views from the cars, accompanied by a carnivalesque atmosphere among spectators. In a bit of intertextual fun, a *Top Gear* type interlude even trained the local slot-car "drivers" in real cars before handing them the plastic controllers for the toy versions. What James May brings to this sort of thing is a determinedly unpatronizing attitude, a tongue-in-cheek quality that nevertheless does not condescend to the people whose enthusiasms he has drawn on for his schemes, including in this instance several "men of a certain age," each of whose attic is suspected of being "the place where his 8-year-old self lives." By taking these attachments to childish things out of cupboards and onto the streets, May achieves a curious sort of recuperative celebration—not so much of the childish things per se as of the sheerly likeable ordinariness of people who are still attached to them, because on this evidence it is really their child-hood selves that they remain affectionately attached to in the end. The communal nature of this recuperative celebration in "James's Great Scalextric Race" is especially apparent and it immerses us in the enthusi-asm, thereby removing the possibility of "othering" these men, while evoking the contemporary elasticity of the term "fan." At the same time, it refuses to elevate the activity in any way: everybody seems to remain blissfully aware that they are doing something very silly. This outs a cou-ple of key academic tendencies in the study of intense popular passions, especially when tinged with fandom as here (the community included a Scalextric fan club): the tendency to "other" and the tendency to recu-perate by elevating. To find things ordinary and to find that they do not harbor "meaning" beyond what they seem to be is to undercut much of what academics write about in these contexts, and indeed we shall not entirely avoid these tendencies in the following pages. We do not entirely wish to, because therein lies another tendency—to see the staging of such enthusiasms as only a microcosm of larger social formations, with people merely acting out their entrapment within those formations where small spaces are defined for largely meaningless expressions of individual taste and interest (with the watching of *James May's Toy Stories* on television becoming then in turn just another one of those circum-scribed spaces). However, "James's Great Scalextric Race" tapped into something else as well.

To ensure that the toy cars would run effectively on the extended out-door track with all its kinks and obstacles, the program enlisted the help of high-speed cameras and computers in order to capture what happens when a slot-car "crashes." With a touch of *Mythbusters* about it, this por-tion of the program included slow motion, ground-level sequences of toy cars sliding off the track, rolling, flipping, and nose-diving into the ground, along with analysis of the forces and dynamics involved. While the underlying technical information was interesting, what lingers in the mind is the imagery. Anybody who has ever played with Scalextric knows that these accidents happen too fast to be seen in any detail; one minute the little car is speeding along its groove, the next it has tumbled off the track. Captured on video in extreme slow motion and from a low angle there is something startlingly vivid, arresting, not a little unsettling, and indeed oddly "realistic" about these moments. Elsewhere, the photographer David Levinthal has created unsettling photographic tableaux by staging plastic figurines and toys in carefully contrived scenes. The same fascination occurs looking at these images and it suggests that something more than meets the eye is going on; at the very least the engagement of an affective response to these small things thus captured. And anybody who has ever played Scalextric knows that something similar in terms of an affective response happens when one has the little plastic controller in one's hand—when the sense of being wired to the thing takes over from visual pleasure and from the represented scene of miniature motor racing as a defining feature of the playful experience. Without access to that tactile fascination, the television viewer has instead in this example the aestheticized slow-motion images of the small objects of fascination. The object is key here. Being wired to the object or being visually arrested in a scrutiny of the object (wired in a different way perhaps) both insist on the object relation itself as central to the disposition of feeling, the *affect*, being generated. That this particular object is a toy racing-car is apposite here.

We will be tracing two paradigmatic instances of this object in the following pages: the Formula One (F1) racing-car and the toy car that transforms into a robot (in an imagined world where all sorts of object can similarly transform, but it starts and ends with the cars). These may seem at first to be rather arbitrary selections but they are not. We want to see whether the affective dimension just hypothesized runs through these other instances and, if so, how. We want to consider how the human relation to the machine as object manifests itself in these very ordinary paradigmatic selections. We want to consider the relation between the boy and the man in this regard. We want to consider the broader kinds of social imagining involved, the imagining of how to relate to a structure of power and a symbolism of difference that can come down in the end to such simple things, in which there is itself a point to be made. And finally, we want to think about the possibility that our two paradigmatic selections reveal the nonhuman object world in its most penetrative mode within everyday life, within leisure, sport, entertainment, and play.

By way of a framework for approaching these questions, we also want to stage an encounter within the habitually troubled but hugely influential French family of European continental philosophy and the social and cultural theorizing it influenced, not least in the very constitution of cultural studies as a field. On one side of a table we have Pierre Bourdieu, Roland Barthes, and Henri Lefebvre. On the other we have Jean Baudrillard (younger by some 30 years than Lefebvre, by 15 than Barthes, and a contemporary of Bourdieu). On one side we have some ideas about how human subjectivity is organized upon, as it were, playing fields where definable strategies are worked out energetically but within tight social bounds, some ideas about how material gets drawn into semiosis (into carrying constructed meanings) around such strategies, and some ideas about how all of this gets anchored in everyday life, not in representations but in lived moments of time. A lot gets erected around such ideas. On the other side, we have the brazen idea that all of this comes down in the end to a system of objects around which meaning implodes and from which no kind of activity is liberating, certainly not any act of consumption, so one may as well just commit to the object. This is not intended to be a comprehensive theoretical discussion but this scene sends its reverberations into every nook and cranny of this small book. By imagining the scene as a doctoral examination, and a generational thing, we have it intersect as well here with the circumstances of our coauthoring. Damion Sturm (younger man) wrote a doctoral thesis about F1 fandom that Dan Fleming (older man) supervised in its final year, a year that raised for both of them some fundamental questions about what is worth studying and writing about and what dead Frenchmen have to do with it.

In light of the above, another way of explaining what this book is about is to suggest that it is very much concerned with what John Urry calls "automobility" (Urry 2000, 59–62), a brilliant piece of writing that we aspired to match in quality when we started but probably failed to achieve in the end. Urry's "automobilised time-space" (59) is the domain of this book but, again, rather than attempting a comprehensive treatment we have focused on the two particular things that intrigued us: the way in which the "mobility" in automobility seems to have got captured, trapped, and sent into closed circuits by F1 (largely for men) and Transformers (largely for boys). In the case of F1, the car's promise of mobility is literally sent in circles, despite F1 like some kind of demented circus uprooting itself every few weeks in a grossly expensive display of literal mobility and shipping its whole apparatus to some other part of the world for its next race. In the case of Transformers, the promise of mobility is representationally released into the object world, but the whole quarter-century franchise across multiple media ends up in a set of Michael Bay films that just as patently seem to capture, trap, and close-circuit it into the regimes of what Michael Ryan and Douglas Kellner, in a different context, called penis-brained militarism. John Urry notes of the complex things that go on around the car, "These complex jugglings are the consequence of two interdependent features of automobility: that the car is immensely flexible *and* wholly coercive" (ibid., 59): flexible enough evidently to appear in the two very different guises we have selected to write about here and coercive enough to become the very model of the Baudrillardian object world. We will be coming back to John Urry's several pages on automobilities in the Afterwords, but we need to flag here that we will end up looking, not at what he terms "the culture of the car" (ibid., 62), but rather at the object in depicted motion—both conventionally at its most intense (as race car) and imaginatively at its most intense (as alien life-form).

In doing this, we will be attending to affect in a particular way. The book's main theme will be the materializing of affect in things and we are interested in a very specific understanding of affect—not so much as feelings of emotion or even dispositions of feeling but as an underlying substrate to these subsequent affective manifestations, manifestations that representational thinking then draws into further constructions, including various narrativized forms. So working back through representations in order to track the affective substrate is a central characteristic of the book's own form. A principal reason for this is that technology seems to have taken hold of this substrate, perhaps especially in relation to masculinities and as an intensification of what automobilized time-space had already begun to do before newer technologies and a pervasive gadgetization also came on the scene. We relate this to the notion of a social imagining of technologies, more specifically to a particular form of such imagining—what we will term an *imaginaire*, borrowing a concept developed by Patrice Flichy to explain how technologies get very specifically imagined as they are being produced and consumed. So in order to develop some understanding of the affective substrate it will be necessary to theorize the particular *imaginaire* to which it lends a particular vitality.

The book will not offer any kind of summary overview or broad treatment of "culture and technology," not least because that has been eponymously done by Andrew Murphie and John Potts (2003) whose book we take as a kind of indispensable primer for the kinds of more focused inquiry we indulge in here (although Murphie and Potts might not endorse our method or our specific conclusions). On the other hand, a particular critical view of "culture and technology" does permeate these pages and should be admitted at the outset. It is Susan Buck-Morss's insightful paraphrasing of Walter Benjamin in her reconstruction of his Arcades Project, the inspirational unfinished project on industrialized, mechanized culture and the crisis in perception it has caused, the project to which we all owe such a debt in this field: "technological *re*production gives back to humanity that capacity for experience which technological *production* threatens to take away" (Buck-Morss 1989, 268). The speed and "shocklike stimuli" (ibid., 268) of technologized culture send us looking for shock absorbers. One possibility is to find this in a special kind of slowing down—Benjamin thought a cinematic mode of perception promised this, though he definitely was not anticipating a Michael Bay *Transformers* film—but another possibility, we will argue here, is to find it in the way that a certain affect materializes in the speeding object itself, at the very heart of accelerating automobilities.

Chapter 1

The Android Imaginaire
(Jacques, Move Your Body)

Things have found a way of avoiding a dialectics of meaning that was begin-
ning to bore them: by proliferating indefinitely, increasing their potential, out-
bidding themselves in an ascension to the limit, an obscenity that henceforth
becomes their immanent finality and senseless reason.

But nothing prevents us from assuming that we could obtain the same effects
in reverse . . .

—Jean Baudrillard 1990a, 7

In order to explain why we want to look at Formula One (F1) racing and
Transformers, especially in relation to the "things" that constitute them
and what might connect them, we have to take a brief detour via
Baudrillard. One does not want to be too interested in Jean Baudrillard
these days. The once prophet of postmodernism had his supposed credentials as the most radical theorist of the postmodern debunked by the
not unsympathetic Douglas Kellner (1989). After he left his full-time academic position at the University of Paris, Nanterre, in the late 1980s, his
prolific theory-fictions became ever more wickedly self-referential, if not
in fact self-defeating, and susceptible to easy dismissal as cynical reality-
denying intellectual puffery. The membership of his 1966 doctoral dis-
sertation committee—Pierre Bourdieu, Roland Barthes, and Henri
Lefebvre—place him in a very particular moment of French intellectual
life. As that moment has faded behind more apparently rigorous ongoing responses to it than Baudrillard's, his highly eccentric response has
come to seem considerably less interesting than it did for a while. But
Baudrillard's sympathetic presence in the sociology department at
Nanterre in 1968 when the "March 22nd" student protest movement, having begun there, took over the University's administration building (their
manifesto calling for "outright rejection of the capitalist technocratic

university") is only one reminder of how unhelpful it has always been to reject Baudrillard's intellectual project as reality-denying per se. In fact, of course, it was always a very particular reality that Baudrillard was denying ("Never believed in reality: I respect it too much to believe in it" (2006, 1)). The logic of Baudrillard's response to that reality (to the accelerating object-saturated "real more real than real" as Douglas Kellner dubs it (1989, 156)) included turning his "theory" increasingly against itself, one last reversal in his project to "reverse" the objects that constituted a reality he wanted strategically to deny. Perhaps one does not want to be too interested in Jean Baudrillard these days, but his unsettling "fatal strategy" still channels potent echoes from the corridors of the Nanterre sociology department of 40 or so years ago. What happens when these echoes faintly reverberate in the pedagogical relationship around a doctoral project in cultural studies on the other side of the world so many years later, where interests in motor racing fandom and boys' toys seem to tell a story, not just of the de-radicalized banality of the humanities in the technocratic university, but of how the field of cultural studies has eventually disappeared up its own trivia? This small book is what happens.

When a boy plays enchantedly with a new toy car that transforms into an alien robotic life-form in his hands and when a man watches on television with a pounding heart an F1 racer in a fast red car putting his life pointlessly on the line as he speeds to overtake another car at a gravity-defying corner, something beyond our older everyday notions of a consumer society is going on. The packaging on the floor beside the boy and the Ferrari-branded shirt the man is wearing (perhaps even in the privacy of his own home in front of the television) remind us of the commodifications involved, but the relative uselessness of these things insists also on their sign-value (as Baudrillard put it). We can almost map the tripartite membership of Baudrillard's thesis committee onto these scenes. Lefebvre is telling us that the minutiae of everyday life and the ordinary spaces where it takes place are worth studying. Bourdieu is telling us that these acts of consumption do indeed carry value over and above any particular use that the object in question might have, and that there will be a socially determined "field" where this value gets constructed and even ranked. Barthes is telling us that such objects of everyday life function within systems of signification where their meanings depend on their positioning in the system, not on any inherent meaning. Older ideas, such as the view that some more straightforward gratification of needs is going on in these scenes, even if merely for entertainment, suddenly seemed incapable of capturing things in the way that these later perspectives did. If the man lifts the toy off the floor, when the boy has finished playing with it, and takes it to a toy collectors' market, he will have entered a field in which, toy in hand, he has not just an easy fit but a "value." If instead he is walking toy-in-hand down the corridor of a university, still wearing his Ferrari shirt, he will have (in the field of academia) a harder task to establish either fit or value, though these days not an impossible one. (If he takes the right turn with his toy into the Psychology faculty, or perhaps Education, he should be OK as play is a respectable object of study there, whereas he can always take his team shirt into Sports Studies.) Thus, something interesting starts to get exposed about the management of passions.

Fandom is a field that recuperates these things in various ways, first as the field where boy and man can maintain enthusiasms around their objects: the boy can outgrow the toy as mere plaything but become a fan of Transformers (with its whole seductive meaning-making media system), and the man as "toy collector" or moviegoer can share that field. Second, as an overlaid field of academic studies: the man is even allowed to be a "fan-scholar" (a fan whose fandom absorbs scholarly perspectives on the object of fan interest) or a "scholar-fan" (a scholar who shares fan interests as a participant observer). The Ferrari shirt in the university setting may then become a statement of ironic self-knowingness. But Baudrillard resurfaces for us here in two ways: he was, for a while, one of those intellectuals who became themselves the object of "theory fandom" (of intense enthusiasm from his academic and artist fans) and, even as this was happening, he developed the cautionary fatalism that still has the potential to turn our sloppier thinking about fandom—and cultural enthusiasms generally—on its head.

From his early position of seeing consumer society as a Barthesian system of signs within which object consumption functioned as an induction into the system (which he did in fact view as a need, albeit no longer for the objects themselves), Baudrillard worked up his theory of symbolic exchange to the point where one key idea became increasingly dominant in his writing: the systemic impossibility of symbolic exchange in an object-saturated world. In relation to reification—the great theme of human subjects becoming things that has coursed through twentieth century Marxist cultural criticism—this idea got Baudrillard into some trouble. He offered, for example, the story of the male seducer who, asked by a woman what part of her he finds most attractive, says "your eyes," and receives a bloody eyeball in an envelope the next day. The object, via this contaminative and invasive reversal, is exposed as dominant. As with most of these provocative scenarios, Baudrillard meant this in a deliteralized way. Not only does this very deliteralization somewhat privilege Baudrillard's own abstracted knowing position and salve the rawness of the real relations momentarily if metaphorically glimpsed in the little horror story, but it describes an impossible exchange and therefore leaves those real relations untouched by the possibility of change, caught in stalemated histories and fixed object relations that fail to admit the unpredictable efficacy of real struggles. Baudrillard's later theory-fictions chased this kind of exchange to and fro across the cultural landscape. All such instances of exchange are perhaps variations on those 1968 students seeming to return the "gift" of their university educations; and all such instances look increasingly impossible at the systemic level where nothing really (ex)changes, where even the real refuses to return anything to the sign, leaving us surrounded by "more real than real" simulations.

One does not want to be too interested in Jean Baudrillard these days, but his distinctive move toward the fatal strategy in response to all of this ("nothing prevents us from assuming that we could obtain the same effects in reverse . . .") has, for us, been the single most potent counter force to the jauntily cheerful populism that infiltrated cultural studies over the same period. Meaghan Morris first raised the alarm about this back in 1990: "I get the feeling that somewhere in some English publisher's vault there is a master disk from which thousands of versions of the same article about pleasure, resistance, and the politics of consumption are being run off under different names with minor variations" (1990, 21); she went so far as to question whether much of this was really even partially redeemed any longer by a populism that at least viewed *any* signs of life under particular reifying circumstances as a prototypically political thing in itself. There have been a lot of variations on the theme (of people making their own "resistant" meanings from what they receive) struck from this master disk—ranging from what Matt Hills calls variations on the "see-saw model" of decoding/reading cultural texts (2005, 64), through various invocations of transgressive pleasures and on to clever forms of cultural consumption as a potential tactic of empowerment or a practice of "poaching" across the cultural landscape under the noses of duped landowners, the old producers of culture whose big houses are crumbling as the poachers sap their strength. The new media landscape even seems to have reconfigured itself more around the activities of the poachers. The "see-saw model" makes it clear that an assumed exchange is taking place between given meanings, on one side, and negotiated (tipping . . .) or oppositional (tipping more . . .) meanings on the other side, whether these meanings reside in "readings" or other anti-gamekeeping practices. Cultural studies scholars (in Meaghan Morris' "thousands of versions") have proved adept at "finding" the elements in cultural texts that encourage the seesaw to tip and this (briefly specialized) ability has been increasingly projected onto people generally, the assumption being that they are doing much the same a lot of the time. So, two decades on from Meaghan Morris' early moment of concern, one can randomly select an academic conference in this field, then randomly select an abstract from the conference papers, and find Lien Fan Shen's paper about Japanese animations and comics (anime and manga) at MiT5 (MIT's "Media in Transition" conference 2007), "Anime pleasures as a playground of sexuality, power and resistance." This took us less than 3 minutes via Google. The abstract says:

> This paper argues that . . . anime images embody the pleasure of evasion and the pleasure of transgression as a form of resistance . . . .. Further, these evasive and transgressive pleasures empower anime otaku (commonly referring to obsessive fans . . .) to go beyond image consumption, actively and constantly changing, manipulating, and subverting anime images in their practices, such as creating amateur manga, peer-to-peer networks and websites, and anime cosplay (costume role-play).

The abstract goes on to say that these practices represent a "playful politics" in which identities and the social structures "in which they reside" are subjected to "deassurance." The appearance of the last term here is interesting, as it was used by political scientists Karklins and Petersen in a 1993 paper to describe how in 1989 popular mass protests brought down the Communist regimes of Eastern Europe, employing what they describe as a complex "deassurance game" in which instruments of state coercion were undermined. The mapping of "rebellious behavior" (Karklins and Petersen 1993, 588) from the situation of a populace under a repressive regime into the field of consumption of popular culture elsewhere and not under explicit repression is an interesting elision of differences in the real circumstances involved (hinging on a generalization of the word "game") but is not untypical of how populist cultural studies has appropriated terms such as evasion, transgression, subversion, and resistance. (Lien Fan Shen does not cite Karklins and Petersen on "deassurance" as these kinds of term circulate freely in cultural studies.)

Now we are being very unfair here to Lien Fan Shen as a randomly selected example, since the point is that so much work in cultural studies is of this sort. Indeed playing the game of institutionalized cultural studies has often required generating this sort of material. But Jean Baudrillard is still capable, from beyond the grave, of "deassuring" this particular game. First, there are no "see-saw" models in Baudrillard's vision of things: "The world is not dialectical—it is sworn to extremes, not to equilibrium" (1990a, 7). We take this, of course, not as an assertion of fact to be accepted but as a rhetorical counterblast to the easy optimism derived from the "see-saw" modeling that has insinuated itself, in a variety of forms, into the very logic of cultural studies as a field (where theoretical debates have been more about the nature of the "see-saw" than about its existence). Second, words such as evasion, transgression, subversion, and resistance in the "soft" arena of cultural consumption, apart from their dependence very often on "see-saw" theory and an increasing vagueness about their "other"—what exactly is there on the other end of the see-saw?—also imply that all the energy invested in these cultural attachments, practices, and enthusiasms develops some sort of negative charge or "critical" reflexivity (somehow knows or experiences itself as "resistant"). In response, we have Baudrillard's reminder that there is "no longer any negative energy arising from the imbalance between the ideal and the real" (1996, 64). And again, we take this only as a reminder that "negative energy" is not to be so easily claimed. Except that, in our preceding half dozen paragraphs here, we want to point out one *moment* where some kind of energy may have been triggered. Ironically, it was when we were quoting Baudrillard himself.

That story about the eyeball in the envelope is the only moment in the preceding text that stood some chance of triggering an affective engagement with the words on these pages, a moment where a certain kind of energy made itself felt. Not only does the little horror story trigger this response but beyond it "Baudrillard" as a name does too, and this (positively) became the condition of his brief status within theory fandom, as well as (negatively) the dominant register within which much "Baudrillard" criticism took place (e.g., a revulsion rationalized as criticism of his "theory"). Baudrillard seems to offer us that scene as a representation, and within representational thought it stages one of those impossible symbolic exchanges as well as seeming to betray the efficacy of real struggles that do not resort to such nightmarish stagings (where "Baudrillard" seemed sinisterly complicit with so many contemporary nightmares in the end). However, there is another way of thinking about such moments—that is, moments rather than representational stagings—and this is to understand them as *nonrepresentational stagings of affect*. It is impossible not to think about how the woman felt when told that the man preferred her eyes, how she felt when she gouged one out and placed it in the envelope, how he felt when he opened it, and—most important of all—how we feel thinking of these things. If we can divest this latter feeling of its particular and antecedent representational details, what lingers is the feeling that we have grasped something.

Only once did Baudrillard come close to being explicit about this in his own writing, and then only obliquely by quoting a modern translation of Chuang Tzu (or Zhuangzi, the fourth century BCE Chinese philosopher). This comes, without commentary, at the end of the essay "Objects in This Mirror" in *The Perfect Crime*. Baudrillard quotes the passage in full but we will briefly summarize it. Chuang Tzu and Hui Tzu are looking at minnows darting about in a river when the former observes, "That is the pleasure of fishes!" Hui Tzu challenges him on how he knew this ("You not being a fish yourself") and Chuang Tzu challenges Hui Tzu on how he could possibly know that Chuang Tzu does not know ("you not being I"). Hui Tzu retorts, "If I, not being you, cannot know what you know . . . it follows that you, not being a fish, cannot know in what consists the pleasure of fishes." Just as we start to feel that this exchange could go on for a very long time, Chuang Tzu says, "Let us go back . . . to your original question" and then: "Your very question shows that you knew I knew. For you asked me *how* I *knew*. I knew it from my own feelings on this bridge" (Baudrillard 1996, 88–9).

The sense of suddenly rolling back the representational schemas here to a specific affective moment of engagement is quite striking, not least when we go back to it in the context of Baudrillard's book and discover that it is Baudrillard the photographer (a "thing among things" (ibid., 88)) who is writing at this point, the Baudrillard who "feels" an object world with a camera in his hands; who, as it were, is photographing the minnows. We intend to do several things from this point. We want to roll back to Baudrillard's doctoral committee and, instead of following a "Baudrillard" forward again with his uniquely eccentric take on that moment, we want to follow our own minnows while (a) still avoiding the "see-saw" models of cultural consumption, (b) focusing on nonrepresentational theory, and (c) tracing the "energy" that surfaces in affective moments.

Deriving the notion of a fatal strategy from Baudrillard will allow us to pursue each of these aims while remaining "fatally" on the side of the object as it were. Indeed our chosen objects—Formula One motor racing and Transformers—are meant to elicit from the outset a certain jaundiced sense of their intractability when it comes to locating any promise of potential for "evasion, transgression, subversion and resistance." There is a certain brutality to these things, a gross materiality, a lack of subtlety, a stubbornness, an obduracy, an inconsequentiality, and there is not going to be some clever sleight of hand two thirds of the way into the book where we reveal them as unexpectedly after all the vehicles of a "playful politics" as Lien Fan Shen put it. Nor will Baudrillard, or any other star from the pantheon of theory fandom put in another appearance two thirds of the way in to tie things up neatly for us. On the other hand, we do want to reengage the discussion with Bourdieu, Lefebvre, and Barthes, or more properly with the bodies of ideas those names represent, in order to develop our three aims in relation to ideas about fields, everyday sites of consumption, and systems of meaning. This reengagement will often be implicit in what follows, although from time to time it will become clearer that we are doing so, not least where there are nonrepresentational alternatives at stake in relation to the more dominant modes enshrined in representational thinking.

Nigel Thrift (1997) provided the first neatly organized summary overview of nonrepresentational theory: "a major change has begun to take place in the way in which the social sciences and humanities are being thought and practised—but no one has really noticed" (126). Thrift, who later wrote a book about nonrepresentational theory (2008), suggested that this emerging theoretical reorientation was about practices (rather than representation), about subjectification (rather than subjects), about spatiotemporal processes (rather than static forms), about material networks with hybrid constituents (rather than things viewed in isolation), and that these practices, subjectifications, processes, and networks involve specific forms of embodiment, spatiality, and temporality: they are lived and take place in everyday life in describable ways, not as theoretical abstractions. Thrift then returned to the question of "resistance" and linked it to play: but not in terms of a "playfully" struggling subject on one end of a see-saw and "oppressive" structures of power on the other so much as, drawing on Larry Grossberg, some other kind of play that is not predefined as oppositional posturing against a real or imagined oppressor. We will derive some helpful sense of context (and endorsement of our style of working) by associating ourselves generally here with Nigel Thrift's depiction of nonrepresentational theory, although we are less confident that the range of theoretical perspectives drawn together in his 1997 paper can cohabit the space so comfortably. Moreover, we gravitate strongly to Mark Hansen's argument that most such theorizing still remains in fact subject to "the contemporary reign of representational thinking" (2000, 103). As Hansen argues very persuasively, it is the question of how we think technology that has demonstrated this, which is to say it is one of the most pressing of contemporary questions for scholarship that has exposed the "major change" evoked by Nigel Thrift as in fact something of a false dawn.

Mark Hansen notes "the celebration of representation common to most contemporary forms of cultural studies" (ibid., 103) in the course of determinedly following Walter Benjamin's lead in attempting to reconceptualize a type of experience (Erlebnis) that is antithetical to such celebration: based on "a corporeal agency sensitive to the inhuman rhythms of the mechanosphere" (ibid., 243). We believe that we recognize that agency in both F1 and Transformers fandom as, in a sense, entirely arbitrary instances cut out of the "mechanosphere" as much for their obdurate inconsequentiality as for their significance, and we will argue that it is a good candidate for occupancy of that "playful" position hypothesized by Thrift. Hence this book. As we proceed, what we mean by nonrepresentational will become progressively more clear, as will an explanation for why it would appear to be a masculinized agency that we are tracing in these particular instances.

"It's about the personality of things": Steven, a graduate student, is speaking about Transformers, the toy range that has had a plethora of accompanying cross-media manifestations since 1985. He has been looking at three "digital stories" about Transformers. These "stories" are short-form videos based on first-person voice-overs. Steven has overseen a "story circle" process to obtain these as part of his research project. The "digital story" and the "story circle" are practices developed at the Center for Digital Storytelling, Berkeley, California (Lambert 2006), and Steven (like other researchers elsewhere) is interested in adapting the form as a potential (auto)ethnographic research tool. At this moment he has three such stories (averaging 2 minutes in length) in which three men reminisce about their childhood attachments to Transformers, illustrated with visual material largely derived from the cross-media franchise (e.g., selected images from comics, animated television series, computer games, photographs of toys, stills from the Hollywood movies). Steven has been thinking about what similarities might link any two of these and distinguish them from the third. This relatively simple task is actually adapted from George Kelly's personal construct theory (1963). Kelly argued that doing this sort of task exposes the "personal constructs" of the person who is doing it and does so more reliably than, for instance, asking them directly what something is "about." So Steven has found that two of his three "stories" concern, in some way, what he is now calling "the personality of things," while the third, he explains, seems "underdeveloped" in this respect: it describes an attachment at a very early age to a specific toy object that is evoked in highly physical and emotional terms but without being elaborated into subsequent evocations of "personality" in the way that the other two stories suggest. This recognition of "the personality of things" then becomes part of Steven's own autoethnographic reflection on his own childhood attachment to Transformers, or a point of reflexive entry into that attachment.

Jaron Lanier (2010), in his manifesto *You Are Not a Gadget*, identifies the gadgetized subject as a distinctive contemporary phenomenon: people, especially men, who in some ways have been encouraged to think of themselves as gadgets in a world of gadgets, a world where indeed things can have personalities. From the so-called new man as "caring" and then "narcissistic," are we shifting into a phase in which the new man is gadgetized, a complex condition that cannot simply be reduced to concern for appearances, narcissism, antisocial tendencies, hollowness, or any of the other supposed characteristics of millennial "new man-ism?"

The car crash and the computer crash occupy important places in the peripheral vision of most of us these days, representing as they do both real risks in the routines of everyday life and symbolic crises in the personalities of things. One can, if one has the money, buy a Volvo car or an Apple computer, with their crash-resistant "personalities," but the possibility of a crash remains endemic despite sensible precautions. For gadgetized men in a world of gadgets with personalities, might the personality crash in some new sense, therefore, also be endemic?

Was Steven "decoding" Transformers? Instead of meaning transparently flowing through channels of communication from sender to receiver, we have come instead, of course, to see everywhere the processes of encoding and decoding that embody the complexity of mediated meaning-making and raise the possibility of mismatches between what goes in one end and what comes out the other in any mediated process of communication. But the concept of "decoding" has its limitations too, encouraging as it does a focus on complexly "encoded" texts in which the decoding takes place. Steven, however, is not only not reading the texts of the Transformers universe directly, but he is not even decoding the three digital stories (texts of a different sort) in any straightforward sense: instead he is handling those texts in a particular way in order to expose a construct in his own understanding, a process that the term "decoding" no longer accurately describes. Steven's "it's about" becomes then quite a complicated pairing of "it" and "about."

Do Steven and the tellers of the short audiovisual stories represent the audience for Transformers? As the late Roger Silverstone put it so succinctly 15 years ago: "An inquiry into the 'audience' should be an inquiry not into a set of preconstituted individuals, but into a set of daily practices and discourses . . . " (1996, 281). A simple enough statement in one sense but he was marking a profoundly important point of self-reflection reached at that juncture by audience study (and in many ways exemplified by the larger volume in which Silverstone's contribution appeared). Since exactly that time, of course, "new media" have massively transformed the range and scale of "daily practices and discourses" with which any inquiry into an audience has to contend. This has been an exciting period for media and cultural studies as a result, the objects of inquiry proliferating exponentially.

On the other hand, old ideas do not simply go away because newer, perhaps better, ones have arrived on the scene, and much scholarship in this field is still shadowed in various ways by the notion of preconstituted individuals, a collectivity of whom then makes up an audience. Indeed, as the fluidity, adaptability, and personalization of daily practices and discourses in the media environment has increased somewhat confusingly, so too has the temptation to seek firmer ground by rediscovering some sort of preconstituted individual as a basis for retaining the term "audience" at all, even if only in relation to some definable and perhaps increasingly small segment of the media ecosystem. This has driven some work in the field into very small niches, where a specific technology or application or cultural form can be matched to tightly defined groups of people. This can be very informative, but interesting and well-founded generalizations about audience in any larger sense are becoming as rare as hen's teeth. We will be dealing with this temptation where it is most likely to raise its head—in autoethnographic contexts where the individual voice is not only allowed to speak but is assumed to have something interesting, if not revealing, to say, though arguably only about him or herself as an audience of one. Our intention, however, is to remain true to Silverstone's rubric, while maintaining that key interest which cultural studies as a field has tended to display when at its best—an interest in spanning textual and sociological thinking in media studies.

Of course, those working in cultural studies are not unfamiliar with the inherent risk in this: that sociologists will be unhappy when cultural studies takes one of its turns toward textual methods, while "textualists" (primarily scholars in the humanities) will tend to be unhappy when cultural studies takes one of its sociological turns. Being caught between a rock and a hard place like this has always contributed to cultural studies' tenuousness in institutional terms (though it has been a relatively short institutional life to date in any case). But if we are to look seriously at a range of practices and discourses in the cultural field, it will always be necessary to focus closely on the texts through which these are mediated, while also being willing to pay attention to the social determinants of the same practices and discourses, in short the important sense in which the latter are not merely implied or produced or required by the texts but are in some discernible and highly significant ways socially constructed as well. In fact, as we proceed, we will look to dismantling this kind of distinction between methods in any case.

Ethnography has been, for quite a long time now, and despite having its own problems, an attractive place to attempt the various balancing acts suggested in the preceding remarks. Ethnography, in several ways, exists fairly comfortably in the liminal zones that seem to arise between the textual and the social, not least because the increasingly important category of "everyday life" both suits the ethnographic stance and is self-evidently populated by both texts and social actors. The introduction to the volume in which Silverstone's essay appeared hinted at how the distinction between "field" work and "armchair" work could too easily be blurred by doing an easy piece of ethnography that seemed to lend some kind of legitimacy to what remained essentially "armchair" theorizing (at best) or commentary (at worst). Autoethnography is often suspected on these grounds.

Reflecting back on the 1990 conference on which the 1996 book was based, coeditor James Hay offers what is almost an aside but is actually a profoundly helpful insight: " 'fields' are arbitrary, not particularly coherent, and constantly crossed by interlopers, poachers, and 'dilettantes' " and he goes on to suggest that "Instead of the loftier aims of interdisciplinary projects . . . what may be needed is something closer in spirit to *bricolage*, the constant invention of new tools for working a changing landscape" (4). Hay and his colleagues probably at that point did not quite fully appreciate (none of us did) how rapidly and in what extraordinary ways that changing landscape was about to change even more; but his point remains if anything an even more useful one as a consequence. (The conference in question, in Illinois, had been called "Toward a Comprehensive Theory of the Audience"!)

So this book is a modest inquiry into certain daily practices and discourses; it is interested in the invention of some new tools for working the media landscape in question, not in pursuit of the definitive tools, much less a comprehensive theory, but in the pragmatic spirit of constant (re)invention to keep up with some slippery objects; and we are unapologetic if suspected at times of being interlopers, poachers, or even dilettantes in relation to any fields that others may work more single -mindedly and in more depth. If nothing else, these characteristics should protect us from hubris, but we think they also have promise in other ways.

Two moments help explain what this book is about.

A stream called Eau Rouge winds through the Belgian countryside, its banks shrouded at times by the wooded hillsides of the Ardennes Forest, an area notorious for its unpredictable shifts of weather. Once a year some of the fastest automobiles in the world disturb the forest calm and streak overhead where a race track crosses the stream before catapulting the machines with their cocooned occupants into a curving high-speed uphill left-right-left sequence of tightly compressed but sweeping bends that culminate in a summit with no clear view beyond. The machines reach the summit at around 180 miles per hour (300 km per hour), a speed that requires not just finely tuned skills to match the finely tuned engines but a repeated act of faith on the part of a driver that doing this is possible at all.

An F1 car hits the Eau Rouge corner on the Circuit de Spa-Francorchamps on a downward slope and then changes both direction and inclination in the blink of an eye, the blind summit just visible at the top right of the driver's peripheral vision as both the bends and the sudden change to a swinging uphill slope implore him (there are no women drivers in F1) to lift almost imperceptibly but measurably off the accelerator for an instant. Some do but some do not. These are cars—at the pinnacle of motor vehicle design and engineering—that rely on massive downforce to keep them from not taking off into the air like jet aircraft. Some of the most sophisticated aerodynamics ever devised essentially invert the principles that get an aircraft into the air and keep it there at high speeds. Turn the same sleek microscopically designed surfaces upside down and the airflow over them presses the machine downwards instead, holding it onto the road. But here is the thing. The faster the vehicle is traveling the more downforce it has. For the fragile, claustrophobically encased but still hugely vulnerable driver in the machine, taking Eau Rouge at top speed, at the absolutely highest speed possible given the technology to hand and the stretchable limits of human confidence, is the key to getting it right. Go too slow, lose downforce, and bang . . .

To the casual observer everything about Eau Rouge's catapulting dynamics says "slow down," even if just by the tiniest margin. Everything that we know from being at the wheels of our own vehicles is telling us this. In our heads, a corner like Eau Rouge has a big road sign warning "dangerous bend ahead," which means take it easy, be sensible, be safe, slow down. Everything that a top F1 driver knows about the aerodynamics of the machine being catapulted into the Eau Rouge sequence of bends, with him inside, is saying exactly the opposite. Push it to the limit.

This despite the aura of death that hangs like the mist in the trees of the Ardennes here. Although today's F1 machinery is the safest it has ever been, the Circuit de Spa-Francorchamps has always killed drivers; two in a 15-minute period in the 1960 race being the worst point on record. Nine years later F1 boycotted the track until some safety improvements were made, while the original track layout was eventually changed to reduce the risks still further. Eau Rouge has seen spectacular crashes in F1 but to date has not claimed an F1 driver's life. No F1 driver will be unaware, however, that Guy Renard died there in a Toyota Corolla GT, and Stefan Bellof died there in a Porsche sports car during other racing events in the 1980s and 1990s. In 1994 the F1 authorities, believing it was only a matter of time before Eau Rouge killed one of their drivers, put in a chicane (an inelegantly contrived narrowing of the track) at the start of the sequence to choke off the speed, but so important was the untarnished—yes, the elegant—experience of Eau Rouge to drivers and fans that this was undone a year later. So the blind summit beyond Eau Rouge still waits there menacingly for F1's human/machine projectiles to top it at foolhardy but technically demanded speeds, the routine repetitiveness of racing, of doing the same thing lap after lap, only slightly blunting the sense that human beings are doing something here that is very special, if in a pointless sort of way. Which brings us to the first moment.

If one F1 driver over the years can lay claim to having refined the art of doing Eau Rouge flat-out it has to be 1997 World Champion Jacques Villeneuve. Unlike the other drivers who could do the same thing technically (and relatively few could), Villeneuve always looked and felt like he had found the absolute edge, that he was only a heartbeat away from total disaster every time he decided to take on the Eau Rouge bends without even a hint of lifting his foot off the accelerator. In fact, in 1999, he did come off at Eau Rouge during a high-speed race qualifying lap, the car disintegrating around him in what Jacques would call "my best-ever crash," a heart-stoppingly spectacular incident in relation to which Villeneuve's subsequent swashbuckling attitude only served to reinforce the feeling that he "owned" Eau Rouge and that its capacity to better him on rare occasions was all part of the game, and of the peculiarly deep relationship between driver, machine, and place.

So the first moment that helps explain what this book is about is watching—and, importantly, listening to—Jacques Villeneuve taking Eau Rouge on any of the many hundreds of occasions on which he did so during his F1 career. The different occasions blur together into one composite moment. Being able to listen, on the television coverage, to the engine note as Villeneuve's race car (different cars with different teams over the years) plunged into Eau Rouge and soared toward the blind summit, was an important part of the experience; because you could hear when the note was unvarying, when he was not "lifting." It was impossible not to imagine an almost maniacal grin on his face under the helmet and balaclava every time he did it, in mute acknowledgment perhaps of the absolute meaninglessness of what he was doing so brilliantly. The technically great drivers, like Michael Schumacher, could achieve the same thing on occasion—but not, one felt, in the same way. Therein lies a crucial distinction to which we will return.

The second moment . . .

"Jacques, Move Your Body (Make Me Sweat)" is a track by Jacques Lu Cont (pseudonym of English DJ, remixer and producer Stuart Price), released under the name Les Rythmes Digitales, one of several names which Lu Cont/Price uses generically for the various band lineups and session musicians he works with. This brand of electro dance music is very much a sound that was in the air in the period when Jacques Villeneuve's F1 career was at its height (the late 1990s). That in itself is not a connection. The two Jacques here are mere coincidence; except that the feel of a funky electro rhythm helping to define the end of the millennium is perhaps not so far from the intangible but discernible "feel" that distinguished Jacques Villeneuve's often rebellious way of doing things from F1's many more coldly technical and decidedly non-funky practitioners, no matter how hard the sport's many marketing experts worked to revitalize the image of a Michael Schumacher or any of the other corporately sponsored young clones that, with their often grim attitudes, had come increasingly to characterize the sport. Try setting a video of Villeneuve repeatedly taking Eau Rouge to a soundtrack of "Jacques, Move Your Body" and it feels just about right. Get the cutting rhythm right, and you will catch something of the sublimely energetic thrill that courses through the mechanical repetitiveness. That is a YouTube exercise worth trying.

Stuart Price became better known as the musical director for three of Madonna's blockbuster world-concert tours and for doing remixes on several of her albums. But "Jacques, Move Your Body (Make Me Sweat)" has an edgier feel than his work with Madonna and on its own became even better known than Price's other work when it was used as the soundtrack for a highly successful car commercial on television, with the punch line "Alive with Technology".

Somewhere in the deep background of a piece of electro-funk like "Jacques, Move Your Body" is the pioneering 1980s electro band Cybotron from Detroit, a connection with what was once the self-styled car capital of the world that the commercial's creators may or may not have been fully conscious of. Stuart Price, however, is an accomplished utilizer of musical nuances, and his combination of a very simple drum machine rhythm with funky bass, mashed-up vocals and a distorted synthesizer melody works together with the track's structural device, of momentarily breaking down and audibly reassembling its layers, in order to evoke something of Cybotron's sound. In particular, what gets evoked is that earlier combination of cold, dry, mechanical strata of sound with a feeling of funky (or soulful) aliveness threading its way through the layers: a quality that is difficult to articulate but easy enough to feel.

This interrelation of the soulful and the mechanical, the funky and the repetitive, does not map neatly onto what we might call an agency/structure distinction—where a quality of aliveness is in contrast with the machinery—for the not-so-simple reason that both sides of this apparent dichotomy have aspects of "agency" and "structure" about them, thus breaking down the distinction before it has proved to be of much use; a point that will be reinforced as this book progresses.

Simon Reynolds has said of Detroit-based Cybotron, one of the most important progenitors of this kind of sound:

> The vision underlying Cybotron songs was Detroit-specific, capturing a city in transition: from industrial boom-town to post-Fordist wasteland, from US capital of auto-manufacturing to US capital of homicide. Following the late sixties and early seventies syndrome of "white flight" to

the suburbs, the decline of the auto industry, and the de-gentrification of once securely middle-class black districts, Detroit's city center had become a ghost town. (Reynolds 1998, 9)

A genealogical line of electro-funk has become a key sound of that ghost town, less specifically Detroit in the end and more a generalized site of postindustrial, dystopian, urban malaise of which Detroit was but one instance. F1 held a Detroit Grand Prix throughout much of the 1980s, Jacques Villeneuve's father Gilles (then an F1 driver for Ferrari) having been killed in a racing accident in Europe 4 weeks before the first one in 1982. Bringing F1 to Detroit was supposed to be part of the city's rebirth but it was never convincingly so, and the race moved at the end of the decade to the more vibrant and sunnier Phoenix, Arizona.

Cybotron-influenced electro-funk still carries some of these connotations. The mechanical rhythms are not the rhythms of Silicon Valley (although Cybotron themselves were eventually signed by a Berkeley, California label looking for something edgier than the locals were producing) but rather of a technoir sensibility bred on the streets of Detroit where the automobile remains as much of a cultural symbol as the computer. Cybotron's track "Cosmic Cars," though heavier, ponderous and more desolate in tone than the lively "Jacques, Move Your Body," nonetheless feeds directly in to the latter's evocation of a technology still largely unconnected with "cyberculture," a technology rather of moving parts, scraping distortions and metallic energies with a certain subliminal soulfulness (the Cybotron track even including synthesized car horn and growling engine sounds).

By the time we get to the repurposing of "Jacques, Move Your Body" in a clever Citroën car commercial in 2004, what we are looking at and listening to seems a long way away from postindustrial Detroit in crisis in the 1980s. But it embeds behind the family-friendly image of the Citroën C4 an unexpected acknowledgment, perhaps especially for those who have taken part in the "white flight" from the inner cities, of a darker urban history behind the blandness of the Vancouver office buildings, high-rise car park and sunny skyline that appear, digitally recreated, as the commercial's backdrop. The sound of electro-funk never quite gets accommodated into a blandly cheerful hard-sell for a new car without carrying some residual echo from street-level of other lives and other ways of feeling. For here the neat, designer lines of the C4 are exploded in the commercial into a humanoid robot, made up of wildly reorganized car parts, which dances spryly to the electro beat. This visual transformation also deliberately and knowingly says "Transformers"—and for a generation of young car-buyers with their newly minted families this is a cleverly playful evocation of their own iconic childhood toy.

So the second moment that helps explain what this book is about is watching—and, importantly, listening to—a very nice looking if plain Citroën C4 family car reveal itself briefly as something else—a hip, streetwise bit of machinery with attitude one might say, in the idiom of the times. Tongue-in-cheek certainly, but witty and delightfully knowing about the multiple layers of significance being deployed.

So the 16-shot, 30-second C4/Transformers commercial shows a "transforming" Citroën car breaking out into robot form and doing a dance routine in an otherwise empty rooftop car park before returning to its original condition as if nothing untoward had happened. Animated by Vancouver-based visual effects company The Embassy for producers Spy Films in Toronto and advertising agency Euro RSCG's London-based Citroën account team, directed by Spy's Neill Blomkamp and utilizing then cutting-edge motion capture and computer-generated imagery (CGI) techniques, the commercial became a popular success in its own right, spawning YouTube spoofs and parodies as well as considerable interest from CGI aficionados and Transformers fans (as evidenced particularly by the sheer scale of unofficial web distribution of the video and ongoing associated forum and social networking chatter). In addition to its international television run, Citroën made the advertisement available for download from their company website, and it self-evidently ended up on a lot of personal computers for its inherent entertainment value. Several more commercials were made in the same vein for the Citroën campaign, as we shall see. Director Blomkamp went on to use the same techniques in his dystopian and politically provocative 2009 science-fiction feature film debut *District 9*, in which CGI brings to convincing life a community of stranded extraterrestrial aliens being confined to a ghetto outside Johannesburg. Blomkamp's ability to suggest dark undertones was picked up in some of the web chatter about his C4 commercial: for example, angelhawk64's comment on one YouTube instance of the video—"cool commercial, but kind of creepy"—which succinctly captures the presence of what we termed above a "residual echo" derived in part from the deep roots of the electro-funk sound but also probably from ambiguities in the Transformers imagery itself that we will be addressing in due course. Something about the dancing car definitely "de-gentrifies" and intangibly disturbs its bland surroundings and this is part of the commercial's particular cleverness.

The dancing car itself was made by having well-known LA-based dance choreographer Marty Kudelka (who has worked on music videos and concert performances with Janet Jackson, Pink, and Justin Timberlake among others) improvise to "Jacques, Move Your Body" while wearing a motion-capture suit (on which illuminated data points allow precise computer mapping of movements). His routine, transferred to the CGI-generated robot, retains much of the subtlety and energy of the original human movements. The moment then has much to do with this subtlety and energy, and on that level it is not so unconnected after all with Villeneuve taking Eau Rouge. Both moments are about our response to extreme machinery that has been charmed by a human touch.

It is possible to look for other connections. The C4 was adopted as the Citroën factory team's international rallying car, with world rally champion Sébastien Loeb at the wheel for a number of years and energy-drink maker Red Bull as the major sponsor. Loeb has test driven for Red Bull's F1 team with a view to entering F1, but, like Jacques Villeneuve, he remains at the time of writing one of the regularly talked about elder talents still on the margins of the sport, after earlier personal glory days and continuing successes elsewhere. However, this is to indulge in a game of "six degrees of separation." The fact remains that, in the field of cultural production, these two moments are widely separated from each other. There are possible institutional, economic, and significatory links, yes, thanks to an inevitable crisscrossing of these factors that allows a "six degrees" game of connection to be indulged in. But it is not in the field of cultural production that the two moments come together. Instead, it is in the field of cultural consumption that they feel most related, especially when we take the fact that both moments are about cars as not really very explanatory at all and look for something more convincing to explain their felt relation.

Now it has to be said before we go much further that these two moments, foundations of this book, do not immediately advertise themselves as either especially important or even intellectually fashionable. At a time when academic attention to the latest manifestation of contemporary cyberculture's addiction to exponential change provides plenty of opportunities to write about "new" technologies, paying attention to (for example) the car seems distinctly old-fashioned, even while acknowledging John Urry's interesting work on automobility. Even Transformers, the 25-year franchise linking toys to television animation shows to comics to big-budget films, may seem decidedly tired or undistinguished to some as a topic for consideration, despite its momentary enlivening by

Neill Blomkamp and the Citroën agency team in our example. But this is very much the point. There is quite often something astoundingly selective in what the academic field of cultural studies "chooses" to look at. Moreover, this kind of selective attention may not be unconnected with the very questions of status that permeate the field of cultural consumption itself—in other words, certain things, and certain attachments to certain things, reflect more social status than others and academic attention may be (more than it cares to recognize?) inextricably caught up in the consequent constraints and dispositions, as we shall discuss in Chapter 4. Villeneuve taking Eau Rouge and the Citroën/Transformers commercial are in many ways low status objects of both consumption and inquiry; indeed even of questionable value in any supposed hierarchy of "taste," incapable of bestowing or lending much "distinction." (Academics unquestionably borrow a degree of "distinction" from the objects they choose to inquire into.) So by focusing so intently on these we hope in the end to expose some of the mechanisms of status-formation. The question of who these sorts of thing matter to and why is one to which we will return.

This inevitably raises the question of the "cultural omnivore thesis," arguments for and against which have been shaping some academic attention in the field of cultural consumption (Peterson 1992; Emmison 2003). The cultural omnivore—the consumer who grazes widely, in relatively unconstrained ways, and more or less indiscriminately across the cultural field—has emerged as a theoretical concept in recent years in reaction to earlier attempts at pinning cultural consumption to class structures or some other deterministic basis. The resulting arguments are not without their nuances. But for the moment it will suffice to offer some preliminary remarks on this topic.

Juxtaposing our two moments here might seem especially appropriate were we to evoke a simplistically pure form of the cultural omnivore thesis. According to this, there would be no reason at all why Villeneuve taking Eau Rouge and the Citroën/Transformers commercial should not be considered together without our attempting to ground both in a specific site of consumption (e.g., defined by particular gendered class characteristics)—because contemporary "omnivorous" cultural consumption is exactly like that. It pays attention to whatever it chooses, whenever, in whichever circumstances. Moreover, the cultural omnivore is perfectly entitled, as a result, to feel that they have freely and, in a sense, even randomly chosen these moments, disregarding the possible effects on consumption choices of the very precise circumstances of their

production. In fact, of course, the particular conditions of cultural production cannot be so cavalierly disregarded; or rather this can only be
done through a deliberate sleight of hand that disguises something more
complex going on. The particular version of Villeneuve taking Eau
Rouge that we have presented here is entirely dependent on a complex
construction of the moment through forms of television presentation,
contextual knowledge of the sport of F1, of Villeneuve's supposed personality, and so on (as communicated through very specific channels).
So too, the Citroën/Transformers commercial as described is an equally
dense cultural phenomenon, as our description of it has already begun
to suggest. Take away its contextual underpinnings in very specific circumstances of production and it means relatively little. More pertinently
still, we might then fail to notice what constitutes the deliberate—or
even the strategic—dimension of cultural consumption as articulated in
relation to those underpinnings. So we are not intending to support the
purest form of the cultural omnivore thesis. Rather, our point will be to
suggest another ground or base for these apparently free-range omnivorous acts of cultural consumption than those more traditionally rooted
in class or even in status (although status will still remain a key concept).
Put more simply, we do not wish to project from our two examples the
image of a specific male consumer, a type definable moreover in class
terms, as the "ideal" subject for which these two moments inevitably take
on the sorts of meaning we have been suggesting.

What is omnivorous about the kinds of cultural consumption in which
we are interested here—the kinds that can embrace and make something
of both Villeneuve taking Eau Rouge and the Citroën/Transformers commercial—is their capacity to decouple consumption choices from the
fixed positioning implied by specific underlying sites of cultural production. It is not even the case that the C4 commercial appeared during
television coverage of an F1 race in which Villeneuve was driving (his last
2004 television appearance in an F1 car was a month prior to the airing of
the C4 commercial in Europe, and in fact he did not drive at the Spa-
Francorchamps circuit that year). So we cannot suggest that there was a
"text" (e.g., a datable sequence of the televisual flow) in which our two
examples were actually juxtaposed and therefore saw a convergence of
their circumstances of production and reception. They remain instead a
deliberate juxtaposition here of two things that were essentially separate
in terms of any framework for describing production, or even in terms of
their specific offering up for consumption. But we want to explore the
idea that the field of cultural consumption floats relatively freely over any

such description of production sites: not totally freely, but with enough of a decoupling to allow us to suggest that Villeneuve taking Eau Rouge and the Citroën/Transformers commercial can cohabit *somewhere else.*

To suggest where this is (if not in a strictly predetermined "audience" defined by a convergence of production circumstances, for example, in a broadcast sequence where automobile commercials are inserted into F1 race coverage, with a highly targeted demographic), we need recourse to a different sort of vocabulary. Hans Ulrich Gumbrecht, writing about athletic beauty, offers a "typology of fascinations": "it contains no unifying principle, no matrix of meanings, no 'grammar' to proscribe the ways in which these fascinations can be combined" (2006, 152). Gumbrecht perfectly echoes here our point about the field of cultural production not proscribing too tightly (not defining an "audience" engaged in) the omnivorous acts of recombined cultural consumption in which we are interested. Fascinations respect no such rules.

In Gumbrecht's typology the operative "fascinations" for us are *tools* and, first of all, *grace.* The vocabulary change here is an abrupt one, we allow, but this break is not without merit as a way of starkly reframing our two moments. On the question of grace, Gumbrecht refers, with surprising relevance, to an 1810 essay by Heinrich von Kleist titled "On String Puppet Theatre":

> Kleist's fictional dialogue opens with a famous ballet dancer confessing how much he has always enjoyed watching marionettes and how he sees in their movements a model for his own performance. This statement, with its implicit admiration of a popular form of entertainment, must have been much more provocative in Kleist's world than it would be today. But the main thrust of Kleist's provocation, in a time when the highest goal of literature and art was to express the most intimate musings of an individual's soul, lies in the counterintuitive reasons the dancer gives for his fascination with puppets. Instead of emphasizing the shapes and movements marionettes share with the human body, the dancer praises them for belonging to "the realm of the mechanical arts". Grace, Kleist makes us understand, is a function of how distant a body and its movements appear to be from consciousness, subjectivity, and their expression. The gracefulness of puppets lies in their inability to become self-reflexive and thus either embarrassed by or proud of themselves. Grace turns upside down all the accepted knowledge about the relation between the human body and the human mind. (Gumbrecht 2006, 167–8)

So what we are doing here is resisting the temptation to propose that there will be a closely definable type of person (defined by gender, class positioning, etc.) for whom our two moments will "naturally" be meaningful, and that having identified this type we will have, ipso facto, both substantially explained the moments and identified the unit from which an "audience" is assembled. Instead, Gumbrecht's powerful notion of fascinations allows us to approach things somewhat differently (which is not to say that gender or class or even audience will be insignificant, just that they will not be explanatory in and of themselves). If we might be allowed to insinuate the first trace of an autoethnographic perspective here, both authors have had to deal for years with the feeling that expressing interest in such things risks immediate pigeonholing as a "type" that is in fact largely unrelated to who we are. The occasional smirk that indicated a lack of borrowed distinction from the object is something we both learned a long time ago to enjoy, even to provoke.

On the other hand, placing our two exemplary moments into the context of Kleist's "realm of mechanical arts" moves the explanation along rather better. First, because the next thing that can be said about Villeneuve taking Eau Rouge flat-out is that the moment leaves virtually no room for conscious thought. It all happens too fast. From this perspective, the repetitive lapping, with cars often line astern, that is so characteristic of F1, becomes part of a real-time, observable training and reinforcement in the "mechanical art" of taking a corner like Eau Rouge. Doing the thing well has to get almost hard-wired into the body. Concentration is required yes, but not anything like a process of thinking one's way round the corner, decision by decision. The F1 spectator/viewer who "gets" this aspect of what is happening is going to be fascinated (in Gumbrecht's sense) by the distance between what is visibly and audibly achieved by the body in the machine, on the one hand, and, on the other, the cluster of subjective phenomena we term consciousness. A state of reverie, a muting of self-reflexiveness, on the part of the spectator/viewer—and we are speaking here from experience—begins to synchronize itself with the "mechanical art" being watched. At the moment that is Eau Rouge, the onlooker has no more time to think than the driver does. And that is the sheer joy of it. It can also be, to all intents and purposes, quite addictive: something sought time and again, waited for, anticipated.

Kleist's ballet dancer goes on to praise the "soul in the elbow" of the marionette. *Soul in the elbow.* There will never be a better phrase than that for capturing the sense of where Villeneuve's soulfulness resides as he drives through Eau Rouge, in sublime memory now more than in reality. It is not just that we are unable to associate that act with any thoughts in Villeneueve's head at that moment—we actually very much do not want to effect such an association and risk spoiling the moment. No real F1 fan would ever, given the opportunity, say to a driver such as Villeneuve, "So, what were you thinking as you took Eau Rouge today?"

Of course, the dancing car in the C4/Transformers commercial achieves the same thing but more transparently in terms of its underlying artifice. We know that Marty Kudelka is not actually there inside the machine—that we are witnessing only the ghostly traces of his agile body. What the extraordinary technology of CGI motion capture achieves is an actual removal, an extraction, of the thinking, self-reflecting brain from the "mechanical art" being enacted and witnessed. Where Villeneuve did not have time to think, thanks to the charmed technology of speed and aerodynamics, the robot-car has no means to think. And yet the grace of human physical presence is still there, thanks in this case to the charmed technology of motion capture. Even the imagined maniacal grin on Villeneuve's face is something that we want to be an automatic thing, not a reflection of thought at that precise moment. Kudelka's mechanical ghost, with its spinning, high-stepping, elbow-popping grace is all soul in the elbow.

So the second "fascination"—the tool—extends the grace, amplifies it, pushes it to a technologically mediated extreme. Yet, the grace survives, which is very much part of what makes such moments so extraordinary. In discussing tools of this kind, Gumbrecht notes two senses in which their "complexification" of the body functions. First, they extend the limits. Villeneuve and Kudelka's bodies get freed by the machines, rather than imprisoned by them. Second, and more subtly, there is a key relationship between the degree of a body's adaptation to the machine and the extent of grace achieved. So there is extension of the body but also an absorption of the body into the tool.

This is important because it immediately raises the question of the "cyborg," which became an influential turn-of-millennium theoretical concept, since an innovative 1991 essay by Donna Haraway developed it, as well as a potent image in contemporary popular culture. To start with an example from popular culture, this is an extract from the 1995 first draft screenplay of *Star Trek: First Contact*, written by Brannon Braga and Ronald D. Moore:

```
She is unlike any of the Borg drones we've ever seen—a
humanoid female with conduits and tubes running out of
```

her body. She has no legs. Her torso is SUSPENDED by a complex rig of CABLES and HYDRAULICS. Her face and upper-torso are much more humanoid, with the pasty-pale white of Borg flesh. Her EYES have a silvery glint to them. Her demeanor is seductive and sensual in contrast to the harsh, mechanical surroundings. She is an eerie blend of two worlds—organic and mechanical.

With the soft HISS of hydraulics, she LOWERS herself down to where her face is very close to that of Data's. Her features are almost angelic, but the silvery glint in her eyes betrays an inner-darkness.

> DATA
> You are the guiding intelligence
> behind the Borg . . . ?

> BORG QUEEN
> Intelligence . . . ambition . . .
> desire . . . I bring order to chaos . . .

She studies his face with a certain child-like quality.

> BORG QUEEN
> It's unfortunate we will have to
> destroy you to obtain the
> information we need. You are a . . .
> unique lifeform.
>   (beat)
> Synthetic . . . and yet far more than
> a simple automaton. You have no
> idea how close to perfection you
> are.

She stares at him intently, and we get the hint that her interest in Data may go beyond simple assimilation. She seems fascinated by him. Data picks up on this.

> DATA
> How do you define perfection?

The Queen opens her arms slightly, clearly indicating herself.

> BORG QUEEN
> A blending of the organic and the
> synthetic. The highest form of life
> in the galaxy.

```
Data eyes her, considering.
                    DATA
          An interesting definition. But it
          is not one that applies to me. I am
          completely artificial. I have no
          organic components.
```

She looks at him as a new thought crosses her mind.

The final shooting script and, therefore, the finished film add some additional expositional dialogue to this version, but this first draft captures the feeling of the scene particularly well. The Borg, who first appeared in the television series *Star Trek: The Next Generation,* are archetypal cyborg characters—humanoid but assimilated into a machine collective, their bloodless bodies merged with various technological parts and synthetic fluids. The character Data is a permanent member of the series' cast—an all-machine android (or humanoid robot) rather than a cyborg, and a crew member of the famous starship Enterprise which, in several variants, has flown across several television series and spin-off feature films over the years, to the delight of "trekkies" as fans are called. What Braga and Moore (key long-term staffers on the television series' creative team) achieve in this scene is perhaps the most knowing, playful, evocative face-to-face encounter between a cyborg and an android yet achieved in popular screen fiction. The "new thought" that crosses the Borg Queen's mind is that she can reactivate Data's emotion chip (part of a fan-satisfying backstory too laboriously complicated to detail here), graft skin onto his artificial flesh and stimulate his (hitherto nonexistent) sexual responses.

Alice Krige plays the cyborg queen, a character then unique to this film (though later reprised in one of the several Star Trek television series), and delivers, with the help of an occasionally exposed, slithering, whiplashing spinal cord, a performance of languorous, sickly seductiveness that considerably outstrips in quality and memorability the film itself. Brent Spiner, as Data, hams it up with a series of knowing nods to his fans, who get the backstory to his character from the television series and, one assumes, like to feel they are "in" on what is happening from his perspective. However, Krige unquestionably steals the scene and makes it worth writing about here.

There is an unmistakably adolescent quality to the way that the scene is handled, other than by Krige herself perhaps. From Data's point of view, strapped to a futuristic operating table, the scene is meant to be titillating, an in-joke to amuse fans. But in fact we end up feeling the scene's significance more from the Borg Queen's point of view, as she circles Data like a predator. So shifting Alice Krige's performance into the framework of Donna Haraway's essay of 4 years earlier may serve it rather better, as the moment has resonances that go well beyond the film as a routine piece of popular entertainment.

Haraway (in "A Cyborg Manifesto: Science, Technology, and Socialist-Feminism in the Late Twentieth Century") calls the differentiation between living organism and machine a "leaky distinction" (1991, 152) of the late twentieth century and offers, as a consequence, the cyborg "myth" as not just a defining myth for anticipated times but a potentially progressive way of thinking precisely because it refuses the many binaries, the category distinctions that have plagued social relations via constructions of race, gender, sexuality, and class, as well as all the consequential dualisms such as factory/home or public/private. The cyborg myth (while refusing to demonize technology) comes to symbolize the leaking of one previously distinct category into another, productive interference across old boundaries, a de-policing of differences that is not a return to something more natural but a dismantling of the very idea that anything is "natural" and, therefore, not open to question.

Alice Krige's Borg Queen, without of course any of the political nuances that enrich Haraway's account, nonetheless unforgettably visualizes a creature whose monstrousness is deeply suggestive, not because of the film's adolescent sexual innuendo, but because it is a monstrousness pitted so obviously against the poor android male who really does not want to be interfered with, if truth were told does not want his "emotion chip" to be activated as this will just make life so much more complicated.

For the point to be made here is that both Villeneuve taking Eau Rouge and the dancing car in the C4/Transformers commercial are almost entirely about the *android* as a way of imagining things and almost entirely not about the cyborg. "What about men's access to daily competence, to knowing how to build things, to take them apart, to play?" asks Haraway (181), unintentionally evoking both F1 and CGI as themselves myths of such daily (unemotional?) competence amplified, technologized, and intensified a thousand fold.

It is an (often ignored) irony of conceptualizations of the cyborg as a boundary-transgressing and binary-dismantling form that in fact the cyborg is always already caught up in its own binary relation with the android, the scene above serving very nicely to remind us of this, which is the main point of its inclusion here. That the android of late has been the poor relation, imaginatively and theoretically, of the cyborg has a lot to do with the attention triggered by Haraway's writing (and with a leaky boundary between academia and culture more broadly). And the cyborg is another example of where borrowed distinction can be derived by the academic. As we said above, Alice Krige's cyborg feels "worth writing about" where the unfortunate android around whom she stalks really does not. But that will not stop us here.

To what extent then are our two opening moments "android" rather than "cyborg" moments and why does this matter? In this context, the words "android" and "cyborg" are ways of imagining, not so much technological advancements per se, as our own relationships with technological advances. As too are our opening moments, our examples of dream machinery at work—and at play—within popular culture. How the terms map onto the moments matters for what this may tell us about the kind of social imagining involved, and then about its consequences for an understanding of how masculinities may align themselves with moments such as those we have been focusing on.

It is not entirely our intention at this stage to set up a gender binary around the cyborg/android dualism, but our Star Trek example serves as a reminder that binary thinking is a given which has to be carefully dismantled; rather than starting with unfounded faith that one's thinking has somehow already evaded binary logic only to find that it has been secretly tainted all along. But we are happy to allow, for the moment, that the android imaginaire in particular has a great deal to do with masculinities (where "imaginaire," as we will see, captures rather more of what is intended than the English term "imaginary").

So we are brought back to the nature of Gumbrecht's fascinations but now to the possibility that a grace where mechanical art, as it were, momentarily switches off consciousness in favor of what Gumbrecht calls a "complex, dehumanizing impression" (169) is absolutely central to what is going on. Gumbrecht sees this "impression" in great athletes, in those moments of peak performance where the body becomes a kind of machine. This, we might now say, is an android moment. Rather than a complex "cyborg" interpenetration of human and machine, a leaking across boundaries, a copresence and mutual infiltration of the thinking human and the acting machine, there is instead a very different, in some ways more direct kind of surrendering of the human to the machine—this is what is challengingly "complex" in the dehumanizing impression that Gumbrecht detects. It has to be admitted in the same breath that Leni Riefenstahl's film of the 1936 Olympics in Berlin comes to mind here, where slow motion and tracking shots begin to establish the basic vocabulary of later television sports coverage; her filming of victorious African American runner Jesse Owens capturing the "complex, dehumanizing impression" of his prowess while complicating any potential Fascist appropriation of this kind of "dehumanizing" for an altogether other, awful agenda. The thought will linger however, that perhaps the appropriation of the cyborg imaginaire for a socialist-feminist agenda leaves the android imaginaire somewhere else—somewhere, in its celebration of a racing car taking a bend in the Ardennes or a dancing car in a computer-recreated Vancouver car-park, not just rather trivial but also disturbingly unprogressive in its ultimately implied politics.

Gumbrecht's work, however, reminds us in effect of how culturally diffident we have been in a post-Riefenstahl world about recognizing the possibility that there may be nothing wrong, in entirely different contexts, and a world away from 1936, with temporarily, and in a particular setting, liking the sight of a dehumanized body in action (although our two opening examples insist that the residual human trace is vital). That any sensitive reader still undoubtedly feels the risks involved in such language—never mind in the conceptual direction implied—only serves to underscore the importance of picking our way carefully across the implications being set in motion here.

So we are embarking on writing about objects of inquiry in the cultural field that lend little distinction to those who choose to find them interesting in this way, and we are setting in train a line of thinking about them that feels at the outset riskily regressive in its possible implications. At worst, we may seem to be already heading toward a point where we will reveal an "android male" spectator, his emotion chip turned off, delighting in the simple pleasures of watching various imaginary re-codings of the android *imaginaire* in popular cultural forms, such as F1 racing or a Transformers blockbuster movie, with all its connotations of regressive adolescent fantasy; perhaps even worse, of politically suspect tendencies. If he listens to death metal music, the picture is complete. Then it would be one small conceptual step to register this figure as a type, pin him down demographically, and build an "audience" from him.

That this picture looms so large, so quickly and so readily is something that in itself intrigues us. A proper rejoinder might be to note that a reductive reading of the cyborg imaginaire is also just as feasible but that alternatives demonstrably exist (as Haraway and writers influenced by her work have proved). But an example might be more convincing.

The cover art for the 2006 vinyl single "Love Don't Let Me Go (Walking Away)" by David Guetta and featuring The Egg carries a yellow sticker showing an ice-skating "Transformers" Citroën C4 with the label "Includes Walking Away (Tocadisco Mix) as featured in the Citroën C4 advert." Guetta, French DJ and producer of house tracks, and The Egg, a British electro-funk band, are listed together here as a result of the kind of complicated hybrid relationship that characterizes so much club music these days (and the evolution of 118–135 beats-per-minute "house" from Chicago warehouse nightclub to global mainstream dance floor includes the absorption and adaptation of the Detroit sound we have already referred to). In fact, The Egg's single "Walking Away" was released a year earlier and one of several remixes commissioned by licensees (in this instance a remix by German DJ and producer Tocadisco) became an electro-house crossover success in the clubs before being itself bootlegged (unofficially rereleased) by Guetta in a version that became a top-selling dance release worldwide. It was cannily picked up by Citroën's agency for their second installment in the C4 "Transformers" campaign. (Because Guetta's release was a bootleg, Citroën officially credits the Tocadisco remix as it appears on The Egg's *Ultra Electro* album.) An ice-skating "transformed" C4 in the second commercial takes the machine out of the city and onto a frozen lake surrounded by coniferous forest, where a small team of technical observers bundled in winter clothing watches it do its routine, to the astonishment of a local woodsman.

This time, instead of dancer Marty Kudelka, it was British speed skater Nicky Gooch who provided the motion-capture material mapped into the CGI environment (by specialist English company Audiomotion). The cheeky electro-funk feel is still there somewhere but its connections back to Cybotron and Detroit are now a lot more tenuous as the disco-resurrecting feel of this strain of house music comes to the fore in the remix. But let us go back, for a moment, to that grizzled woodsman.

Only appearing in the longer versions of the commercial (a more tightly edited version aired in some time slots), the woodsman is something of a caricature of an axe-wielding, unshaven mountain man, and his somewhat disbelieving glance at the skating car-bot as it whizzes past his lakeside vantage point bespeaks a playful acknowledgment of the rather camp version of masculine interests being depicted here. As Simon Reynolds has pointed out, a transition from Detroit-style electro-funk to house tends often to imply a segue from straight black male to gay black male. A certain camp suggestion was already present in Marty Kudelka's routine for the original commercial but it was held in check to a degree by the slightly harder electro-funk sound, and possibly by Blomkamp's grittier sensibility. Here the French directorial team of Bardou-Jacquet, Houplin, and de Crecy (who call themselves H5) find a style that is less redolent of the streets and more evocative of performance for its own sake—even more a preening display of prowess than an expression of attitude. (In the longer version, the car-bot even glances over its shoulder and straight to camera before taking off, in a conspiratorial wink to the audience.)

As a result, the trace of Nicky Gooch in the machine (derived from 4 hours of motion-capture filming on an Olympic-size skating rink) delivers an even more extraordinary impression of grace in Gumbrecht's sense. The especially memorable moment in the commercial is when the car-bot corners athletically at speed (in the longer version it also leaps an obstacle on the ice). The power and balance in Nicky Gooch's high-speed skating get unmistakably reexpressed despite the heavy reworking in CGI (and the slightly more mechanical quality of the original commercial's animation gets consequently muted). Like Villeneuve taking Eau Rouge, the speed-skating car-bot cornering on the ice is joyfully, pointlessly all about speed and grace and smoothness and the subsuming of the still detectable human trace in the machine's own moment.

The next commercial in the series (in 2007) makes the link with our Villeneuve moment at Eau Rouge even clearer. The so-called Runner commercial for the Citroën, directed by Trevor Cawood, shows a C4 leaving a workplace in the city and arriving back at a distinctly affluent sun-bathed hilltop home (shot in South African locations that provided a suitably idyllic if geographically unspecific backdrop). Taking off from its starting point in the city like a sprinter off the blocks, the car-bot transforms a couple of times along the way as it negotiates a winding road in the scenic foothills on its way home. In the middle of the commercial the "runner" does a parkour move when it leaps momentarily at speed onto the barrier on a curve and slides along before rejoining the road. Now in one sense, of course, this should be a readily forgettable moment—the commercial is just a clever piece of selling and the CGI techniques (again by The Embassy) are already by this point so familiar as to have lost some of their surprise value. Even the choice of music— this time it is "Echo" from Luke Dzierzek—should have become predictable by now. (A version for German television dropped the Dzierzek track and tried to surprise by going semiclassical instead, but the effect was flat.) In fact, though, the parkour moment is perhaps a small high-light of the whole campaign and Luke Dzierzek's track, though pushed into the background this time by an obtrusive (if commercially predict-able) sales voiceover, has a tremendous energy.

The fleeting "quotation" of a parkour move in the C4 "runner" com-mercial is an interesting touch. Free runners and parkour practitioners, called traceurs (male) or traceuses (female), use their athleticism to move at speed through cityscapes where walls, fences, gaps between buildings, and so on are obstacles to be gracefully negotiated. Free run-ning and parkour (the latter the more exhibitionist version) exist in a liminal zone between youth and adulthood and typically reclaim the cityscape for a pure form of playfulness. The cityscape is reduced to obstacle course, largely undifferentiated by socially determined mean-ings (Fleming 2009).

The music video produced by the Paris-based Gum Prod label for David Guetta's remix track "Love Don't Let Me Go (Walking Away)," the soundtrack for the second C4 commercial, uses parkour in a distinctive way, with well-known practitioner Danny Ilabaca in a central role. The video provides a concrete example of what we are going to call a nesting loop, a concept we want to generalize from and apply more broadly to the examples charted in this chapter, and more widely as the book proceeds.

Shot by director Marcus Adams in a Paris banlieue, a suburb of low-income apartments in the kind of area that has spawned persistent social unrest and occasional riots in recent years, the video has a flat, unobtru-sive visual style and is shot in muted naturalistic colors that counterpoint the explosion of physical energy on which the video depends for its impact. Two young men (one of them played by Ilabaca, or perhaps he is just being himself) are lethargically hanging out in a fenced ball court surrounded by gray apartment blocks. Two young women approach on the other side of the wire, their dress and demeanor suggesting they are smart, worldly, no-nonsense inhabitants of the banlieue with a sense of style that has nothing overtly consumerist about it. Looks are exchanged and then the video sets in motion its central conceit—the transference of a special kind of energy via a touch. Ilabaca's companion and one of the girls touch through the wire fence, triggering an instant transition into dance moves in which, moments later, Ilabaca gets caught up, set-ting him off on an astonishing parkour routine through the banlieue. In the course of the video, the "energy" gets transferred to several other people (even conducting along a metal barrier rail on one of the concrete walkways to affect another group of initially aimless looking young men), while Ilabaca continues on his high-energy excursion, ending up back in the ball court with his friend and the girl who are locked in a passionate embrace.

What is especially clever about the video's combination of parkour and the Tocadisco mix of "Walking Away" that is embedded in the larger Guetta track is the use of a nesting technique. Guetta's track is distinctive for the way it borrows the high-energy electro sound provided in the Tocadisco mix and places it inside the much blander, more pop-orientated "Love Don't Let Me Go," the lyrics for which continue to run over the "Walking Away" segment of the remix. The transition to the staccato, elbow-popping electro sound is matched, in the video, with the transition from lethargically, even wistfully, hanging around in the banlieue to the parkour-based high-energy explosion of—yes, grace, in precisely the sense in which we have been deploying the term throughout the present chapter.

The framing of one set of musical connotations with another, and the elaboration of this in the "story" that the video tells about the momentary enlivening of its banlieue denizens through sheer physical energy and grace, provides a good example of a nesting loop. This concept occurs in various contexts (from computer programming to neuro-linguistic programming) to identify the way in which interdependent frames are nested one inside the other with feedback relationships looping through the frames as a result. These frames might be computer code or frames of reference in communicational exchanges, but here we intend to appropriate the term to describe the loops that this chapter as a whole has been tracing through its examples.

It can be argued that the C4 commercials depend centrally on such nesting loops. Within the frame of sophisticated—indeed cleverly manipulative—pieces of contemporary advertising are nested subsets of content and connotations that can be selectively responded to without necessarily feeling that one is "buying in" to the commercial (though one can equally well buy-in if one wants to of course). Within each of those subsets is nested material, especially in the form of the music, that in fact may run counter in its associations to the consumerist hard-sell of the ostensible outer frame. And where is that outer frame in any case? Beyond the confines of the particular television commercial we have been hypothesizing a field of cultural consumption in which the neatly separated frames delimited by the field of production may break down or prove to be highly fluid when viewed from the perspective of the fascinations that we are tracking, fascinations that run somewhat more freely across the cultural field (parkour-like in their own way?) in search of their defining moments, irrespective to some degree of "original" text or context.

Just to repeat in the interests of clarity, the two fascinations we have become concerned with in this chapter have been grace and tools. Our series of nesting loops have sought to demonstrate how these fascinations play across a broad field, even though the isolated moments singled out so far have in fact been very narrow and specific; from F1 driver Jacques Villeneuve taking a corner called Eau Rouge to the athletic bodies of Marty Kudelka or Nicky Gooch acting like traceurs within the machine, from a melodramatic encounter between cyborg and android in a Hollywood film to a series of television commercials for a French-made family car, from the fusion in a banlieu ball court of an electro-house sound with free running to the evocation of childhood memories of Transformers toys that now come "alive with technology" (as the Citroën slogan goes).

The fascinations of grace and tools—the achievement of grace through tools—find satisfaction in the apparently simplest of ways: in waiting with bated-breath for Villeneuve to arrive at Eau Rouge or getting caught up momentarily—perhaps even unintentionally—in a clever bit of dancing CGI animation that transcends its commercial message and at the same time brings back to life a childhood toy. What the tools of F1 and CGI facilitate here is a realization of what we have termed an android *imaginaire*: the realization of Kleist's dancer's fascination with marionettes in the distancing of thought from (mechanically projected) body.

> Whereas the frame of functioning of a technology is developed primarily within the technological community and in research laboratories, the construction of the frame of use involves more diverse actors and is manifested in more varied discourse not only by technicians but also by "literary persons": novelists, popularizers, journalists, and so on. All this discourse contributes to the formulation of a social *imaginaire*. (Flichy 2007, 125)

Patrice Flichy's formulation of this process perhaps does not quite leave as much room in social imaginings of the frame of use as we are taking to accommodate the sorts of example discussed in the present chapter, but once admitted the notion of a social imaginaire in relation to technology seems to want to expand to include just such instances. For social imaginings, in a profoundly important sense, do not have any existence independently of the many instances in which they are constructed. But Flichy is writing more of a unified technological *imaginaire*, such as the ways in which, at the end of the nineteenth century, novelists and social utopians to a great extent converged in their visions of emerging technologies (as freeing people from drudgery and opening new vistas for exploration). We need to ask whether a contemporary *imaginaire*, or specific form of social imagining of technologies is as likely to be a unified one (or indeed whether the late nineteenth century's was really as unified as it may have seemed). Our cyborg and android *imaginaires* already start to split the field and an early suspicion may persist here that the question of masculinities will exacerbate, rather than mend, such splits as the argument develops. Finally, of course, to Flichy's "literary persons" we shall be adding the governing bodies of a sport such as F1, the agencies behind automobile commercials, the toy designers, the film studios, and so on. A greater diversity of agents recognized as being involved in the imagining decreases the likelihood that they will all be found to act in mysterious synchronization.

Six questions begin to take shape out of the foregoing material.

How can we translate the notion of fascination into a less metaphorical vocabulary, in order to identify the practices that constitute its practical application in the field of cultural consumption? It is in relation to this question that we shall be developing a theory of interlinked intensities and strategies in order to map such practices (in short, a fascination in Gumbrecht's sense may be constructed by a specific interaction of intensity and strategy as we shall later define these).

If fascination with the grace entailed in a particular kind of physical performance involving machines ("tools")—one where there is no gap into which consciousness has much time or inclination to insert itself self-reflectively—is a key contemporary phenomenon, to what extent and in what ways may this be linked to masculinities in particular?

If a helpful alternative to pursuing reductively a type as ideal viewer/ spectator/consumer projected, as it were, from these forms of cultural production (and from which a supposed audience may then be generalized) is instead to develop a modified cultural omnivore thesis, to what extent will our interacting intensities and strategies be found to ground or anchor that "omnivorous" cultural consumption in nonetheless definable ways? And is the free runner or parkour in fact a better image than the omnivore?

If, as proposed, nesting loops are a key (and nonreductive) structural feature of the cultural field from the perspective being developed here, where do these cultural loops register on a consuming subject, especially given the hypothesis about lack of self-reflective opportunity or inclination; that is, if there is no process that mirrors the conscious detailing of intertextual connections we have undertaken in this chapter? It is in relation to this question that we will be developing the notion of affective materializations.

To what extent, then, is the hypothesis of an android *imaginare* a defensible one, as a way of updating Kleist's marionette and its contemporary implications, given that this seems to be potently at work in the fascinations we have identified? And might this not be so much an exclusively masculine preserve as, rather, somewhere where masculinities only tend to gather?

Finally, will it be possible to link the distinctive technological *imaginaire* we are focusing on here to a wider set of concerns about gadgets, so-called boys' toys and a broader view of contemporary masculinities in relation to technologies within which our specific focus on F1 and Transformers can take its place, and to what extent may an autoethnographic style of thinking be helpful with this?

Chapter 2

Intensities and Affective Labor

Autoethnography remains very much the poor relation of other longer established (if themselves not unproblematic) ethnographic methods. Methodologically, it looks especially sensitive to antipositivism's valuing of situation-specific understanding over suspect claims to ultimate extra-situational objectivity and so autoethnography should be a valuable tool at our disposal. However, it is often suspected of tending toward the other extreme—of paying too much attention to situational specifics grounded in the particular understandings of one or two people to be a method that can encourage much widespread confidence. We do intend to deploy autoethnographic perspectives in this book though, for reasons that will become clearer as we proceed.

As a first step in this direction, there follow two extended sections written separately and in the first person by each of the coauthors. We are holding back our methodological discussion proper for a conversation in the next chapter.

Dan's Story

It was in 1995 (approximately 2 years after the term "information super-highway" really began to enter public consciousness as one way of imagining new technologies) that the seeds of writing something about the largely non IT-related high-tech of F1 and Transformers got unexpectedly planted for me. The world's major telcos at that time were running expensive trials of video-on-demand (VoD) systems to see if people would want to watch movies and television programs that they could access via their telephone lines, enhanced by interactive menus and other services. It was not at all apparent then that the web would eventually let people do essentially the same thing, but using largely open standards rather than proprietary ones controlled by the big telcos. So a prodigious amount of money was being spent developing and trialing the technologies for phone-line based VoD. The concept was pretty much right—just that the platform turned out to be wrong and the timing perhaps premature. BT (British Telecom) in the United Kingdom was in the forefront of these developments and, at that time, I was working in the BT Human Factors Unit, where a team was tasked with researching consumers' responses to the new systems and content. BT had run a small trial a year earlier with 60 households (of BT employees) in Suffolk, England, and had bedded in the technology nicely—so the much larger 1995 trial (several thousand households) was very impressive in its technical robustness. At a point when the dial-up web, for most people, was still text-heavy and slow by today's standards, reliable, effective interactive access to high-resolution audiovisual content on-demand was something of a revelation. A deal with Columbia Pictures had put some attractive movie content onto the system alongside complete television series.

The BT Human Factors Unit at the near-legendary Martlesham Heath research laboratory in England had been partly staffed with a new generation of young graduates (largely in Psychology and Human Computer Interaction) and innovation was in the air, not just in terms of the new technologies but also methodologically. Every second desk when I was there seemed to sport a copy of David Morley's book *Television, Audiences and Cultural Studies* (which had appeared 3 years earlier), as BT's gung-ho young researchers tried to get their very smart heads around some of the new ways of thinking about "audience" (not a concept that telcos had dwelt much on to that point). This was in the shadow of the big Illinois conference "Toward a Comprehensive Theory of the Audience," at which Morley had presented a paper. Futurist Peter Cochrane was, at that time, heading the lab's overall research department, with more than 600 staff working on future technologies, and he was bringing an unexpected blend (for staid BT) of hyperbole, speculativeness, and risk-taking to the whole enterprise (while alienating a few people along the way who saw unfounded optimism and more style than substance in some of the emerging emphases). The facility would later join forces with MIT's Media Lab, as part of a powerful "technology triangle" that included the University of Cambridge, to research what they would then start calling "disruptive technologies" (in the sense of disrupting long-established ways of doing things).

The point now, however, is not to report on the research I was doing in this setting but to reflect on some of the other things that were going on at the time. Most of the people I was working with were about 10–15 years younger than me and their late teens or student days had precisely coincided with the emergence of rave music and rave culture in Britain in the late 1980s (whereas for me, rather differently, it had been punk rock in Belfast over a decade earlier). In the first half of the 1990s large-scale almost impromptu rave events were happening throughout England, with numbers at some of the bigger all-nighters topping 20,000 at a time, to a musical accompaniment described as "sounds wholly or predominantly characterized by the emission of a succession of repetitive beats"—in the wording of the 1994 Criminal Justice and Public Order Act that sought to codify the circumstances in which the British police were then being authorized to break up such events. Despite Peter Cochrane embracing new styles of techno-utopian thinking at BT, its corporate culture remained profoundly conservative (Cochrane himself remained at heart an engineer) and many of the young staff in the Human Factors Unit were genuinely fearful that their weekend activities would come to their employer's attention, especially as the law tightened its grip. I saw at least one peremptorily fired, his desk cleared into cardboard boxes by BT security who escorted him out through the security barriers on the main gate. Such was the climate in Britain in the immediate afterglow of Margaret Thatcher's years in power as prime minister.

I was lodging in the basement of a house full of these young, male BT Human Factors Unit employees (in Ipswich, England). I saw their lifestyle at close quarters, inevitably heard a lot of the music and got a passing taste of the club scene on weekend trips into London, but it was not until Simon Reynolds' book *Energy Flash* came out a couple of years later that I was able to join the dots more fully and grasp something of the bigger picture of rave culture thanks to his documentarian's acumen (hence our quoting of Reynolds as an authority in the previous chapter). When I eagerly got hold of *Energy Flash* in 1998, one thing in particular that Simon Reynolds said immediately brought back to mind the distinctive rhythm of life and work among those young high-achievers at BT Labs: he described "the whole magic/tragic cycle of living for the weekend and paying for it with the midweek comedown" (1998, xv). I was immediately able to translate that observation into memories of attitudes and bodies, of moods and atmospheres, of intensities and strategies, as they played out week after week.

The main point I want to make here, though, is that Sundays spent lazily in front of the television watching F1 Grands Prix races were very much part of that rhythm. English driver Damon Hill was heading toward the peak of his F1 career and was hugely popular among my housemates and their friends. Hill had a cerebral quality that appealed to them but still effected a laddishness then fashionable. Watching them (and consequently watching myself) watching F1 races should have told me as much about "audience" as the research we were all engaged in at the lab. But it takes a while for that kind of unintentional participant observation to filter through into one's intellectual consciousness, at least in my case. When it did, it turned out to be more informative than any of the formal research I had then been engaged in.

Simon Reynolds writes insightfully about the "liberating joy" of surrender involved in rave music, where the names of tracks and artists were largely irrelevant and "meaning" was not to be found in any particular example so much as in the crowd and in the culture as a whole, which means in the larger amalgam of lived practices and discourses. What I saw my younger companions at that time do with F1 had an unexpectedly similar quality of surrender about it, though I was not at all sure at the time what it was they were surrendering to—in fact the preposition is misleading, as I will argue that they were surrendering something not surrendering *to* something. As with rave, there was a secondary level of elaboration where magazines and other sources of information fed a curiosity about what went on behind the scenes, but this material was to all intents and purposes filler between the moments of primary engagement. While the rave scene was not mine, and I remained decidedly an interested observer there, I did recognize common ground in the forms of engagement with F1. But it became much clearer in retrospect and only when contrasted with the weekday lives we were living.

Let us be clear about the risk of misunderstanding here. It would be easy to characterize the lazy Sunday hours watching F1 on television as "mindless," even as a caricature of dumb male surrender to a pointlessly repetitive entertainment, divested of much intelligence (at least as a practice of cultural consumption) and marked by a shutting down of much deliberative activity in favor of staring blankly at a screen. In that mental picture, putting a beer can or two into the hands of the viewers more or less completes the caricature. It is a tempting caricature, not least because reinforced by endlessly repeated stereotypes of this sort generated by popular culture itself, as if to disclaim any responsibility for there being more to it than that. As an aside, I do not actually remember much beer being drunk in my example from the mid-1990s, not least because those particular people were typically trying to rehydrate after an all-night rave the night before. Two-liter bottles of Evian were much more in evidence.

Looking back, it seems quite ironic that those particular F1 viewers with their big bottles of Evian water and their quality of often mute absorption in the screen on a Sunday were spending their weeks doing expensive, multi-technique research into television viewing that connected in just about no ways at all with their own lived practices. There were three key differences. First, the weekday research was focused on preconstituted individuals who were assumed to have reasons dominating what they did, if only we could refine the research techniques that would capture these, while at the same time adequately defining the individuals themselves (so that other similar people would become predictable in terms of their reasons and, therefore, choices, preferences, interests, spending). Expressible reasons in that sense had very little, if anything, to do with the weekend practices. Second, the weekday research had a strong tendency to isolate television viewing from other cultural practices whereas the weekend blurred these in all sorts of ways, but initially in terms quite simply of the lived rhythms of everyday life (a few of which we evoked in the previous chapter). Third, the weekday research was largely uninterested in the small details of content or the granularity of the experience, whereas the weekend seemed to be all about that granularity, all the way down to the rhythms of drinking and breathing and moving (or not).

It was not that the weekday research into the VoD audience was unsophisticated (it triangulated its object of inquiry with a good mix of quantitative and qualitative methods, ranging from telephone surveys through automated data capture via a set-top box to fly-on-the-wall observations in people's homes). It was sensitive to many of the issues raised by Morley about how meanings are constructed in the context of family viewing and household dynamics. In fact, in some senses, it was possibly too sophisticated in its pursuit of both rational behavior and meanings, too ready to over-interpret for meanings, too convinced that reasons could be articulated, and, as a consequence, relatively insensitive to other things—such as rapture.

Rapture is the only word I have ever been able to find that captures both what I understood (largely at second hand) to be the experience of rave and, if somewhat less intuitively, the experience of watching F1 in the way I saw it watched at that time, which is to say the way I was watching it as well. Rapture in this sense is a quality of engagement grounded in affect, where "affect" refers to what Patricia Ticineto Clough defines (in one of the best recent collections of writing about affect) as "a substrate of potential bodily responses, often autonomic responses, in excess of consciousness" (Clough 2007, 2). This is where the android *imaginaire* that is focused around technologies may get grounded in specific practices and lived experiences: not a mindlessly automatic condition (therefore preconscious one might suppose) but a condition beyond or after or "remaindered" in relation to consciousness where the autonomic refers to a kind of intensity and engagement that does not need so much of the paraphernalia of consciousness in order to be felt. That paraphernalia includes the conscious narrativization of emotion or feeling that often passes for the "expression" of affect, but affect as conceived here is not expressible in that sense and indeed may only very loosely, if at all, relate to any such narrativization as a representational device.

To explain this more clearly requires a fuller description of the contrast between weekday and weekend rhythms as they characterized the particular mid-1990s example being recounted here. Office cultures were changing at that time. "Hot-desking" was becoming fashionable and the Human Factors Unit at BT Labs at the time was a very large open-plan space in which people had their own desks but worked in an unmistakable ambiance of potential motion, with fluid boundaries. Popular representations would catch up with this within a year or two, when the much-imitated pairing of writer Aaron Sorkin and producer-director Tommy Schlamme invented their "walk and talk" style of television situation comedy and drama. In fact, when the first Sorkin/Schlamme example of this appeared (*Sports Night*), the style immediately and recognizably captured (if in exaggerated form) a good deal of the rhythm of daily activity that was coming to characterize actual work environments at that time, with the disappearance of many office walls and the emphasis on near-constant communication. (After *The West Wing*, which even achieved this effect in the corridors of the White House, Sorkin and Schlamme's third series, *Studio 60*, captured the feeling, the ambiance, and the rhythm definitively.) So the unit at BT Labs in the mid-1990s did not feel at all like a factory environment, staffed by cloned operatives working to a synchronized beat. Those old Fordist and Taylorist characteristics were long gone; replaced by an often high-energy flow of mobile interactions, a blurring of throwaway interpersonal exchanges and serious work, an unpredictability, and a requirement of the participants that they stay alert, multitask, and often monitor several overlapping conversations at once. Nothing so heightened as the Sorkin/Schlamme version, but the main characteristics were definitely all there.

Now the importance of this is the high level of conscious, cognitive participation it required. Though fascinating, it is often tiring just to keep up with the invented Sorkin/Schlamme creations as the camera retreats in front of them or dodges other people to keep up, their walking pace and quickfire dialogue demanding more or less constant alertness from the viewer. In the real work environments being exaggeratedly mimicked by Sorkin and Schlamme, the level of conscious engagement was no less high, if the unit at BT Labs can be taken as typical, especially for ideas-based workplaces staffed by smart young professionals. The contrast between these always-on states of consciousness during the working week and weekends given over to something else becomes an important and revealing one.

Rapture is based on an entirely different rhythm—and ironically perhaps it is one that may almost return to the repetitive, mechanical beat of the factory floor, where the individual is subsumed back into the machinic, is reincarnated as autonomic. This was present in rave music and it is also the rhythm of F1 with its endlessly repeated laps (rather than loops), the same corners being taken at high speed over and over again, with relatively little emotion-stoking excitement in the racing itself, which is often criticized by outsiders as processional. If we take the demonizing legal language of the time—"predominantly characterized by the emission of a succession of repetitive beats"—and enlarge our sense of what the term "beats" might mean, we have the beginnings of a way to think about affect in these contexts, and for relating this to the unpacked moments in the previous chapter.

This brings us in a roundabout fashion to Transformers. In the mid-1990s I was also preparing to write a book about toys and television (*Powerplay: Toys as Popular Culture*) that had grown out of a fairly casual remark to an editor about being interested in robot toys in particular, which seemed to reflect in intriguing and under-researched ways the development of twentieth century technoscience. Weekend breaks from BT Labs in London at that time also took in the toy museums (Pollocks on Scala Street, the Bethnal Green Museum of Childhood and the museum at Craven Hill that would close not long after, when its toy collecting Japanese owner died). The Craven Hill museum had perhaps the world's best collection of metal toys, from tinplate onwards, whereas the other museums tended to place more emphasis on dolls and whimsy. So this interest came up casually in conversation with the BT Labs' staffers and I was struck by how many of them then talked, largely unprompted and often at surprising length, about having had Transformers toys as boys. A few even cropped up at the labs as desk ornaments, though frequently in little contrived tableaux with other objects that deliberately flagged an adult sense of irony rather than merely a childish attachment. A Lego F1 car (made from small plastic bricks!) was also a feature of these in one instance and I recall one desk that had a row of Transformers robots whose heads (with some effort I presume) had been replaced by miniature die-cast racing helmets in the colors of the then popular F1 drivers (a common collectable). I wrote about Transformers in that earlier book, but the thought niggled away for a long time that young men talking about and recalling Transformers (or hanging on to the objects themselves) was in some ways even more interesting than the toys per se or indeed even than the children playing with them, at least in relation to the sorts of interest being pursued here. So the present book is especially interested in *recollections* of Transformers.

Somewhere at the back of my mind I knew there was a connection between rave music, F1 and the memory of Transformers, a connection that was not going to be accessible to superficial thematizing ("it's about the body in the machine") or allegorizing ("it's about surrendering to impersonal power") but it just refused to take any sensible sort of shape for me at that time, so compartmentalized was my thinking. The appearance a decade later of the Citroën "Transformers" commercials only served to tantalize further—as the creative team behind those ads seemed to know about the connection, or at least to grasp it intuitively (as well as the likelihood that 10 years on quite a few of those young BT Labs researchers and their ilk would have families and be in the market for cars like the C4).

There is a remarkable chapter entitled "The Aesthetics of Force" in Paul Souriau's 1889 book *L'esthétique du mouvement.* There is also a relatively recent Deleuzian elaboration of this phrase (e.g., Ronald Bogue's essay "Gilles Deleuze: The Aesthetics of Force") that I want to bracket off for the time being, while picking up some original ideas from Souriau instead:

If, metaphysically, force is only the unknown cause of movement; and if, geometrically, it is measured only by the acceleration that is communicated to a given mass, in practice it is impossible for us not to picture it as effort. [. . .] The impression will be the same with an inanimate object. If I push it, I imagine it opposes me with a force of inertia, that is, an effort to cling to the ground. If I raise the object, it seems to me to be making an effort to fall. [. . .] If, finally, I witness a collision of heavy masses, if I see a body push or crush another, it will give me the idea of a conflict of forces which I will picture to myself as antagonistic efforts. [. . .] Is there not already in this notion of force, however primitive, a kind of poetry? [. . .] We have a kind of sympathy for every force in action. (Souriau and Souriau 1983, 97)

Souriau evocatively describes the difference between experiencing a substantial building and looking at a painting of it. The painting might capture or reveal all sorts of nuance, but being there in the presence of the building itself affords an often intense experience of force: "I do not picture these stones as geometrical solids, but as hard, weighty masses, piled one on top of the other; the entablature weighs down on the column which makes an effort to support it; the vault weighs down on the facings which in turn lean against flying buttresses, to resist this pressure" (98). There is, suggests Souriau, an "understanding" between these forces. The steam engine (this is the 1880s we should remember) puts this apprehension of effort in force into dynamic play and occasions what Souriau calls a "complex feeling" made up of "imagination and dizziness" (100). The apprehension of effort in this manner does not necessitate anthropomorphism. The architectural column does not have to come alive in that sense in order to make an effort to support the entablature that weighs down on it.

Can this be the basis of the kind of rapture ("complex feeling") we are trying to explain here—a poetry in the involuntary apprehension of effort in sheer (clinging, pushing, falling, crushing, speeding) force? Does the rave crowd, pressing against the music with its collective "mechanical" movement, signal effort in force? Does the corner at Eau Rouge resisting the F1 car signal effort in force? Or, even, does the Transformers toy, momentarily resisting its manipulation into another shape, have the potential to embody for the child the very apprehension of effort in force, and does this get remembered (it certainly got represented in the Michael Bay films)? Palpably the answer may be yes in all three instances and we come a good deal closer to identifying the connection as a result: a connection based on Souriau's prescient "sympathy for every force in action," though the contexts in which we are now recognizing this sympathy would have been unimaginable to him. Bianco (in the Patricia Ticineto Clough volume) describes force in much this sense as "materializing affect" (Clough 2007, 50). Souriau's "effort" is essentially an affective phenomenon—not something that exists where there is only force but something that is affectively apprehended and it is through this process that force materializes affect.

The racetrack corner, the rave crowd, the still unrealized thing that a Transformers toy is not prior to its transformation—these embody an apprehension of effort where there is force. The racing car and driver, the rave music, the thing that the Transformers toy wants to be—these all embody real effort, were designed, built, composed, constructed, performed. In all three instances a muscular effort—a "soul in the elbow"—is required to articulate one with the other, car with corner, beat with crowd, toy with transformation. Endowing whatever this real effort is directed against with "effort" of its own is where affect shows its hand. So, looking at a Transformers toy, it furnishes an image of the other thing it can be, but the manual dexterity then required to realize this other thing meets the inevitable resistance of friction, of articulated parts that move in various ways (there is a Rubik's Cube quality to this at times), of machined complexity, and thus a small but tangible force is encountered and apprehended as "effort," stored in the object and straining against the effort being put into the thing by the manipulating hands. When an F1 driver and car hit the bend at Eau Rouge on the Spa-Francorchamps circuit, all the human effort expended in getting to that point meets a force embodied by the corner itself and by its interaction at the level of physics with the small projectile being launched at it, and this is apprehended as "effort" too. When a rave crowd surged as one, it realized a physical force in response to the effort expended on music production, a force apprehensible as an impersonal, collective "effort" transcending the individual. Even the law apprehended this effort in force and found itself having to define a musical rhythm that presented a threat to public order.

It will be helpful, in terms of furthering the book's larger argument, if we return these materializations of affect to the specific contrast between weekday and weekend rhythms for the young researchers working on the VoD trials at BT Labs in the mid-1990s, while all-night raves and Sunday F1 races on television helped define many of their weekends and they were easily rendered talkative about memories of their Transformers toys from childhood (all evidence of nesting loops in action, crossing boundaries, affect looking for places to settle). The point to be made about this is that our three instances of materialized affect are precisely that—only three instances. I am not suggesting that they are the defining instances; merely that they are the three which came to my attention when I was working there, given my own specific predispositions and interests at the time.

What can we do with this? With Paul Souriau's example in mind, we can suggest, for example, that affect is there in our immediate response to a substantial piece of architecture, to its forces and moments, prior to any representational meanings that the particular building then more or less instantaneously takes on (as school, cathedral, shopping mall or office tower). There is a materialization of affect in our response to the building's forces, where we apprehend a kind of effort on the part of the building's elements in relation to each other. The further suggestion here is that this recognition of force and apprehension of effort (which together constitute what Souriau meant by the aesthetics of, and "poetic" sympathy for, force) exist in other things too, some perhaps that seem quite trivial in themselves. What becomes detectable here is the basis of a rapture—an absorption in these things—that contrasts sharply with the workaday sorts of attention—rational, fluid, meaning-seeking, communicative—that characterized the kind of workplace described in my particular example, and undoubtedly still characterize a great many today. Such rapture is far from trivial, especially when we eventually make specific the connection to masculinities.

Of course we have been holding back what is perhaps the most important point—the link with technologies, and with ways of imagining the machine. Here it becomes much easier to see the connection that links rave, F1, and Transformers: all three instances put the body into play in relation to machinery marked by the distinctive characteristics of modern technology, though not Information Technology as such, reminding us that IT is not the only kind of cutting-edge technology being imagined and realized. It is important to recognize the materializing of affect first and then the link around things "techno," secondarily; because it is in the latter that a rapid slippage into thematizing and allegorizing then occurs. ("Techno" was a catchall buzzword in the mid-1990s, extending well outside techno as one current of club music.) This takes us into the universes constructed around each instance (the "idioverses" in Schwartz's (1978) terminology), around an elaboration of histories, personalities, characters, institutions, economies, where the articulation with contemporary life is based more on meanings (on semiosis) than on affect.

The BT Labs' staffers who have been the subjects of my extended anecdote here were nothing if not preoccupied with technologies in their workaday lives. But their focus (often under pressure to perform) was on rational assessments of technology, on figuring out what things mean when people use technologies in particular ways, on bringing their own intelligences to bear on explaining technologies as deployed in specific, ring-fenced, planned ways. Indeed the VoD system on which they were working at the time was nothing if not an extremely rational system, based on carefully built tree-structures of content, precisely conceived categorizations and front-end menus that had a lean-forward effect on users who had to focus on making clear choices and "navigating" the options successfully. Combine this highly rational day-to-day work with the workplace rhythms already described and it is not difficult to see how the weekends might surrender all of this in favor of affect rather than rationality.

What these bright young men were remembering when they talked about Transformers toys were earlier moments of affect materializing in their lives through things, something that the Transformers toys were especially good for because of their unique way of deploying a particular manipulability in the hands of the child. When these young men transitioned from a night's clubbing or a rave by watching F1 they were experiencing a similar materializing of affect. We might conclude that affect typically finds its expression in just such ordinary moments of everyday life, where the rush to make meaning is considerably attenuated because the thing in which the affect is materializing does not seem worth the bother in terms of any grander interpretive ambitions: it's just a toy, it's just motor racing, it's just a bunch of flailing young people jumping around while a DJ's remix of a decade-old Cybotron track intones in a rasping mechanical accent "Oooh oooh Techno city, Hope you enjoy your stay, Welcome to Techno city, You will never want to go away" ("Techno City").

Of course this takes some degree of strategy to achieve, a seeking out of the right opportunities for the materialization of affect, and we will develop, in due course, a fuller consideration of strategy as a dimension of what is going on. It also involves a second dimension that we might now introduce as "intensity."

Charles Altieri (2003) has written the most careful and insightful account of intensity in relation to affect. He calls it a basic aspect of affective states, one that is key to "significant affective satisfactions" (186), though Altieri also notes: "For a state so enticing to modern consciousness, intensity has not elicited much theoretical discourse" (187), perhaps because, he goes on to suggest, it seems a little "naked" when isolated from its carriers. Altieri's first significant insight is that we do not have to tell ourselves that something like a sporting event is intense in order for the intensity to be there in our engagement with it—this chimes nicely with what we have been saying above about the contrast between the rational and self-reflecting on the one hand and affective engagements on the other. But Altieri's most important contribution to a theorization of intensity perhaps comes when he identifies its three component dimensions: "There are dimensions of magnitude established by the kind of elements brought together, dimensions of compression established by the forces of resistance engaged by the act, and dimensions of sharpness established by how the act comes to appear distinctive in its particularity" (187).

Magnitude, compression, and sharpness. Adapting these descriptive concepts to our present contexts, it becomes possible to see how two phenomena that were interacting—Reynolds' "magic/tragic cycle of living" and the law-provoking "succession of repetitive beats"—then got formed across those characteristics into a rhythm of life, an embodiment of what we have termed the android *imaginaire*, within which seemingly mundane moments revealed a particular materializing of affect. Magnitude: the sense of a machinic culture at large, beyond rave music, F1, Transformers. The particularity, transience or at times relative insubstantiality of these instances does not prevent that magnitude from making itself felt and, therefore, underpinning the intensity of affect available for materialization in things (rave crowd as thing, F1 car/driver/corner as thing, toy as prototypical thing in this sense). Compression: the sense that there is "soul in the elbow" occurring in all these instances, as human or humanlike effort meets force apprehended as effort. Sharpness: the very granularity of particular practices, where magnitude and compression do not interfere with being able to say "it's only dance music, it's only motor racing, it's only a toy"—it is what it is, nothing more. The intensity generated invests Souriau's "sympathy for every force in action" with its affective charge, prior to any "more" getting produced—as inevitably happens—through all the proliferating secondary elaborations that build meanings representationally via institutionalized practices, economic investments, cultural fabrications, interpretive interests, and that turn our instances into complicated cultural productions staged for consumption in elaborate ways.

Damion's Story

Supplemented with flash forwards to more contemporary occurrences, my story begins in the late 1990s. At this time, Formula One had been adopted as my favorite televised sport and I had entered a "naïve" fandom phase (the one where naïve F1 fans increase their knowledge and display their support through purchasing merchandise, devouring information derived from specialist magazines, and avidly watching races). I should note that two other sports had had a longer history in my televisual fandom (stemming back to the 1980s): New Zealand international cricket matches and cheering for the Balmain Tigers (or Wests Tigers since 2000) in the Australian rugby league competition. While both of these sports continue to provide affectively powerful moments, Formula One operated on a deeper plane of intensity for me in the years under consideration. Although I had disjointed childhood memories of cars barreling through the tunnel at Monaco or hearing various driver names such as Nelson Piquet or Nigel Mansell, it was the 1998 French Grand Prix that marked my entry into Formula One fandom.

Like many other times in 1998, I had gone to my uncle Noel's house to watch the Sunday night movie "blockbuster" on television. When the film ended, he flicked channels to catch a replay of race qualifying prior to live coverage of the French Grand Prix. Initially uninterested, I was about to bid him farewell and leave him to it. Instead, I lingered and then sat awestruck: here were these superfast cars with the drivers visibly throwing their machines through corners, catching slides, and correcting the car to stay on the tarmac. The sheer velocity was amazing, an almost incomprehensible pace that was maintained throughout the twists and turns of the track. As I continued to watch, what was even more astonishing was that all these drivers were within split seconds of each other: 19 of the 22 cars were separated by only 3 seconds. I was hooked and rushed home to view that race. After watching the next exciting televised race in Britain, I felt that I needed someone to cheer for (as has been the case with my other sports, such as Paul Sironen and Tim Brasher for the Tigers, Andrew Jones for New Zealand cricket or Steve Young for the San Francisco 49ers). Although I had already heard of Michael Schumacher, the name Jacques Villeneuve for some reason stood out. As I began to investigate, I discovered that he was the current world champion and therefore obviously talented. However, it was upon first seeing Villeneuve's image that I was sold; here was a guy with bleached blond hair, spectacles, and stubble contrasted with the impossibly clean-cut images of the other drivers (who, in F1 more than other motorsports, are groomed corporate representatives and make frequent PR appearances for their sponsors). Within a few races, Villeneuve's performances had solidified my choice with two podium finishes, while his aggressive driving style enthralled me, as he seemed to get his car more "sideways" than the others, that is, put more personality and risk into his driving.

Having fallen into the naïve fan habit of gravitating toward the champion at the time, it was over the course of 1999–2000 that my knowledge of and engagement with Formula One really increased. Aspects of Villeneuve's maverick personality, as they became apparent, began to firm up my allegiance. Here was the scruffy rebel, the macho risk-taker, the reluctant commodity, and anticorporate dissenter who apparently operated in a distinctive manner from his peers. First, his appearance was literally and visibly bereft of those corporate grooming practices. So, with messy hair often bleached an assortment of blond, pink, red, and even blue at different times, baggy rather than tight-fitting apparel, spectacles and regularly sporting a beard or excessive stubble, Villeneuve, symbolically at least, resisted the expectation of a clean, cookie-cutter image. Villeneuve the macho racer was frequently demonstrable through an on-track display of bravado, fearlessness, and aggressive driving in which he bounced furiously off the Monza track's kerbing in Italy or kicked up dust from his offtrack, unconventional and high-speed driving lines at, say, the A1 Ring in Austria. On Formula One's return to the "Brickyard" at the Indianapolis Motor Speedway in 2000, he was also the only driver to attack the famous curved banking at full throttle on his first lap. With Villeneuve I got to see a driver who had mastery over the machine (executing a 900° spin at full throttle after being clipped from behind, before then re-performing a 180° spin to continue racing at the 2000 German Grand Prix) and who had a proclivity for danger, risk-taking and brushing off big crashes, illustrated by his self-imposed annual challenge of taking Eau Rouge "flat" and the resultant wrecked cars in 1998 and 1999 that would constitute his self-proclaimed "best crashes" at the time.

Finally, although he was operating in a transnational, corporate sport which positioned Villeneuve as always already a commodity, I found his apparent reluctance and forms of resistance to sponsors' requests and their associated publicity duties and marketing expectations quite intriguing. Thus, despite its obligatory contractual status for the drivers, Villeneuve refused to perform extensive public relations duties by reducing his PR days to, for example, only 4 in 2000 (most drivers provided 30, while McLaren drivers provided over 80). Villeneuve also demanded contractual stipulations that limited his press commitments and, more broadly, resisted overt attempts to manufacture his star image in compliance with sponsor expectations or excessive forms of branding, including the refusal to endorse some products. Moreover, he was a dissenter on the prevailing norms within Formula One, regularly and publicly attacking the sport's corporate ethos, orientation, and structure, while deriding various attempts by the governing body to regulate safety or to "improve" the racing with new rules. This dissent was also directed at the broader complicity of his peers, with Villeneuve scathing about what he saw as the collective lack of nonmanufactured character among his fellow drivers, while deploring the voracious demand for young and compliantly groomed drivers from many teams.

I should note that my focus on the years 1999–2001 is also important contextually, with Villeneuve having already secured his status as

Formula One World Champion in 1997, in addition to his former glory days from American racing as the IndyCar Champion and Indy 500 winner in 1995. Villeneuve had left the British-run Williams team to join the newly formed British American Racing (BAR) team in 1999, a team funded by tobacco giant, British American Tobacco (BAT), and comprised of key bought-in motorsport figures, most notably Adrian Reynard (with some of his handpicked technical staff), who had designed chassis that were dominating the American CART series in the 1990s. Most significantly, Villeneuve's manager and friend Craig Pollock became the BAR team principal and was paying Villeneuve double his previous Williams salary. Surrounded by key allies, funded by BAT's multimillions and with Pollock by his side, this looked very much like Villeneuve's team, with the entire operation based around their champion driver. Such an individually focused organization is not commonplace in contemporary Formula One. In fact, I can only recall the restructuring and hiring of key personnel around Michael Schumacher's clear number one status at Ferrari (1996–2006) or Honda's creation of Super Aguri in 2006 so that the winless and crash-prone driver Takuma Sato could remain in F1 and keep the Japanese flag flying there. So there was some irony in Villeneuve's projection of that particular personality at a time when BAR exemplified a high-cost corporate organization focused around him. On track, though, BAR would be a source of disappointment, as despite its corporately self-proclaimed "tradition of excellence," the fragile and often slow car itself let them down and failed to yield many results, with Villeneuve accruing 39 points over five seasons, compared with his 180 points in just three seasons with the winning Williams team.

Nevertheless, Villeneuve's on-track bravado and skill remained visible, while his offtrack image arguably provided even greater allure over the 1999 and 2000 seasons. Often publicly labeled a rebel, Villeneuve's scruffy appearance led two *F1 Racing* magazine writers to proclaim that "JV is motor-racing's answer to rock'n'roll" (Clarkson 1999, 84) and that "Jacques Villeneuve remains a rebel, remains his own man, and F1 is better for it" (Bishop 2000, 46). Of course, Villeneuve's nonconformist image was also being encouraged and capitalized upon by BAR, BAT, and key sponsors as a marketing ploy to promote their "rebel" star, whose image might be even more saleable offtrack than on, especially at a time when tobacco companies were beginning to get squeezed out of sports sponsorship (BAT's tobacco brands had been advertised on F1 cars since the 1980s but this was their first purchase of their own four-wheeled billboard). Nonetheless Villeneuve *seemingly* had a freer rein in terms of his conduct and (non)compliance with sponsor expectations and obligations outside of the cockpit.

During the same period that my fandom was developing with Formula One, I returned to university to complete a Postgraduate Diploma in Leisure Studies. Much of the emphasis was on research methodologies, theoretical approaches, and mapping these ideas into the domain of leisure with a future research project in mind. Unsurprisingly, I drew on my burgeoning interest in Formula One when I contemplated applying what we were learning (not that I was considering going beyond a diploma at this stage). Two aspects captivated my attention. One was the idea of the postmodern, offering an apparent openness in research possibilities, including notions of multiplicity, difference, and the foregrounding of the researcher's own position. This was in contrast with any of my previous university studies, while the promise of ethnography, a narrative focus, even autoethnography sounded interesting, and even slightly unconventional as academic research if combined in a distinctive way. The second academic "moment" occurred during weekly sessions where a range of concepts and theorists were discussed in order to broaden our grasp of sociocultural issues relating to sport and leisure. While ideas like the civilizing process or Marx's analysis of superstructures and ideological relationships made some sense to me, they also seemed too reductive and sometimes even too "obvious" when applied to sporting examples. In class I found myself wondering whether recognizing Formula One as a transnational and corporate-dominated business meant labeling its fans as merely duped consumers and whether the civilizing process is always positive, especially given the contradictory mediated, commercialized, and global "scapes" of contemporary sport's construction.

What did focus such reveries, however, was exposure at that time to a string of work by Jean Baudrillard (1983a, 1983b, 1987, 1988, 1990a, 1990b, 1994, 1998). Although on one level his ideas about simulation and hyperreality seemed nonsensical (what do you mean that the social and reality no longer exist?), somehow they still felt relevant to Formula One's strange reality. What's more, like Villeneuve in Formula One, Baudrillard seemed to embody the "rebel." Baudrillard rattled many academic cages with both his fatalistic vision of the social as a brutally impersonal object work that exchanged nothing with the real and his repudiation of many of the key theorists and concepts then still lauded (Marx and production, Freud and desire, feminists and liberation, and Foucault and power). He had even derided sociology as redundant in the 1970s, despite being a university Professor of Sociology. I experienced an echo of the Villeneuve appeal here, with links to Villeneuve's outspoken attacks on the Formula One that owned him: in Baudrillard's case here was a professor prepared to throw rocks within and at his own ivory tower. I was attracted to this seemingly maverick quality in his work, while also naïvely assuming Baudrillard was my best way in to postmodern thinking. I too readily bought into the notion that in a depthless (i.e., postmodern) world "all that remains to be done is to play with the pieces" (Baudrillard 1984, 24), and this—along with some vague notions about hyperreality—seemed to give me an early purchase on theorizing F1.

Then there was the soundtrack to these engagements with F1, Villeneuve, academia, and Baudrillard. Despite—or perhaps because of—its often maligned status, extreme forms of metal, most prominently death and thrash have been my music of choice since before that period of my life. Of course, some of the appeal may again reside in the rebellious and out-sider status that such musicians have, with some of my favorite long-established American bands, Slayer, Suffocation, Cannibal Corpse (or more recently The Black Dahlia Murder), shunning pop-metal markets and the more commercial orientations of mainstream popular music pro-duction (e.g., major record labels) or circulation (e.g., radio/TV airplay), although commodified merchandise, branded equipment and endorse-ments remain just as salient. These musicians avoid "hits" or "catchy" mel-odies in favor of aggressive, fast, and often highly technical musical structures where particular patterns, such as the "killer riff," virtuoso gui-tar solo, vocal "death growl" or drummer's blasts or fills are the hooks for their appreciative audiences. This kind of metal also has limited popular appeal or mainstream exposure, often playing to small audiences in under-ground clubs or venues (Nile and The Black Dahlia Murder separately toured New Zealand in 2010, playing to only a few hundred people in Auckland). This contrasts with mainstream "metal" bands, such as Metal-lica who sell out large venues, although this literal "selling out" polarizes the metal community. Metallica is arguably *the* band that most readily divides metal fans, with many (including myself) disappointed that they moved away from their pioneering thrash origins in the early 1980s to a radio-friendly rock sound in the 1990s (Metallica is castigated as Sellout-ica, Metallicash, and a pop-metal band in many extreme metal circles). My fandom resonates with bands that stay "brutal," display a degree of "integ-rity" in relation to their (grass)roots, and play an uncompromising musi-cal style that, fans like me believe, mainstream audiences simply don't get and most likely never will (chances are, widely known or familiar "metal" bands are not considered metal in these extreme metal circles).

Metal's rebellious and uncompromising stance works as a double edged sword in terms of its reception, status, and appeal. For many, metal in its most extreme forms can be written off as staged aggression and mindless noise which may be supposed on occasion to promote violence, racism and sacrilegious views (see the moral panic and court cases over MTV "metal" or Slayer accused of promoting/glorifying Nazi/Aryan themes—primarily around the song "Angel of Death"—in a controversy in the United Kingdom, both in the 1980s). Like the stereotype of the beer-guzzling, couch potato television sports fan, such over-simplified assumptions require some redress though certainly not defensiveness. Like any musical form, metal operates within its own tightly defined genre which delimits and contains it on several dimensions. Frith (1996) traces five "genre rules" pertaining to musical form (instruments used and sound), the semiotic (meanings conveyed), the behavioral (performance), the social and ideological (offstage connotations and reception), and the commercial/juridical (production companies and legality). These rules play out in complex ways. Death metal's instrumentation is generally stripped of harmony and melody, a key convention for most popular musical genres, relying instead on an abrasive wall of sound and flurry of speed not shared with many other styles (I want to return to notions about technicality and high intensity beats per minute). Metal focuses on elements of the macabre, the obscene, and the occult in a manner that intentionally operates outside the mainstream commercial landscape. Imagery also reflects this orientation, with the stereotypes of black clothing, heavy tattooing, macho aggression, long or shaved hair, and grotesque band names and song titles generally holding true. So bands like Slayer, Suffocation, and Cannibal Corpse fit this image, dwelling on often reprehensible themes and non-PC politics (Cannibal Corpse arguably being the most extreme with its almost comical, cartoon-violence descriptions of bodily dissection and mutilation). There are always exceptions to the rule, such as Nile's idiosyncratic focus on Egyptian mythology or The Black Dahlia Murder not looking or acting like a death metal band despite their name, lyrics, and sound fitting the bill. While sometimes unquestionably objectionable, reducing metal to a reprehensible *message* ignores its complex construction around its own genre rules, which position it strategically as extreme for mainstream audiences, while semiotically and behaviorally deploying the grotesque, the macabre, and the offensive to achieve this ideological effect. It is also important to recognize the role of metal subgenres. Within death metal, some of the subcategories include "melodic" (rediscovering traces of melody or harmony, such as The Black Dahlia

Murder), "brutal" (explicit, gore-obsessed or antireligious content, such as Cannibal Corpse and Deicide), "technical" (comprised of intricate and complex musical structures, such as Nile) and even blurred classifications, such as Suffocation's brutal-technical-death metal. These subgenres reinforce the subtle yet distinctive means for distinguishing oneself as a fan within the broader field of metal and determine why certain images, sounds, and content "matter." It is important to have explained this background in order to communicate something of the way that this formed a soundtrack to my life even as I was discovering F1 fandom and academia at the same time. Normally these things would be held apart, represented as obviously separate, and with this separation would be lost the possibility of exploring how a specific kind of embodiment ran through them all.

The point I want to make is that Villeneuve, Baudrillard, and metal all had a certain naïve *representational* appeal for me at a certain point in my life, organized around a semiotic and social "rebelliousness" that I sensed their images had in common, though in vastly differing ways and in different social domains. A kind of general fandom managed to embrace all three in some way that I was less conscious of at the time, an attachment to that common element as well as to the particularities. But the realization that my intense engagement with metal had a nonrepresentational, a physical and—we will want to emphasize here—an *affective* dimension, poses the question of whether a nonrepresentational attachment was not also deeply at work in these attachments, in the case of F1 and metal a direct attachment to something nonrepresentational and in the case of Baudrillard an indirect attachment via an intuition that he had something accurate to say about how the object world is experienced. Metal promotes some aggressive forms of dancing—stage-diving, crowd surfing, moshing, circle pits, and so on—and, stereotypically, mainstream media coverage typically focuses on the visibly violent behavior of a few attendees while overlooking the pleasures most other participants also get from going "sick in the pit" or that not all participate in the same way: if possible, I like to jump around at the front of stage, appreciate the performances but refrain from slam dancing in the pit. Moreover, despite the often violent appearances, I do not recall personally witnessing any real physical aggression—despite jumping on one another in convincing mock aggression, people tend to help anyone up who actually falls to the ground. So "aggression" is more the manifestation within physical activity of the representational thinking that is operative throughout the larger imagery constructed around metal. Reversing our attention here allows us to see the physicality itself much more nakedly.

The "rebelliousness" becomes the explanatory superstructure for rationalizing such attachments but does not capture the intensity of the materializing of affect *in* the attachments. Dyer again provides a useful first framework, arguing that intensities in popular entertainment offer "the image of 'something better' to escape into, or something we want deeply that our day-to-day lives don't provide" (1981, 177). For Dyer, this want is very much affectively apprehended, as "what utopia would feel like rather than how it would be organized" (ibid., 177). And this involves a certain intensity. Dyer uses the term to mean the "experiencing of emotion directly, fully, unambiguously, 'authentically', without holding back" (ibid., 180). However, he is also aware that this conceptualization remains unfinished, noting,

> A little more needs to be said about "intensity". It is hard to find a word that quite gets what I mean. What I have in mind is the capacity of entertainment to present either complex or unpleasant feelings . . . in a way that makes them seem uncomplicated, direct and vivid, not "qualified" or "ambiguous" as day-to-day life makes them. (ibid., 182)

If we eschew the vocabulary of feelings and emotions which tends to fill these terms with representational content, the "direct," "vivid" and "uncomplicated" materializing of affect emerges independently to some considerable degree.

Formula One and metal materialize affect via their intensity and, at this level, both have about them the quality of a Baudrillardian object world. Both offer a wall of sound and a flurry of speed that does not need to be representationally elaborated, although of course it is: their intensity first grips people in an uncomplicated, direct, and vivid manner. Affect materializes as an intense soundscape and spectacle of speed. At a Grand Prix circuit, the high-speed racing cars confront me both at a distance (the unsighted yet pervasive shrillness of a V8/V10 engine getting closer), or in close proximity blasting past me in a blur (with the intoxicating smell of brakes and engines remaining as the cars disappear). Television mutes this sensorily but compensates by providing continuity—instead of the fragments experienced trackside—and still makes the less muted sensory aspects available for imaginary recovery. Formula One's affectivity offers intense, uncomplicated, direct, and vivid materializations. Extreme metal operates in a similar manner.

A materialization of affect occurs during the concert via the direct impact and intensity of the screaming guitars, thunderous drums, and guttural vocals. These sounds, visuals, and the flailing bodies surrounding me enliven my physical sensibilities and compel me to respond in an automated and instantaneous manner, involving movement and vocalization of my own. So, despite my body being twisted, crushed, and dehydrated, there is the compulsion to jump around in what rationally is a claustrophobic space and should be an unpleasant experience. But as with Formula One, listening to metal music I get lost in the intensity of a succession of moments. Despite being musicians, my friends and I are rendered briefly inarticulate and reduced to "wow" in the postconcert period before gradually returning to any capacity to discuss and analyze. As a drummer, I also find that the objective of accurately playing a piece of music gets entangled in the intensity moment: I "transcend" to observe my arms operating the sticks but cannot always cognitively process what is going on. Gumbrecht, evoking the grace of runners, eloquently suggests, "their bodies and legs, instead of following instructions from the brain, seemed as though they were commanded by some higher force—or perhaps by some mathematical formula" (2006, 169). My drummer friends and I have similarly discussed our experienced intensity as out-of-body moments where we watch ourselves in the flow of the music before returning to an awareness that we are actually making these sounds and need to reenter our bodies to control the sticks.

One of the key similarities F1 and metal share is the intensity carried by velocity. Both the Formula One driver and the extreme metal drummer become metronomic and seemingly mechanical in their application. The drivers need repetitively to deliver quantifiable times of astonishing precision over miles of track through uniformly tight driving lines as they continuously lap a race circuit. Likewise, drummers need to be precise and "in time" as they negotiate a given song's nuanced structure (much like the racer varying his driving tempo through chicanes, slow corners, and on fast straights). Of course, we are also talking about high tempos—Formula One, the pinnacle of open-wheel racing, exceeding speeds of 200 miles per hour on many circuits, while some death metal songs are reaching 280 beats per minute (bpm). This bears repeating, as I laughed while listening to Dan talk of "up-tempo" house music that, at even 135 bpm, pales by comparison. I used to think Slayer was the pinnacle of technical-speed with 235 bpm, but George Kollias' (Nile) current blast beats (essentially one hand snare rolls) at 280 bpm are beyond my comprehension or ability. I'm not aware of many other musical forms matching this combination of speed and technicality in terms of the complex time signatures and cymbal patterns metal drummers also incorporate; arguably, only some forms of jazz bear any similarity (an abundance of drum cam footage of Kollias, Mike Smith, Derek Roddy, or Shannon Lucas can be accessed on YouTube). This takes "soul in the elbow" to yet another level.

Of course, despite the machinelike requirement of sustaining a precise, technical, and complexly layered fast tempo while either repetitively lapping circuits or playing metal drum tracks, these two forms also support the re-instatement of representations of the human, or "personality." In Formula One, Villeneuve remains metronomic like his peers but also becomes *for me* readily identifiable through his hard-charging style, unconventional driving lines, and exceeding of the apparent boundaries of what should be contemplated in a Formula One car. The Eau Rouge challenge immediately springs to mind, with Villeneuve evidently using this particular section of the Belgian circuit to test his individual mastery over fear, racetrack, and the machine in a manner not shared by any other drivers. Despite the mechanical drumming of extreme metal, *for me* it is still desirable to recognize the signature features and styles of certain individuals among their peers: Dave Lombardo's (Slayer) thunderous use of double kicks and tom rolls, Mike Smith's (Suffocation) immense power achieved by seemingly blasting harder and louder than anyone else (he looks like a machine in that muscular body) or the insanely fast technical complexity of George Kollias (not surprisingly, he has released an instructional DVD entitled *Intense Metal Drumming*). And finally, *for me* Jean Baudrillard's "personality" had so much to do with his apparent capacity to recognize that these intensities are bound up in the recalcitrance and opacity of the object world, allowing me back then to effect the switch from experiencing those intensities to studying them.

* * *

What both these "stories" highlight is the matter of affective labor (Hardt 1999). For the BT workers, for Villeneuve as a working driver employed in F1 and for Damion as an apprentice academic contemplating doing a doctorate, there were questions about how they all felt when engaged in that labor and what solutions they found to deal with any tensions around how they felt. To focus on the representational features of those solutions may be useful in passing, but it risks missing the affective substrate to those particular representations. Music has emerged as an important lens onto this problem, including the challenge offered by the representational side of something like extreme metal, not least its construction of a masculinity. The very real tension between BT as employer and rave as leisure activity for employees also posed a challenge, in the context of

English legal moves at that time to regulate the latter. And it is unclear whether Jacques Villeneuve's "maverick" attitudes within the corporate system of F1 served the larger marketing interests of the tobacco company that built a team around him or were signs of his own affective labor struggling to find some emotional dignity in that kind of workplace. In fact the undecidability of the latter probably tells us that all such instances are going to be similarly marked; that there is likely to be some such oscillation within affective labor between the interests of a "system" and the interests of those doing the work; also that there will be different "agents" involved (tobacco company BAT was not the same kind of agent as the F1 administration, so Villeneuve as agent was not positioned in relation to one coherent "corporate" system).

As Michael Hardt points out, this is caught up in larger changes, which he and others (such as Benjamin Coriat 1994) articulated in relation to auto-manufacturing as a shift from Fordist to Toyotist models: "Toyotism is based on an inversion of the Fordist structure of communication between production and consumption" (Hardt 1999, 93). Instead of standardized production determining consumption, the consumer market communicates its wants to production for satisfaction through flexible production systems that can adapt quickly (even "just in time") to meet those wants. This, of course, is now a familiar way of thinking about postmodern production. As Hardt suggests, it puts communicative action into play in new ways and as an integral part of these processes alongside the instrumental action of production, albeit as "an impoverished notion of communication" (Hardt 1999, 94). However, as entertainment media, the culture industries and "symbolic-analytical services" (Reich quoted by Hardt, 95), represented by BT Labs and the university in our "stories," take over more and more of the economy, so the immaterial labor generated around those forms of communicative action takes on increasing significance, and Michael Hardt argues that within this the affective dimension to labor is "the binding element," while more of the economy is given over to "the creation and manipulation of affects" (ibid.). Hardt notes, "This labor is immaterial, even if it is corporeal and affective, in the sense that its products are intangible: a feeling of ease, well-being, satisfaction, excitement, passion . . ." (ibid., 96).

Chapter 3

The Scene of Autoaffection

*The scene is the Cook bar and café in the city of Hamilton, New Zealand. The second oldest building in the city, dating back to colonial times, the Cook is spacious and warmly clad with kauri wood from native trees. **DS** and **DF**, perched on broad and comfortably padded wooden stools, have spread piles of photocopies, printouts, and books across a large high wooden table by a window, a table that also becomes increasingly littered with cups and bottles.*

DF: So, we have both just written partly autobiographical "stories" relating to the interests we are exploring in this book. I guess the first question we should put to ourselves is whether that constitutes autoethnography. Or is autoethnography something else?

DS: This is an interesting question to ask. For some the autobiographical or anecdotal material would certainly be too arbitrary, personalized, and a distraction from the seemingly more significant theoretical questions that could be pursued without that kind of interruption. Indeed any form of autoethnography might be deemed a waste of time in that regard. For others, the autobiographical would not actually constitute autoethnography in any case as we don't go "deep" enough, even in terms of evocative and emotive content. In point of fact, to turn the question on its head, by even choosing autoethnography as a concept and methodological approach, aren't we simply falling into a process of academic navel gazing; that is, producing simple, autobiographical, self-indulgent, descriptive, and in the end irrelevant accounts of the self that do not constitute "proper," rigorous or valid forms of academic research?

DF: That's clearly the big risk, and the assumption that critics of autoethnography always make. But for me the key question is whether we are thinking of ourselves as preconstituted individuals, with exposure of those selves as the object of autoethnographic attention, or instead we are thinking of a set of daily practices and discourses that constitute the site of "self." If it's the latter then there is no "navel gazing" involved (though there's a bit of a Freudian slip going on here as we'll legitimately want to think some more about the body), but the question becomes how to write these sites in ways that do have rigor, if indeed "rigor" turns out to be what we want. I'm mindful, though, that you've raised the question of "depth" too. From one side, our autobiographical excursions can be accused of lacking rigor, from the other of lacking depth. Is moving away from the more recognizably autobiographical a way of then addressing either or both of these criticisms?

DS: Freudian slips aside (navel gazing or self-indulgence are common descriptions used by autoethnography's detractors for repudiating its validity), I don't think . . .

DF: I meant that anybody using that phrase in relation to autoethnography is exhibiting the same slip, as the body remains important.

DS: OK, but I don't think that the autobiographical dimension is quite so easy to move away from given its prevalence in much of the existing work of this kind. For example, it would be easy to summarize many autoethnographic works as producing an essentially autobiographical account of the self as both the *researcher* and the *researched*. Authors such as Spry insist that "in autoethnographic methods, the researcher is the epistemological and ontological nexus upon which the research process turns" (2001, 711), while many of the American authors have tended to favor a combination of looking at social and cultural factors around "personal experience" with exposing what's been called a tragic self through the autoethnographic process. So, I think addressing this material (in terms of its strengths and weaknesses), as well as clarifying our position, needs to be something that we do right here.

DF: But Susanne Gannon (2006) points out that there is a paradox in this, around the presumption that subjects can speak for themselves, which may be in doubt even when the subject is in fact the researcher. Evoking experience and exposing a sensitive or tragic self both presuppose that subjects can speak for themselves and thus express experience in some manner or open up some normally veiled, protected, private, or disguised aspect of self to expression. If, however, we start to question that presumption—on grounds that we can initially label post-structuralist—then a question immediately arises about the realist claim that is implied, that is the claim to be expressing something that preexists its expression rather than something being constructed inside the very expression, perhaps even invented there. More specifically, from this broadly post-structuralist angle, there is in fact a likely attempt at "expressing" oneself as a more coherent, unfractured, unfragmented subject than one is in theory: the potential use of autoethnography both to secure this "undeserved" coherent speaking position and, as a corollary, to effect some kind of satisfying closure on the proffered autoethnographic narrative. In short, there can be a romantic yearning to know the self despite what we know about the "self" as subject, even where this may be disguised as a strategy to know a culture via a "self." A couple of other things tend to go on too. First, there is what Susanne Gannon calls the "aversion to analytical academic writing practices" (ibid., 476) that the more simplistically "evocative" styles of autoethnography seem sometimes to be motivated by. Second, there is the feeling of self-therapy that is sometimes present— not just an exposure of the normally veiled or tragic self but an exposure directed toward some sort of palliative treatment. These features can interact, so that writing as a coherent subject takes on the palliative function of counterbalancing any theoretical recognition of the subject position's fundamental instability, and does so in a vocabulary that reflects some sort of weariness with, or seeking of respite from, the theory-heavy language necessary to express such a recognition. If there is, as it were, an alternative social self to be written about without slipping into this pattern, then autoethnography may still be one means of describing it, but it is likely to require a form of writing that is (a) non-averse to the language of theory as a necessarily troubling presence amidst the evocative, and (b) a refusal of the univocal in favor of speaking in multiple voices.

DS: To support your line of thinking to some degree, throughout my own early immersion in this field of writing I observed that, despite the multiple and diverse representational styles (e.g., Ellis and Bochner (2000) noted approximately 60 variations 10 years ago), two thematic orientations did seem most pertinent. You have intimated the first; the highly emotive, first-person accounts (often with an aversion to theory) that advocate an emphasis on deep emotion (typically vulnerability, pain, suffering, and even "breaking hearts"—in short the tragic self as we've started calling it) in order for autoethnography to be effective, with the work of Carolyn Ellis being the most obvious example. The second thematic strand explores tensions and/or contradictions in relation to the sociocultural constructions and experiences of identity, power relationships and, as you've suggested, the body. By and large, both represent a coherent "self" for analysis and draw on the knowing subject-author as the locus of study. I "confess" (a gesture I think we'll both need to address as we proceed with this conversation and with the book generally), that I like the feeling of including thick description, evocative accounts and other emotive literary devices as possible writing strategies. However, my professionally adopted preference is for more concrete contextualizations of the sociocultural dimensions that structure practices and processes of daily life, which then may allow for the integration of the social self into this field of inquiry, via the combination of limited agential capability and recognizing a fractured selfhood. So I agree with the central premise that you are setting up through Gannon, in terms of recognizing that theory "matters," especially a theoretical articulation of the broader sociocultural factors, rather than authors assuming that they have the tools and capacity to conclusively deal with (their own) subject/object relations and tensions (but I'll return to this point later if an opportunity arises). Do you have a particular position on (1) the existing research more broadly and (2) your favored orientation or approach to autoethnography and everyday life?

DF: I suspect you'll find the opportunity to come back to that other stuff. My favored orientation would have to combine characteristics (a) and (b) from my last remark, which is to say that there will be something necessarily experimental about the writing (which does not preclude the autobiographical). Actually, in due course I will want to introduce a (c) which is writing focused on something about the body, but we'll get to that. Now we have to be quite careful with the word "experiment." In one sense it might suggest a literary or artistic experimentalism for its own sake. But in a research context it is useful to remind ourselves of the obvious—that the experiment has always been a research method in some fields. Thinking of experimental autoethnographic writing as a research laboratory of a sort is quite different from thinking of autoethnography as a site of recovered subjective coherence and evocative non-theoretical language which, according to a realist paradigm, expresses some preexisting real. In terms of existing research, or really more of a gap which that research might have filled, I am very much drawn to the relationship between racing cyclist Lance Armstrong's autobiographical book and Ted Butryn and Matthew Masucci's paper "It's Not About the Book" which proposes a counternarrative to Armstrong's own. Neither of these can in isolation be characterized as autoethnographic but their interaction if juxtaposed is fascinating and does suggest something of a strategy for an experimental autoethnography that reworks the autobiographical in a space between these two kinds of telling of the same story. So that's the thing that I'm going to come back to here.

DS: I sense I am circumventing the transition you are attempting to make here to the "experimental" or to whatever might fill that gap. Nevertheless, it is also worth pointing out that one of autoethnography's features (whether it might be the "exposed self" or "context-laden self" variant) was to offer new forms of knowledge and an epistemological challenge to preexisting social scientific research methods, especially those steeped in positivist or realist traditions. In this vein, autoethnography is commonly associated with the "narrative turn" in social sciences which, Sparkes suggests, recognizes that "writing is a method of inquiry, a way of knowing, a method of discovery and analysis" (2003, 60). Hence, autoethnography is defended by its proponents as introducing an alternative voice to knowledge construction, while also undercutting the traditional criteria for either constructing or evaluating such work given its challenge to traditional ways of representing the subject/object. Such autoethnographic works reflect the dual crises of representation and legitimation in qualitative research (Denison 1996; Denzin 1997; Sparkes 1995) where notions of rigor, validity, and "proper" research are deemed problematic. The experimental that you suggest in your previous remark would, therefore, be embraced but not privileged as no one style or approach is elevated as the most useful for conducting autoethnography. Moreover, as there are no universal or even traditional criteria to evaluate such work, many of its practitioners suggest that literary aesthetics and values might be more appropriate given its (first-person) narrative orientations, in which "coherence, verisimilitude, and interest" (Sparkes 2000, 29) seem like useful enough benchmarks. So can you elaborate on this broader epistemological shift and whether those sorts of benchmark are acceptable for judging the kind of writing you seem to be advocating? **DF:** I think we have to start with the two things that we know we are not going to get out of any good autoethnography: the first is reliable self-understanding, and the second is revelation of a unitary subject. Looking to expose either or both of these is to look for a knowledgeable speaking subject—the presumed "I" in autoethnography—who constructs some kind of authority in the telling from a unified point of view. If instead we tell ourselves at the outset that we have no interest in, no confidence in, no epistemological grounds for accepting that kind of authority then immediately we have to think of autoethnography in a different way. But is it then possible to write autoethnography oneself at all and not believe in the possibility of reliable self-understanding and in the authority of one's own seemingly coherent, unified voice (autobiographical authority?) as the place where that self-understanding might find expression? Of course, this problem besets a lot of ethnographic work in general. Even if not "speaking" autoethnographically, one might be "listening" ethnographically, for example, to what some audience members are saying about their own behaviors and choices, and there really is very little reason to believe them, not because they are lying but because there are no solid grounds for their self-understanding being considered reliable, never mind what they choose to reveal to us. In this light, autoethnography might in fact be a theoretically more honest method so long as the unreliability is admitted and dealt with in some useful way. A shorter way of expressing this is to ask, is it possible to write autoethnography as a knowingly unreliable narrator, which suggests some criteria other than nineteenth-century "novelistic" coherence, verisimilitude, and interest but criteria that more experimental literary practices have in fact already investigated? So while you are right that, by and large, no one style or approach is privileged as the most accurate for conducting autoethnography, what I've characterized as nonetheless a "traditional" impulse here is the viewing of all these alternatives as having legitimate claims to reliability; whereas I'm interested in foregrounding the unreliable narrator because of the argument that unreliability is not just inevitable but proper, in the sense of being theoretically mandated.

DS: Well, although positivists and realist researchers will of course refute any such assertion, isn't this the central epistemological issue (and an ontological issue to some extent) that shapes all social research? Are we not merely returning to a question here of academic authority and legitimacy, where some academics hide themselves within their preferred methods and/or theories but still "spout wise" on the social world, or pass off their opinions and interpretations as somehow theoretically mandated facts? Perhaps I may be asking for unachievable clarification at this point, but I thought that there were some key ideas floating around when you talked about Susanne Gannon's paper earlier, a paper that we both evidently like. The first one was about the multivoiced scholar—although not wanting to reimpose strict methodological boundaries on autoethnography, I can see how this could slip into inconsistent, even incoherent and unstructured rambles that might distract from rather than illuminate the research topic, at least if not contained in some way that isn't quite clear to me in what you suggest. I agree that the notion of the "knowing subject" is indeed tricky since, despite whatever deserved or undeserved collective wisdom and confidence we academics have acquired, clearly aspects of "our" social reality antedate both subjective understanding (language, visual cues and codes, stratifications/frameworks of identity) and indeed our personal existence (structured forces of history, culture, economics, and relations of power). The second seems to be the notion that expression may only construct or invent itself within the actual "moment" of expression. Is that what you're really suggesting?

DF: I want to quote Laura Jewett who says,

> The pedagogical desire of autoethnography . . . might be seen as an example of play in which the exaggeration of the everyday, embodied, joint action of its coupled modes of representation (autobiography and ethnography) contains the capacity to hint at "different experiential frames, 'elsewheres' which are here" (Thrift 1997, 150). This sort of play is the un/real: the fictional work of autoethnography's double desire. (Jewett 2008, 68)

Now play can clearly be thought of in terms of your "trivial, unstructured rambles" and ignored or dismissed as such but it is not too difficult to see, not only that some very interesting things go on in play, but that the concept of "play" might provide the container you're looking for, the boundary within which moments of expression happen. Without being too literal about it, we can recall how children often adopt multiple voices in play, slip across different experiential frames, and so on. Once "unreliable" becomes "playful" we have something to look at that is less slippery, and Laura Jewett has already suggested here that exaggeration is one aspect of this playfulness, in particular the exaggeration of something in autobiography and in ethnography when they are coupled in this way, an exaggeration that ultimately has something of the fictional about it in the sense of representing an un/real or "elsewheres" or an as-ifness (including your things that antedate us) within the everyday, the here and now, as play does. Autoethnography's desire for both autobiography and ethnography has the potential to spawn this elsewhere, or to produce *semblances* as Nigel Thrift calls them. And Jewett's emphasis on the pedagogical is important, as we know that academics "spouting wise" as you so colorfully put it (I always worry that you've been sitting in at the back of my lectures) is not what pedagogy is about, although the former is often passed off as the latter. So there is an epistemological, and as you say perhaps also an ontological, stance in play thus conceived. What it particularly means for us, in this "here," which is to say this book as context for a conversation, is the need to ask whether autoethnographic writing can be a thing, an object, in which affect materializes, since we are beginning to suggest that such materializations are vital to play. Moreover, we may want to conceive of such writing as a writing "machine," which is perhaps one way of thinking about what a whole book is in effect and how it relates to the other machines we are interested in.

DS: Do we have a primary site of inquiry for us to focus this writing machine on?

DF: And is that site outside or inside what we are up to here? One of the things our book is about is fandom, albeit with an acknowledgment that everybody can be a fan one way or another. When academics in our field—media and cultural studies—write about fandom from the inside, that is as fans of something themselves, the "something" is always in the field of popular culture and never in the academic field itself. And yet it strikes me that so many academics come across as fans of this or that major theorist—that European continental high theory in particular has been culturally constructed as itself a site of, or medium for, fan-type relationships and attachments that are deeply felt and yet go largely unacknowledged as such. The dense theoretical justifications for—the insider knowledge justifying—attachment to this or that theoretical star comes across on occasion as not unlike the arcane knowledge that the nonacademic fan has about his or her attachments. Could it be possible, one wonders, that media and cultural studies as a field has actually constructed itself, in some measure, around fandom by replicating fan-type behaviors within academic discourse itself? Matt Hills talks about the "discursive mantra" that fans of a particular television series, "event" film, comic book, or whatever typically display when pressed about why they are so attached to it—a common, recognizable, repeated set of justificatory statements. Haven't we all, as academics, sat at conferences and in seminar rooms and heard such "mantras" when somebody wheels on their favorite theorist? And you just know that they've consumed all the relevant material (the book as object where fan affect materializes) so you're never going to best them by going head-to-head over insider knowledge, even if you wanted to. Doing your doctorate, you have described your attachment to Baudrillard in quite rational terms to do with his maverick status in your eyes at the time, but do you think this played out for a while as a replication of deep fan-type attachments, in the guise of becoming an "expert?"

DS: It is interesting that you make this connection, as apprentice academics and the scholars they become, despite whatever distanciation, guise of objectivity, or vocational defense they will produce ("it's just my job"), clearly gravitate to theorists for a range of reasons, while castigating others. And, as you say, they also demonstrate not only a cultural literacy in their complex and intricate knowledge of a specific theorist's work but sometimes seem to be operating on a deeper plane of affective attachment to or with a deeper investment in their particular theorist(s).

Matt Hills has talked about this, while Alan McKee's term "theory fans" (2007) is useful for considering the pleasure that integrating these theories and theorists in everyday lives evidently gives certain academics (self-titling, collecting, attending like-minded conferences) which McKee asserts is an active, emotional, and passionate reading (and reworking) of these fan-type characteristics in their daily practices as scholars. There is also a celebrity connection that sometimes becomes pronounced, with star-theorists garnering attention and the adulation of others, such as the scholar of film stars/celebrity, Richard Dyer, being himself treated as a star performing for his "fans" at academic conferences, replete with standing ovations (Holmes and Redmond 2006). Of course, I am very much an early career academic trying to get my foot in the door, but my everyday working activities over the past 5 years have allowed me to recognize in a short period of time the theorists that other academics in my field gravitate to and who they reject (quite often if I mentioned Baudrillard many would give me the rolled eyes or a throwaway comment about the futility of theoretical postmodernism in that vein and I even recall being told by another doctoral candidate that she had been pulled aside and advised never to read that "French wacko"). What is intriguing is that you also come to associate some scholars' writings with their "pet" theorists and know that within a few pages, his or her theorist's name and concepts will permeate the entire text, no matter what the topic. This is not a slight on those scholars, as often their theorist has convinced them of a particular theoretical tool for prizing apart and investigating a sociocultural phenomenon. I may be going offtrack here, but this is arguably part of my interest in Baudrillard. Despite at times offering insightful explanations of the contemporary mediated landscape (even though contemplating some of these things nearly 40 years ago as he was), at other times he is engaging in absurd diatribes that frustrate the apprentice scholar looking to glean just the right quotation to resolve some conceptual and rhetorical conundrum in their own writing. So, yes the "rebel" element was always part of the initial intrigue, as well as Baudrillard having something useful to say but not always in a straightforward or expected way (and, as we suggested in the previous chapter, with a resultant "rattling of cages"). But we've shifted Baudrillard into an odd position in this book, by imagining him on the other side of a table from Bourdieu, Barthes, and Lefebvre as we said in the Foreword. I'm not yet sure exactly what that imagined scene is doing to my early Baudrillard fandom, if that's what it was, but it certainly shifts the ground.

DF: It seems to me that "theory fandom" is precisely the sort of thing that an experimental autoethnographic writing might very usefully explore, although perhaps I don't mean "explore" so much as be aware of in its own construction as writing.

DS: Can you elaborate, in terms of your "theory fandom" and if you see any of the theory fan in your own work?

DF: Well, I'm not sure that I do want to elaborate too much because what I am suggesting is that experimental autoethnographic writing might be the best place to explore theory fandom (for the concept itself you're right to be referring specifically to Alan McKee's essay), rather than doing it within a discussion of method. The reason for this is that there is going to be an inevitable slippage, here, toward then explaining or justifying one's theory fandom, as you've just demonstrated a little, which is perfectly acceptable of course but may become a distraction from the methodological discussion. What the latter needs is perhaps just an acknowledgment that theory fandom exists and that autoethnography might be able to expose this further because it is probably more important than we like to admit. But you are about to accuse me of sidestepping the question so, yes, I have long been in thrall to Walter Benjamin. I think Alan McKee has given us the test for this—it's whether one uses the books by these thinkers as favorite bedtime reading. I don't much anymore. But our book, for me, is one half of a current project derived from Benjamin, and I mean the form of the book just as much as its content, something that I "owe" in some sense to Benjamin theory fandom. And Benjamin stands outside the room in which we've put our French theorists, although I'm not sure quite why I'm remarking on that.

DS: McKee's test is not entirely reliable then, and certainly bedtime theory reading has never been my hobby. You are right, we risk going off-track by foregrounding theory fandom but I take the point that our writing might remain usefully self-conscious in this regard; recognizing that it could be a useful site for autoethnographic reflexiveness. Outside and inside get very confused here don't they?

DF: Absolutely. That's an excellent way of expressing it and it also raises the question of turning inside out to reveal something. In cultural ethnographies where the unreliability of the insider-narrator is recognized, the task for the ethnographer entering from the "outside" becomes one of gradually and progressively peeling back the layers of unreliable "self-understanding," the "discursive mantras," the concealments (perhaps for fear of embarrassment), in order to reach a point of explanation, like discovering how an elaborate magic trick was done despite the magician's many misdirections. The ethnographic scholar-fan is then a bit like the magician who gives away the secrets of the Magic Circle (in fact, London's Magic Circle has as its motto *indocilis privata loqui* or "not apt to disclose secrets"). This installs the idea of disclosure, almost as a generic convention, at the very core of much ethnography. Autoethnography then hosts the same convention, but perhaps more damagingly, in the sense that there is an expectation of disclosure, whether consciously (reliable self-revelation) or fortuitously (the unreliable narrator who slips up and gives something away). Writing about your F1 fandom (I see you're wearing an F1 shirt today), have you ever felt under pressure to "disclose" something, to give something away?

DS: I can recall two apparently "obvious" explanatory frameworks that I had to consider. The first I chose to address as a means of developing a broader discussion of masculinity and mediated gender relations in my thesis: that is, consideration of whether the homoerotic informed my viewing and fan practices. I was resistant and, if truth be told, extremely annoyed that other, older scholars of both sexes were convinced that there was a "deep" reading that (to them) obviously explained my apparent attraction to Jacques Villeneuve. In fact, informal discussions with my friends (was that ethnography?) ultimately convinced me of the sheer banality of these academic "deep" readings using outdated modes of theorization—*all* of my male friends were accustomed to having *always* formed fanlike attachments to male sport, music and film stars in the course of media saturated upbringings—but not reductively explicable as submerged fantasies of "sniffing jockstraps," as one especially uninsightful scholar has encapsulated the male sport fan/star relationship. I like the image of the magician revealing the rabbit in the hat, because homoeroticism was the rabbit I was expected to "reveal." That's how it was all to get turned inside out. However, I argue against there being an "inside" in this way, that the combination of Formula One's mediated conventions, technologies, garb, absent-present representation and the fragmented, concealed, and commodified sporting body (the things I explain in my thesis) all militate against homoerotic identification as a secret to be revealed. The second disclosure has links to the first. Back in 2001, I did a graduate presentation on my upcoming Villeneuve-focused doctoral project and was asked if this was about the homoerotic. I suggested that the relationship was probably more to do with an absent father (who died when I was young) and that there was an identificatory attachment to Villeneuve going on around this, although I also pointed out that this was about constructions of masculinity and how various male celebrity figures probably fed into my personal embodiment of "being a man." This subdued any further questions about homoeroticism on the day, but throughout my thesis writing I became increasingly unconvinced that this really was *the* correct explanation. Of greater concern, I sensed that readings of Villeneuve as an absent father figure or the idea that Villeneuve (who also lost his father when young) was my identificatory figure for living without a father would come back to haunt my work (apart from anything else, in mundane personal terms this inappropriately marginalized my stepfather's pastoral role in my upbringing). So, submerged, deeper, in fact *psychoanalytical* readings were seemingly required and would unlock for examination my preconstituted selfhood while reducing my fandom to phases, transitions, and complexes. I'm thinking though, that a middle-aged academic with no children who writes about toys may not be unfamiliar with these pressures?

DF: Right. This brings us to a crucially important point about the normative oedipal narrativization of subjective identity and the tenacity of its hold on how we tend to think about "depth" or "disclosure" in autoethnographic as well as autobiographical writing, and also about narrative closure. The closure that is culturally mandated as a consequence of this interest in disclosure is deeply tied in to the continuing hold that oedipal narrativization has on our ways of thinking about identity. So attachments of the kind that we are interested in in this book can be explained as failures or ruptures in the oedipal narrativization to which our "stories" should be subject. Disclosing that your interest in Villeneuve derives from your early loss of your father (as Jacques lost his), or that my interest in toys derives from my being childless, is to suggest that our subjective identities are marked by those failures of, or interruptions to, the "deep" oedipal story in our lives, which should have been structuring our identities differently, and that we are (regressively?) compensating for gaps in that structure. Disclosing this autoethnographically offers a confessional, conventional, and reassuring narrative payoff, a satisfying little tragedy. Now, and it is very important to register this, those autobiographical facts are indeed important, but for a different reason. They help explain why we have noticed certain things, why we paid some attention to these things and not to others, why we are so curious about them. But the step from curiosity to accepting a psychoanalytically informed "explanation" of that curiosity is a huge one, as it recuperates that curiosity within a normative framework, reinstated by a palliative disclosure. That step back needs to be resisted because it binds autoethnography back into an endlessly repeated story, a cultural narrative the dominance of which needs to be queried not reinforced yet again. So in this light autoethnography becomes a crucial site—and there are relatively few such sites available to us—for such querying. We are both "odd" (fatherless or childless) in relation to the normative oedipal narrativization of subjective identity but, instead of disclosing this as an answer, a solution, an explanation of the clues, and having our curiosity recuperated by that explanation, we want to deploy this "oddness" strategically in order to query the normative explanations. Of course we know full well that the cowriting of this book, and the particular manner of its writing, can be tied to that normative explanation too (the book and the academic relationship remediating that fatherless/childless dynamic in yet another context) but again, we'll want to argue, this is not an insightful disclosure—in fact it is a profoundly banal observation because it fails to note that we are leveraging our recognition of that disclosure's appeal in an entirely strategic way here. Sometimes, I find myself imagining an autoethnographic "machine" that is like a Big Brother set, with multiple cameras, but it is oneself that's being watched and the "cameras" are one's own writing. I wonder if autoethnography can be pursued as itself a fatal strategy, a seeming effort to "restore" the subject but knowing that what one is doing is pushing toward a breaking point instead? Derrida used a term—"autoaffection"—to describe this attachment to the subject, this voicing or staging of the subject's experience as one's own, even in the face of theoretical deconstruction of the subject. Any display of autoaffection (and we'll have plenty of them in this book) then has to be done perhaps as either a banal or a fatal strategy, which raises the question of how to distinguish one strategy from the other. Patricia Ticineto Clough has said,

> The autobiographical revision of ethnography and of the social sciences has seemed both a symptom and a dull or slow response to teletechnology. It is a symptom in that it is a performative practice engaging the vulnerability of exposure to media event-ness; its melodramatic focus on the personal, especially the tragic, is televisual. But it is slow precisely because it repeats too closely levels and kinds of exposures common to television without much interfering with them or redirecting them. (2000, 16)

So is there a fatal strategy of autoethnography that is not simply autobiographical ethnography, that pushes past the "tragic" personal and interferes with or redirects the televisual kind of exposure? Autoethnography that is not just unreflexively like the video diaries in a reality TV show but where any added reflexiveness is not just a reinstatement in a different voice of an authoritative self-knowing? You've staged this dilemma nicely for us around the questions of the homoerotic and the identificatory. To what extent are we meant to trust you or your friends on those matters?

DS: Well, that is the question, and to re-approach that question from a different direction I want to go back to Susanne Gannon's paper again and to suggest the outlines of a theoretical—and itself autoethnographical—perspective on autoethnography, clearing the ground as it were for your question.

DF: This sounds like there's a lecture coming and a long one at that. I'm ordering more coffee.

DS: You do that. Meanwhile (as I shift into lecturing voice), it's worth my repeating that one of autoethnography's central tenets conceives of blending the personal with the cultural, placing the self within a social context as a writing strategy. For many, this does constitute an emphasis on the autobiographical and exposure of a supposedly "tragic" self which, at its most personalized, follows the example of Carolyn Ellis (2004, 2007), dealing with intimacy, introspection, and emotions in a highly evocative way. These assumptions about a tragic self that can be (1) written about evocatively in a still coherent manner and (2) "healed" through exposure, confession, or revelation are challenged by post-structuralism as Susanne Gannon demonstrates. Also, as I said earlier, a second more "context-laden" approach, while possibly still reliant on some core emotive and evocative content, seeks to provide a wider sociocultural context for exploring the self through fluid and interchangeable formats such as personal narratives, diary-type accounts, ethnographic fiction (again the point is that numerous variants of autoethnography now abound). In this vein, some useful examples draw on the teaching and daily life of an academic (Holt 2001; Pelias 2003), of the postdoctorate experience (Humphreys 2005) or, most especially, sport-related case studies (Markula 1998 and 2003; Pringle 2001 and 2003; Sparkes 1996; Tsang 2000) which discuss the intersection of the evocatively described "subjective self" in sociocultural spaces with practices, identities, embodiments or dynamics of power. As a generalization, these forms tend to develop and make more prominent the sociocultural contexts and aspects of daily life over and above any introspectively evocative content, rather than concentrating on the emotional "depth" and intimate details of a personal life (while recognizing varying degrees of connection between the social and the personal) . . .

ASM: (*prompting*) Picking up what we were talking about . . .

DS: Picking up what we were talking about earlier around distrust of traditional forms of knowledge making, and reflecting the orientation of most qualitative researchers, autoethnographic proponents start with the idea that "facts" are value laden and heavily dependent on the judgment, perceptions, and interpretations of the researcher, as well as on an awareness and understanding of the social conditions behind their formation. Hence, a broader methodological approach that allows for divergence in knowledge construction, interpretation, and representation is championed as a means to recognize, explore and convey the multiple realities, meanings, and subjectivities (including that of the researcher) that permeate the social world. The apparent paradox that emerges between a championing of multiplicity and a reliance on a singular realist vision of researcher subjectivity that writes the autoethnography is often the result of mis-conceptualizing what is being done, but we can come back to that point. So we might want to say that autoethnography constitutes part of a broader postmodern challenge to research methods and paradigms. Research done within a postmodern mode of thought is arguably governed by a philosophical position of doubt, refuting the notion that there is a correct method as well as disavowing the privileging of any particular viewpoints (Bruce and Greendorfer 1994; Rail 2002; Richardson 2000). Of course, evocations of the postmodern are often ambiguous these days. As Lyon asks, "is postmodernity an idea, a cultural experience, a social condition or perhaps a combination of all three?" (1994, 4). So, while many proponents of autoethnography will evoke the assumptions of a postmodern moment to secure their positions, the mapping of this onto the details of research and writing practices is often more tantalizingly difficult to trace and appears to have assumed considerable latitude.

DF: Latitude?

DS: Indeed. Commenting on autoethnography's diverse forms of reflexivity and voice, Wall observes that "there is considerable latitude with respect to how autoethnography is conducted and what product results. Autoethnographers tend to vary in their emphasis on *auto-* (self), *-ethno-* (the cultural link), and *-graphy* (the application of a research process)" (2006, 6; see also Ellis and Bochner 2000; Reed-Danahay 1997). Although these differences can be used by proponents to legitimize an array of approaches, these three distinctions are not arbitrary. So work such as

Sparkes (1996 and 2000) incorporates all three aspects by including personalized, emotive narratives, the broader social contexts of elite sport, an academic career, daily life, embodied pain and Sparkes' sense of inhabiting a "flawed body." Moreover, his own research process is interrogated to determine how to write his "story," whether autoethnography is an appropriate representational method and the potential problems for publishing and acceptance in academia.

DF: Of course we benefit from people like Andrew Sparkes having already won some real legitimacy for autoethnography. So today's doctoral students aren't going out on quite such a shaky limb as they once were if they go in this direction . . .

DS: (*digging into the pile of papers on the table*) That's why Wall's autoethnography of learning about autoethnography (2006) is very interesting. As a doctoral student, what she writes about chimes with much of my own pre- and early career experience. In fact, reading her article invoked memories of the various early writings I did where my "naïve" academic period was marked by an almost celebratory undercurrent around this methodological approach, supplemented by an equally dogged, almost apologetic exposition of its legitimacy and applicability. I wanted it but I still felt I had to justify it.

DF: Are we doing the same here I wonder?

DS: Well, maybe that moment has to keep repeating itself after all. Sarah Wall captures it vividly:

> Quite unexpectedly, my curiosity turned into a foray into postmodern philosophy and critical theory, reflexivity and voice, various vague approaches to autobiographical inquiry, validity and acceptability, defenses and criticisms, and a wide range of published personal narratives, the typical product of autoethnography. I was confronted, challenged, moved, and changed by what I learned. (2006, 2)

A lot of the stuff we've got on the table here that we're grabbing and talking about is marked by the traces of the same kind of foray. Like Sarah Wall, my initial feeling was that autoethnography furnished something worth pursuing, tempered with an awareness that its methodology and styles of representation might always be mired in a struggle for legitimacy and acceptance. Sarah Wall and I (we've never met) both sensed that there were problems with the expressly autobiographical works that can be criticized as "self-indulgent, narcissistic, introspective and individualized" (ibid., 8), although my naïve academic phase was more willing to embrace such an approach for capturing my own fandom, an objective that seemed particularly well matched. It was my later work that would move away from such an explicitly subjective orientation to a wider recognition and contextualization of my limited agential capacity within broader social, mediated, and commercial structures, such as those of Formula One as a cultural phenomenon. Sarah Wall says "how the self is used is important" (ibid., 10). She concludes, "I see autoethnography as a research method that is part of, but delineated from, the broader realm of autobiography. By conceptualizing it this way, we can use self in a methodologically rigorous way, but personal stories can coexist with autoethnographic research," while advocating "principled, disciplined choices" (ibid., 11) in how such connections are developed.

DF: I immediately warm to the notion that it's really all about *how* connections are made. Let's not lose that thought.

DS: OK. As I've said, like Sarah Wall I have a preference for connections that trace broader sociocultural dynamics. In turn these can be fed into and will recontextualize the autobiographical style. I find the claims of many of the more purely autobiographical accounts difficult to substantiate. Two key authors, Ellis and Bochner suggest that "back and forth autoethnographers gaze, . . . focusing outward on social and cultural aspects of their personal experience; then, they look inward, exposing a vulnerable self that is moved by and may move through, refract, and resist cultural interpretations" (2000, 739). In principal some of these claims have validity but as I've suggested with my earlier account of the "tragic" self that I ended up repudiating as a trope, there is a style of narrative writing here that is less likely to make the broader social connections or theorize their importance because it so actively *favors* the inward gaze. Such accounts tend to privilege literary techniques and devices that elicit empathic reader responses over the establishment of contextual frames. The word "resist," as used by Ellis and Bochner in the passage I've just quoted, suggests another move being effected too: such accounts being used to position the subject as an active agent resisting dominant cultural forces through the manner of an emotionally narrativized occupancy of his or her social position. As such, the promise of personal empowerment derived from many autobiographies becomes a dubious trait in appropriations of the form for the purpose of autoethnography.

DF: (*leaning sideways as more coffee gets delivered, and slightly distracted by what appears to be the smell of the waitstaff's hair as it wafts by his face*) So that becomes the point of the autoethnographic story? Are you suggesting that this also leads to other things getting left out?

DS: Right, because they may disrupt the particular representation of self being narratively constructed, there is always self-editing going on. It's obvious it has to happen but the question is why it happens in a particular way, and then what the particular consequences are. So, for example, daily chores or minutiae of daily life that don't contribute to the narrative, the selectivity involved in how to frame a particular issue in a PC world where one doesn't want to be too unguarded about uncensored everyday thoughts, seeking to elicit certain responses from readers or not to position the author too unfavorably: these all coalesce around the representational style used and what gets disclosed. But you seem to be tuning out, if you don't mind my saying so?

DF: Not at all. You said earlier that there was stuff you wanted to come back to.

DS: Yes, it's this quotation from Susanne Gannon—I've marked it with a yellow highlighter. We have to look at it to see the use of brackets in the punctuation. She says, "although autoethnographic research seems to assume that the subjects can speak (for) themselves, post-structural theories disrupt this presumption and stress the (im)possibilities of writing the self from a fractured and fragmented subject position" (2006, 475). So, while the inclusion of embodiment, memories, thoughts, and feelings is not untypical as subject matter for autoethnography, what starts to matter is whether these things are made to coalesce or allowed to fracture. Or used to "destabilize the authority of the self who writes and knows himself or herself as a discrete and autonomous subject" (ibid., 477). I'm going to keep on reading this:

> In these texts, although personal stories are still privileged and the body and memory are sources of knowledge, theoretical texts thread through autoethnographic texts and author-ize different writing technologies. We do not abandon theoretical or critical frames in pursuing evocative provocative effects in the texts we write. Rather, genres and speaking positions proliferate. Texts foreground the dialogic relationship between the self and his or her tenuous and particular social/cultural/historical locations. (ibid., 477)

DF: As Susanne Gannon's has become another voice at this table, I think we need to acknowledge her more recent work, like the fascinating collaborative writing project *Doing Collective Biography: Investigating the Production of Subjectivity* (Davies and Gannon 2006).

DS: Have you read it yet, because I'm afraid I haven't managed to?

DF: No.

DS: All right then.

DF: But it really sounds like we should.

DS: Especially if the orientation is toward theorizing the self as a temporal and disjointed project perpetually under construction, emphasizing the disjunctures to "eschew seamless linear stories of coming to 'know' our hidden selves" (Gannon 2006, 480).

DF: Absolutely. I'm feeling really guilty now that I haven't read that new book. We should read it and then edit this section out of the conversation before publication.

DS: OK, but just to sum up what I've been saying: life is disjointed and fragmented, made up of eclectic memories, embodied spaces, ever-changing, complex, and contradictory images of a self (particular temporal/spatial "snapshots") intersected by formations of varying subjectivities that are contextually and discursively framed (through lived experiences, our interrelations with others in specific social frameworks, and familiar genres) but never cohesively comprehended. Avoiding an overemphasis on the "feelings" that have stymied some of the preexisting work, a reorientation to the context-laden autoethnographic approach is what I'm proposing, but with a post-structuralist sensibility thrown into the mix.

DF: In place of feelings in that sense we have the affective though, don't we?

DS: Our project is interested in the materializing of affect in things, with autoethnography furnishing the textures, the color, the moods, of specific sites of materialization (machines, toys, F1, mediated/commercialized masculine cultures) and specific people (boys, men, the authors).

DF: So what seems to emerge for us here is a step beyond the simple juxtaposition of the expressively personal and the more deliberately context-laden autoethnographic voices (tending to look inwards and outwards, respectively, from the autoethnographically inhabited position) to a post-structuralist autoethnography that recognizes the auto-ethnographic "voice" as only the temporary, situated sound of subjectivity in process, in flux and engaged in attempted self-representation but momentarily freeze-framed where it inhabits a particular position? The initial juxtaposition maps itself onto the distinction between reflexively observing one's own experience—the subjectivist orientation—and reflexively observing or analytically reporting the context in which one is having an experience, where one is perhaps a representative self in some sense (where context may mean group or setting or institutional circumstances, for example, but also bigger stuff). This distinction between two kinds of reflexive observation has been very hard to maintain in a good deal of actual autoethnographic writing, where a sliding to and fro tends to happen between self as autonomous/expressive and self as representative/observational. The third view, where post-structuralism queries the stability of either speaking position, promises to transcend these options by destabilizing the subject positions implied in both and recasting the autoethnographic "voice" as necessarily an act of contrived self-representation.

DS: Is it going to be this straightforward in a sense? Is that really a third and better methodological place to be?

DF: Well, it's not necessarily as new a place as it seems. Context-laden autoethnography, as we want to call it here, is often really a version of symbolic interactionist ethnography (with its particular interest in doing micro-level sociology), where the observer is very much a well-integrated insider and self-consciously observes and reports from that point of view while maintaining the dual personality of participant and researcher. The "auto" here just exposes rather more of what actually goes on in maintaining the dual personality, so that, for example, the influence of the researcher's emotions (let us say in a hospital as research setting) might be introspectively detected and their influence admitted rather more clearly than is otherwise feasible. This seems like a good thing. But of course one might suggest that, in its most carefully delimited and executed forms, what we have here is better thought of as reflexive symbolic interactionist ethnography rather than autoethnography per se, so careful is it to ring-fence and contain the "auto," to maintain a disciplined analytic observational stance and not let too much of the subjective erupt onto the scene. At the very least, this is the respectable face of autoethnography, holding back the subjective density that interests the more expressive or idiographic form. What is suspected of being lost, of course, should this holding back fail, is the analytical interest in explanatory generalizations which would get swamped by nongeneralizable detail. If writing autoethnographically about illness, for example, what is to be gained by admitting that sort of detail? Well, the problem is, as soon as one asks the question in this way it becomes not too difficult to start thinking of reasons why that sort of detail actually would be of real interest. Suddenly the tables can get reversed in favor of the more idiographic form, precisely because we might suspect that this is always what tends to get repressed by institutional knowledges (such as medicine or health policy) and so as social researchers we should not be replicating that kind of repression, or at least not doing so unthinkingly. The very sensible form of reflexive symbolic interactionist ethnography that calls itself auto-ethnography suddenly looks like it might still be insufficiently open to the often marginalized, ignored or silenced voices with all their insistent particularity. More broadly, this interest in the writings of the silenced voice has informed some excellent work from postcolonial contexts, migrant groups, ethnic minorities, and so on. Now we lack that immediate sense of respectability here, of course, as we are only writing about fast cars and toys after all. But what we might share is a critical intention.

DS: And by idiographic you mean the specific, the idiosyncratic, the local . . .?

DF: Yes, our narrow choice of fast cars and toys here definitely reflects a rather stubbornly idiographic focus. A nomothetic approach on the other hand couldn't conceive of how so narrow a focus might ever add up to anything more.

DS: But you're suggesting that there's a particular critical intention which somehow deals with that worry? Is this a way of challenging the assumption that the idiographic can't encroach on the nomothetic's claim to generalizable validity, that the idiographic can only document the particular element whereas the nomothetic deals with the larger set?

DF: I'm going to call it a nonrepresentational critical intention, which I'll explain in a moment, although we're going to need our book as a whole to work it out. Even before the jump to a post-structuralist autoethnography, it's important to note that by no means all autoethnography of the two preceding types has any critical intention, or certainly not as the dominant factor. Reflexive symbolic interactionist ethnography intends, typically, to be as descriptively and analytically accurate as possible. Idiographic autoethnography, typically, intends to be as thickly expressive as possible. There would be critical versions of both of these, where critical interrogation of the context-laden nature of the moment or of the personally experienced nature of the moment would be the dominant factor, except that this shift to a critical perspective tends to be concomitant with the move to a post-structuralist perspective in the sense that the latter includes a critical interrogation of the autoethnographic impulse itself, especially the stability of its speaking positions, thus "completing" the reflexivity. And what this critical post-structuralist autoethnographic perspective brings with it is not just a recognition that the autoethnographic subject has far too often been essentialized, has rendered itself as too static and fixed in the interests of some implicit claim to authenticity, whether this is being staged as an authentically personal voice, as authentically representative of a group or community, or as authentically "native" in the sense of being a previous object of ethnographic interest now discovering its own reflexive voice (and that it can study itself, thank you very much). The critical post-structuralist autoethnographic perspective also wants to tell us that there are operative forces at work in that fixing, that rendering static, which have to be exposed and identified; this is what it means to be critical. Yet here comes a further twist. It comes when one begins to think about the possibility of one's criticism being an accomplice of the object it is directed toward.

DS: Shades of Baudrillard I think . . .

DF: To some extent, yes, but there are various ways in which such complicity might manifest itself, and we should be especially interested in one in particular. This relates to what Mark Hansen has called the "fetishization of representation" (2000, 139), and we need to acknowledge that Hansen's work has been very influential on what we are doing here. What the word "criticism" means in this context is entirely bound up with the overwhelming dominance of representationalist thinking. We need to be very clear about this for three reasons: first, representationalist thinking still largely characterizes the post-structuralist turn in autoethnography, so in this sense it may not be such a radical alternative after all to the preceding forms of autoethnography; second, if our particular autoethnographic interest is in technologically informed things (machines, gadgets, toys, etc.) then Hansen's critique of representationalist thinking is especially important, because he links the latter to certain key failures in our conceptual grasp of technologies; third, if we want to write autoethnographically in or with these pages we have to ask ourselves to what extent our writing can and should be freed from representationalist thinking. Is there a critical form of autoethnography that is less bound to representationalist thinking, or turns it inside out, at the same time retains the "post-structuralist" destabilizing of subject positions, and is context-laden but still allows something otherwise unspoken to reemerge? The problem, of course, is that we cannot simply point to examples because they seem not to exist yet, at least not in any formats appropriate to the present purpose.

DS: You're reaching for Lance Armstrong's autobiography. I wondered when we were going to come back to that.

DF: What we might do is construct an example where two existing forms of writing can be juxtaposed to suggest unrealized nonrepresentationalist autoethnographic potential in the "space" between them. If we can take as object here something very pertinent to the book's overall concerns, then we can really start to focus our preceding methodological discussion in ways that will underpin what we do with the rest of the book. In fact, this is possible thanks to the availability of these two very interesting texts: Lance Armstrong's autobiographical book *It's Not About the Bike* (2000) and an article in the *Journal of Sport and Social Issues* called "It's Not About the Book" in which Butryn and Masucci (2003), two sports sociologists with cultural studies interests, offer what they term a "counternarrative" to Armstrong's own. Neither of these is strictly auto-ethnographic, although Butryn and Masucci do foreground the circumstances of their own writing and Armstrong's book, thanks perhaps to cowriter Sally Jenkins' assistance, is a considerable step up in terms of reflective depth from most celebrity autobiographies. But when we read the two texts together it becomes possible to generate, as it were, an imagined autoethnography in the gap between them. If, in due course, we can begin to realize this form of imagined autoethnography then we have something to take forward in our own book. What I am going to argue here is that both Lance Armstrong's book and its academic counternarrative get pulled rapidly into representationalist thinking about the "machine" at the center of both—which is Armstrong's own body on a racing bicycle. The gap left between them is then the possibility of non-representationalist thinking about that machine. When we start looking at these two pieces of writing, what we mean by "representationalist" will also become more clear.

DS: Do we need to explain who Armstrong is?

DF: Lance Armstrong is the American road-racing cyclist who won the prestigious Tour de France race seven consecutive times. Competitive cycling at this level is a highly technologized sport, which often surprises people who have difficulty imagining how a body on a bicycle can be quite so technologized. But Armstrong even spearheaded an F1-style consortium called the F-One group, which emulated the practice in F1 motor racing of bringing powerful sponsors, technology companies, aerodynamicists, sports physicians, and so on together for integrated thinking about the overall system that produces a winning package of man and machine. When Armstrong rode a racing bike, every aspect of that package, from the aerodynamics of his suited body and shaved skin or the bicycle's onboard digital monitors to the high-tech materials used in the bicycle's construction or the earbuds through which his team fed him data about his body's performance, combined into one highly integrated and superefficient high-performance system.

The light from the window is at a low angle now. Across the floor it is starting to illuminate a fast-looking racing bicycle leaning against the wall.

DF: This technologizing started early. Armstrong explains:

> When I was 16, I was invited to undergo testing at a place in Dallas called the Cooper Clinic, a prestigious research lab and birthplace of the aerobic exercise revolution. A doctor there measured my VO2 max, which is the gauge of how much oxygen you can take in and use, and he says that my numbers are still the highest they've ever come across. Also, I produced less lactic acid than most people. [. . .] Basically, I can endure more physical stress than most people can. (2000, 3–4)

The bike is fully illuminated now.

DF: This 16-year-old body, measured, probed and statistically assessed as superior, would go on to become the core organic component within the winning machine—but only after it had been reshaped by cancer that struck when he was in his mid-20s. Armstrong's survival of cancer is the main story in his autobiography and the reason for its bestseller status, but ironically it also exposed his body to intrusive, long-term technological intervention—much more so than a healthy athlete's body would have been exposed to—from which it emerged more energy-efficient thanks to changes in body mass relative to strength. This post-cancer body, successfully achieved in part precisely because Armstrong could already "endure more physical stress than most people can," became the turbine in the machine. At the same time, as a careful reading of the autobiography makes clear, an affective change grounded in that body underpinned the determination necessary to win and win again, a change obliquely but revealingly captured in Armstrong's startling statement: "The truth is, if you asked me to choose between winning the Tour de France and cancer, I would choose cancer" (259). He does not say "defeating cancer" here. He is talking about cancer itself, having it in his body, experiencing it, surviving it, changing as a result of it.

The pool of light around the bike is slowly, almost imperceptibly widening.

DF: For Butryn and Masucci there is a relatively seamless continuity between the remaking of Lance Armstrong's body by medical technology and the technologizing of his body as racer (indeed they even include the technology of in vitro fertilization on which his fatherhood depended): together, in the counternarrative offered by Butryn and Masucci, these constitute the "cyborgification" of Armstrong. The counternarrativized Lance Armstrong that emerges in their parallel retelling of his autobiography, is a completely reshaped body fitted into an expensively designed machine package with a corporatized persona shaped by sponsors such as Nike. Butryn and Masucci comment on the expensive medical technologies that Armstrong had access to during his cancer and imply some continuity between these and the technologies (of materials science, aerodynamics, sports medicine, etc.) he accessed (or that had access to him) as a racer. They discuss the persistent—and persistently unproven—allegations that Armstrong used performance-enhancing drugs. Although not suggested by the authors, the undercurrent informing many of these rumors has been suspicion that high-tech drugs exist for which tests do not as yet; in short that Armstrong's body has been so much the result of advanced medicalized technology that it exists at the cutting edge of scientific advances. The implication is also that Armstrong's sense of self became so thoroughly technologized that he would no longer have had a "normal" sense of where he ended and a technologized other began. At this point the "cyborgification" of Armstrong seems complete.

A man steps into the pool of light around the bike. He is shaven-headed, thin and wears white pajamas. He looks frail.

DF: Now the key point about both these narratives—Armstrong's autobiography and Butryn and Masucci's parallel counternarrative—is that they shift so rapidly into representational thinking about the body on the bike. The contested term in this representational thinking is "human being." The book cover for *It's Not About the Bike* features this list, after "Winner of the Tour de France": "Cancer Survivor, Husband, Father, Son, Human Being." Butryn and Masucci are suggesting, in some quite fundamental sense, that "Cyborg" might be a more accurate substitute for the last term here. (In fact the Australian edition of the book dropped "Human Being" from the list on its cover, but this is more likely a reflection of default Australian cynicism about bombastic prose than a recognition of cyborgification.) If we accept that the body on the bike is the central image in all of this, Armstrong's autobiography can then be seen to focus on all the ways in which this figure becomes understandable as a "human being"—the human interest in the account of his unknown father, his close relationship with his mother, his family, and so on. The medical, technological, and racing accounts weave through this other human interest material but always with the same process at work: the unpacking of various interconnected representations of the "human being" from that more austere central image of the body on the bike, because after all "it's not about the bike." Butryn and Masucci do much the same thing with that central image, except that, instead of a "human being," their counternarrative constructs a representation of a "cyborg." Both narratives are concerned with achieving these representational projections.

The gaunt man bends slowly, unsteadily, to pick something off the floor—a plastic box with levers and an aerial.

DF: What is the unrealized nonrepresentationalist autoethnographic potential in the "space" between them? Butryn and Masucci unintentionally tap into this potential when they quote Lance Armstrong's response to one of the many doping allegations. On his website in June 2002 he wrote that "intense and calculated training . . . has been the key to my success on a bicycle" (quoted by Butryn and Masucci 2003, 141). Were we to strip the representational projections of a "human being" out of Lance Armstrong's autobiography what we would find is not a "cyborg" (which is just an alternative representational projection) but a body on a bike that is understandable in terms of intensity and calculation, where the intensity and calculation (or "strategy" as we will also call it in due course) fold the body and the bike together into a machinic assemblage and where affect is located. The book's strongest descriptions of riding evoke the intensity and the strategy involved (the rhythms, the monitoring, the rapture) and in these vividly depicted moments there is never any question of daydreaming about all the other projections of the "human being" that the autobiography aspires to. At most, these descriptions note the passing landscape in which the cycling is taking place. In these moments, beyond that horizon there is nothing. Despite the book's title, in these moments it really is about the bike, with the caveat that bike and body are in machinic unison.

DS: But as you've said, Armstrong's writing is not autoethnography, so where's the model of autoethnography here?

DF: I'm saying that it's in the gap between two bodies. You're frowning, but this is where Lance Armstrong's autobiography is at its most interesting, and where it offers access to things that nobody else could have written about. It comes nowhere near to being a critical nonrepresentationalist autoethnography of course—why should it?—but it helps us to imagine what such a thing might look like. At the same time, Butryn and Masucci offer the sort of critical context-laden account that you would want to see integrated into such an autoethnography, but I'd want it without the reintroduction of so much representationalist thinking in the form of their alternative representation—of cyborg rather than human being. Armstrong's autobiography also has one largely unexpressed but palpable theme: the persistence of something—personality?—through all the changes. The human-interest story is located more in the changes: beyond the corporeal transformations were profound changes in relationships, location, and family life, all documented in the book. But, perhaps a little unexpectedly, the persistence of something did not seem to reside in "personality" or in any fundamental stability afforded by such circumstances. Instead, it becomes clear that the rapturous times on the bike provide this persistence. While the authorial voice—Armstrong's helped by his cowriter—wants to suggest that it is about personality, one begins to feel that it is more about the persistence of an affective layer unifying bike and body, more a matter of how it feels to be on that bike, moving rhythmically and at speed. That is what persists, and the projection of "personality" from that affective layer is just another manifestation of representational thought. There is a curious moment in the book that suddenly makes sense in these terms (Armstrong and Jenkins 2000, 134). Now, you are going to argue against our leaving this conversation hanging in the way that I'm about to, and we'll probably argue about this all the way into print. You'll want us to say something about the following moment, to explain what it's doing here, but I'll want it just to be what it is and for its inclusion here to demonstrate something about a way of writing inside a gap or an interval but also that creates the gap or interval at the same time.

The light fades on **DF** *and* **DS**. *In his own pool of light the gaunt man presses buttons on his little plastic box. There is a mechanical buzzing noise off stage. It gets very loud.*

DF: Amidst all the personality-projecting vignettes and in the middle of the cancer treatment, Lance is at home regaining strength between chemo treatments. Not able to be on a bike or to do much of anything, he is playing with a high-tech remote controlled toy car capable of doing 70 miles per hour, when his chemo nurse calls:

"What's that loud buzzing noise?" she said.
"I'm in my garage," I said.
"What are you doing?" she said.
"I'm playing with my toy car," I said.
"Of course you are," she said.

Chapter 4

Containment 1:
The Strategy-Intensity Field

In Chapter 2, one "story" revealed a Formula One fandom orientated around the driver Jacques Villeneuve. Focusing on fan strategies and intensities, this chapter fleshes out how such intensities are strategically deployed in terms of individuals constructing, activating, and demonstrating their fandom, but in ways that affectively anchor them in specific concrete contexts of lived reality. In part, this is a recognition that fandom is not always "on" but, rather, is multifaceted, temporally differentiated, and multidimensional in its actualization. Moreover, strategies and intensities shift and transform rather than remaining static, reflective of the varying degrees of reflexivity fans utilize in their practices and their accompanying strategic imperatives at specific spatial and temporal moments. As a means to map the trajectories and anchorings of fandom, the dimensions of intensity (ranging from the reflexive to the nonreflexive) and strategy (from the banal to the fatal) will be explained, and then transposed onto what we term the strategy-intensity field, where the term field is intended to have associations with Pierre Bourdieu's theorization of agency and consumption.

The work of Dyer (1981) on utopian impulses and entertainment and Grossberg (1992b) on affective relationships and popular culture help us to consider the nature of the intensity invested in particular activities and that underpin engagements in media consumption. That is, these authors trace the notional level of "emotion" or energy that either activities or engagements entail and, for our purposes, can usefully be referenced to help map in specific ways the intensities and practices fans engage in with their subject/object of affection. More specifically, Dyer and Grossberg "quantify" the emotional dimension of intensities in terms of elaborating what sensibilities are enacted via mediations and, in turn, extrapolate the degrees of intensity on a continuum of low to high (inclusive of the emotional investments and levels of energy these experientially involve).

Archer's (2007) articulation of reflexivity furnishes a further theoretical layering as, potentially, the *quality* of such intensities can be mapped through integrating the reflexive deliberations and designs of individuals. She points to the mobilizing effects internal conversations have in allowing individuals to select courses of action within the options offered by the social world (recognizing that the dual composition of "external" sociocultural and "internal" atomized deliberative dimensions construct reflexivity). Archer suggests that "it is agential reflexivity which actively mediates between our structurally shaped circumstances and what we deliberately make of them" (2007, 16).

This conceptualization has clear links with Grossberg's central premise of the structured mobility of individuals who use their affective relationships to anchor, move and re-anchor themselves in an ongoing way within specific temporal and spatial circumstances. That is, the processes of both affect and reflexivity are seriously atomized in their temporal and spatial occurrences, while such practices are infused with both fluctuations in intensity and strategic dynamics as individuals devise projects that matter to them in their daily lives. Archer elaborates: "what reflexivity does do is to mediate by activating structural and cultural powers, and in so doing there is no single and predictable outcome. This is because subjects can exercise their reflexive powers in different ways, according to their very different concerns and considerations" (ibid., 16). While a shared or collective dimension may occur (e.g., the "shared" affective investment in a media sports star, such as Villeneuve), reflexivity and affect are bound in the contextual specificities of an individual's circumstances and his/her particular practices and equivocal experiences, thoughts, feelings, and sensibilities within any given temporal and spatial moment. So there is an atomistic containment of the shared at the *moment* of its impact, as the attachment to Villeneuve will demonstrate shortly.

Understanding intensity only in relation to its emotional content or degrees of energy does not take us far enough, though, since individuals will be further qualifying their intensities through variations in reflexivity. The quality of the intensity will be marked by the degrees of reflexive deliberation, as are the carefully considered courses of action undertaken which assign significance to a particular sociocultural object (F1 as worthy of affective investment by a fan), which distinguish this object from others (why Villeneuve is more worthy of investment than other drivers) and which further construct particular practices (the expense of Grand Prix attendance, regular late night televised viewing of races, or committing to a doctoral project as fan-scholar). Again, such designs may themselves be ineffective, either directly for the individual or as deemed so by external opinion (the sums of personal money "wasted" on F1 merchandise or hours "lost" playing computer games). However, by (re)investing intensity with a qualitative rather than merely quantitative property we come closer to understanding both the prominence of reflexivity as part of the process and, more significantly, how the quality of the intensity is underscored by the reflexive element of those designs that shape the concerns, actions, and mobilities of individuals in their daily lives, as they move from moment to moment over often long time frames.

To re-ground these theoretical perspectives in particular concrete, context-specific examples of fandom, the preference here is to marry conceptualizations of intensity with the strategic and then to plot these as constitutive of a particular field—offered as the strategy-intensity field. Aligning these two terms acknowledges that internal conversations are simultaneously always inflected both by strategic imperatives and by variations in the intensity of the reflexive deliberation (such as oscillating from the perfunctory to the profound in our quotidian existence). The terms strategy and intensity operate as vectors within the strategy-intensity field onto which the specific reflexive and strategic dimensions of particular practices can be traced. For our present purposes, Archer's reflexivity and Baudrillard's (1983a, 1988, 1990a) distinction between banal and fatal strategies are combined and transposed unto the strategy-intensity field as a means to explore the sociocultural phenomenon of fandom. This field also allows us to explore various phases across a fan's career, herein characterized and plotted as the "naïve" fan (origins and initial phase), the "insider" (high in affective investment and forms of cultural capital and literacy), and culminating, in this specific instance, in the "scholar-fan" (deploying fandom as a cultural resource for potential career advancement).

Comprising the intensity vector are the distinguishing terms reflexive and nonreflexive intensity which are intended to mark out the quality of the intensity underpinning the reflexive design and its concrete realization in specific fan practices. In particular, the intensity vector maps the nonreflexive as orientated toward affect (with whatever associated emotional dimensions) while, conversely, the reflexive is characterized as guided more by cognition and intellect. Such a means of organizing the field will be supported by embedding Archer's three modes of reflexivity (the communicative, autonomous, and meta-reflexive) within the broader theorization of these nonreflexive and reflexive intensities. The strategy vector comprises Baudrillard's notions of the banal and the fatal, in order to recognize that the activation of specific social practices (here Formula One fandom) and their preceding reflexive designs are marked by the differing dimensions, meaning and "depth" to the strategies individuals deploy. Nevertheless, rather than being constituted by a static set of distinct binaries, this field should be recognized as fluid and dynamic. By doing so, the fluctuating degrees of mobility afforded by the intensity of reflexive deliberations, strategic imperatives and the resultant actions (e.g., the overlap between strategies and intensities) can also be plotted onto this field. In fact, as Figure 4.1 suggests, within each quadrant the overlapping intensities and strategies are inflected by broader social dimensions and/or implications (see labels). It is onto this field that a particular F1 fandom is now transposed as a means for revealing how such strategies and intensities are embedded and actualized in particular, concrete practices. This approach also makes cognizable Grossberg's notion of *structured mobility* by mapping the routes, trajectories, and temporal/spatial anchorings of an individual, through the processes of fandom, within and across this dynamic field.

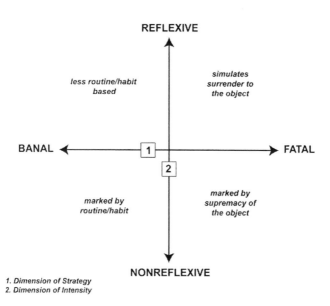

FIGURE 4.1   The strategy-intensity field.

Banal/Nonreflexive

As our first plotted trajectory on the strategy-intensity field, a banal/non-reflexive strategic-intensity can be characterized as being both obedient strategically and less critically informed reflexively. While the banal/nonreflexive nexus can be emotionally driven or dependent (though conversely, it may not be, as some oscillating examples will demonstrate), it tends to privilege routine and to be activated by habit. Archer suggests that for individuals surrounded by their "similars" (a network of close family and friends) and "familiars" (contextual continuity in terms of location, vocation, existing socio-cultural structures, etc.) the intensity of reflexive deliberations is weakened. Classified by the "communicative" mode of reflexivity, such individuals often have reduced internal conversations as they turn to their interlocutors to check, clarify and/or confirm any ruminations, reveries, or deliberations externally. A by-product of this mode of reflexivity is immobility, as these individuals (often guided by their interlocutors) privilege contextual continuity by falling back on existing habits and routines. This has clear links with Bourdieu's account of individual dispositions and the *habitus*. Nevertheless, Archer refutes any overly determinative relationship between larger social formation and modes of reflexivity, arguing that the reflexivity of her own research subjects in interview was deliberative (not a mere reflection of circumstances) and was actively used as a means to maintain a close proximity to these actual similars and familiars.

Routines and habits shape the banal/nonreflexive nexus for fandom as, strategically, individuals are obedient to these external factors to some considerable extent despite their own deliberative capacities. As a prime example, an individual's *habitus* shapes the particular formation and mode of his/her fandom. Nationality and the nationalistic are a clear example of this, hailing socially constituted individuals to recognize their cultural identity and interpellating them into associated practices and processes (Althusser 1977). With sport remaining one of the primary sites for staging contests between nation-states, nationalistic sport fandom is often a banal/nonreflexive process with fans drawing on habitual routines to manifest their support. During his childhood and early adulthood, rugby was the locus for DS's sport fandom as a New Zealander. This fandom was clearly inflected with nationalistic sentiments and characterized by the habitual, routinized processes, practices, and formations that accompany nationalistic fandom (and shaped his grassroots rugby participation). So, the communal gathering and viewing of rugby by similars, the evocation of the familiar through imagined communities and the habitual reinforcement of this social context (articulations of national pride and unity) were the routinized and habitual components of "his" New Zealand rugby fandom. Through the repetition of these communal activities, such fandom can also constitute a form of banal nationalism (Billig 1995) which has the potential to become mundane and drab through the recycling of habitual routines (regular and regulated viewing of test matches, displaying or wearing nationalistic symbols, singing national anthems and so forth).

These characteristics can be transposed, with sociocultural and contextual refinements, onto other nationalistic fan cultures, such as baseball or basketball in America, cricket in India, soccer in England, and ice hockey in Canada although, of course, not all social individuals are hailed and interpellated in the same manner (and certain individuals may respond through indifference, atomization, or even disdain, as much as through collectivism and communality). Strategically banal and reflexively uncritical in its obviousness, its level of expectation and its obedience to the socio-cultural status quo, the banal/nonreflexive nexus may be affective in its emotional investments and intensity but, it would seem, privileges an awareness and activation of habitual routines in the realization of specific concrete practices of fandom. Indirectly, Archer captures this perspective by surmising,

> What the practice of communicative reflexivity does is to privilege the public over the private, shared experience over lone experiences, third-person knowledge over first-person knowledge . . . In short, the speculative realm is severely truncated in favor of common sense, common experience and common knowledge. In the process, "similars and familiars" become still more similar to one another as well as familiar with each other. (2007, 273)

At this juncture we have viewed the banal/nonreflexive nexus only through a nationalistic lens. Such a lens for nationalism in Formula One is blurred or distorted because of the amalgamation of diverse team, driver and staffing nationalities (and localities). For example, there is no New Zealand driver, team, or race catering to nationalistic identification for the particular fan in question here (DS).

The banal/nonreflexive nexus has particular applicability to the initial stages of fandom. New to a particular sport, for example, fans rely on habitual practices and routinized processes to develop what we might term their cultural literacy and, in time, their cultural and symbolic capital. Such practices may be marked by the initial "compulsive" forms of consumption which people engage in to quickly (and symbolically) acquire forms of capital to demonstrate and display to others. This is afforded and encouraged by the commercialized processes built into sport which, collectively, treat fans as consumers, transform events into commodified experiences and imbue consumer goods with broader socio-cultural significance within specific fan communities (Crawford 2004; Giulianotti 2002; Grossberg 1992a; Gruneau and Whitson 1993; Rinehart 1998; Sandvoss 2005; Schirato 2007); see also our discussion of Ferrari in Chapter 6. Collectively, these commercialized and commodified processes cater to both the ephemerally "casual" viewer/spectator and the more culturally literate fan, while facilitating entry into the cultural field (or subculture) of specific sports for what we have labeled the "naïve" fan. Due to his/her relative degree of cultural illiteracy, the naïve fan finds routinized and habitual practices of consumption in order to *become* a fan, for example, via purchases. Still developing their cultural literacy, naïve fans deploy an initially banal strategy by obeying the expected consumerist rules and are largely nonreflexive in their designs. So, as they collect merchandise they will be generally thoughtless of the distinctions embedded in consumer goods as cultural capital and their own "duped" practices or status.

The initial selection of particular sportspersons to support arguably follows similar routinized and habitual lines. Star athletes are central to the televised sport spectacle and to forms of media fandom, often being given textual prominence and marked as exceptional in sport mediations. Both casuals and naïve fans may be culturally illiterate in certain sports but soon perceive who the star athletes are through their continual coverage, circulation, and exchange which, usually, are founded upon some genuine degree of success. In contemporary men's sports the leading, winning, and "champion" athletes are renowned; most obviously in recent times, Roger Federer in tennis, Tiger Woods in golf, Lance Armstrong in road cycling and, prior to 2007, Michael Schumacher in Formula One. Unless another avenue is constructed for identification, such as nationality (or other "traditional" social classifications such as race, gender or class), it is fair to extrapolate that most casual and naïve fans will gravitate toward the star athletes in their respective sports. Lacking intensity of deliberation and being strategically obedient to the predominant mediated images and privileging of star athletes within certain sports, such a process is orientated by the banal/nonreflexive nexus. As recounted in Chapter 2, DS's early Formula One fandom was shaped around Villeneuve's status as reigning World Champion (the aura of the current star driver). Naïve and culturally illiterate in, for example, how central the car itself was to driver performance, DS's deliberations lacked any intensity of rational engagement with the sport's subtleties. DS equated Villeneuve's status with ability and although, through viewing of races, it became apparent that Villeneuve would not be a contender for the championship, he was regularly scoring points and had his status sufficiently evoked in the global telecasts (and on the associated PlayStation One video game) to reaffirm a fandom. This was not the only reason for selecting Villeneuve and such strategies and intensities of reflexivity would be refined over time, especially as F1 cultural literacy and the affective relationship with Villeneuve subsequently increased (these refinements will be tracked as trajectories in the strategy-intensity field). Tracing this experience of naïve fandom reveals that, although the obvious habitual process of selection based upon nationality was not afforded DS in 1998, another routinized practice of affinity—toward the prominent and pre-eminent sport star—was being followed. This provides a pivotal first anchoring on the trajectory of a specific F1/Jacques Villeneuve fan.

Fatal/Nonreflexive

The banal/nonreflexive nexus reveals a process of fandom often steeped in routine and habit which can reduce at that point the strategic and reflexive possibilities and perhaps too the salience of affect. By contrast, while the fatal/nonreflexive may also become a habitual and routinized process to some degree, it tends to privilege both the supremacy of the object and the intensity of affect for individuals. In relation to fatal strategies, Baudrillard notes, "the object is always the fetish, the false, the *feiticho*, the factitious, the lure" (1990a, 184) all of which, strategically, fascinate but confound the subject (surpass the subject's understanding) through the object's deployment of its own fatalistic strategies of cunning, ruse, and artifice. Positioned by the dual fatal strategies of object and subject, individuals lack at this point in what we might term more rational, objective, or even intellectual internal conversations while privileging the supremacy of such objects. For Archer "the internal conversation is not an area where instrumental rationality has hegemony; it is just as much an arena for reviewing the emotional commentaries on our concerns, which are registered internally as we contemplate doing this rather than that" (2007, 285). The argument being made here is that, within the fatal/nonreflexive nexus, these deliberations tend to be less inflected by reflexive intensity and to be characterized more by affect. By conferring supremacy to the object, the relationship and nature of such deliberations is predisposed to a higher affective intensity in the relation with the object and a truncated critical reflexive deliberation around any rationale for bestowing such a status.

Archer's second mode of reflexivity, "autonomous," demonstrates some of these tendencies while conflating others. For example, although the "autonomous" are highly reflexive individuals (which we will be returning to in the remaining trajectories), their orientation toward acquiring procedural knowledge and a proficiency or skill in subject/object relations seems to marry with the fatal/nonreflexive nexus. Vividly present in this subject knowledge and proficiency, the object retains its primacy as the locus for the subject's associated affective fascination. Archer notes,

> What the subject knows, and only he [*sic*] can know it, is the intimate satisfaction that he derives from *using his skills*, in the ultimate privacy of the subject/object relationship . . . these sources of satisfaction are matters of first-person knowledge. Ontologically, they exist only by virtue of the person experiencing them and constitute a deeply intrinsic source of satisfaction experienced by the proficient. (ibid., 288, emphasis added)

While this may also retain traces of a banal strategy, in terms of the subject still assuming they have mastery over the object, that they can take it or leave it, ultimately it reveals itself as fatal since, strategically, the object retains its preeminence in any course of action undertaken by the individual engaged by that object. Moreover, in a reflexive mode, the affective clearly shapes and molds the deliberation and orientation of the person toward his/her specific object. These constitutive components of the fatal/nonreflexive nexus can be transposed onto fandom, with DS's trajectory as a Formula One fan affording some specific insights here.

Formula One deploys its own strategies to fascinate and seduce subjects. Lacking in cultural literacy of the field, these ruses drew DS in and corralled his support in 1998/1999. So, the publicly communicated images of Formula One's elite status, underscored by its extravagant costs and hi-tech sophistication and supplemented by the televised race commentaries of Murray Walker (glowing and hyperbolic) and Martin

Brundle (technical expertise of an ex-driver) were important aspects for initially acceding supremacy to the sport/object. What is also discernible in this naïve phase is that such deliberations were essentially nonreflexive in kind (internal conversations lacking in sophistication) and strategically fatal (marveling at and conferring a supremacy on the object). Although a very generalized assertion, we might assume similar patterns emerge in other forms of sport fandom for naïve and less culturally literate fans who are lured or seduced, in varying degrees, by the public myths, the persuasive role of commentators, and the broader structures and strategies deployed by specific sports. With the commencement of a doctoral thesis post-2001, DS's fandom became by definition more critically informed through enhanced levels of cultural capital and literacy (as well as symbolic capital) bringing a resultant academic "depth" to reflexive deliberations. However, in spite of the "researched" knowledge and awareness of some of the sport's paradoxes and contradictions (dubious evocations of national pride, questionable degrees of driver agency, problematic gendered representations), DS's fandom was still strategically fatal in stubbornly retaining the primacy of F1 as object. That is, the continuation of DS's Villeneuve fandom for several years from that point was underscored by a sustained acceptance of Formula One as a preeminent object. The reflexive deliberations may have developed in intensity to match the accumulated academic knowledge and sport-specific cultural literacy but, simultaneously, such intensities remained affectively colored in terms of an orientation toward and emotional investment in Villeneuve as the supremely fatal object and locus for fandom, over and above Formula One itself as object.

To demonstrate how the fatal/nonreflexive nexus inflected DS's trajectory as a naïve fan, we reproduce an "internal" moment, that is, his affectively oriented ruminations on watching televised coverage in 1998, staging deference to Villeneuve as supreme object, supreme, that is, in the emotional life of the fan.

Italian Grand Prix, Monza 1998

Lap 37, *finally* the cameras cut to Villeneuve. "About time!" I remind the television screen. I have hardly seen Jacques all race, although he is running in a strong fourth place. A wave of nervous excitement washes over me as I view Jacques negotiating the Lesmo turns.

He appears to be quite close to Eddie Irvine too. "Come on Jacques" I urge, "push, get another podium." Jacques runs very wide on the exit of the first Lesmo, exciting me with his ragged style of driving. Split seconds later the coverage cuts to another camera as Jacques flies off the track in the background. "No!!!!!" I scream. Replays and Brundle's commentary reveal Villeneuve running wide before getting sideways through the corner, careening into the gravel runoff area. I leap to my feet, kicking the table in front of me while searching for something to throw. I want to see Villeneuve win or at least get podiums, not crashing! The replays cut to an onboard shot of Villeneuve getting sideways and bouncing through the gravel. "That was pretty cool," I think, watching Villeneuve's helmet frantically bobbing from side-to-side as his car jolts across the uneven surface before coming to a gentle stop. Back live, Villeneuve is televised out of the car, flanked by track marshals as he removes his helmet. My anger at the missed opportunity quickly evaporates. "Cool!" I say to myself. Anger has turned to fascination as I now look at him with some awe. I've hardly ever seen Villeneuve filmed out of the car during my first year of watching F1. But here he is clearly visible: the baggy red overalls, bleached blond hair, nose strip, stubble, and determined look in his blue eyes searching for an escape from the crash scene. His face betrays his self-annoyance. Villeneuve rips off his nose strip and throws it to the ground. He looks over to the crowd, giving them an appreciative but half-hearted wave, seemingly acknowledging their support but also recognizing his own fallibility before turning to walk away in shame. And with that, Jacques was gone, replaced by the televised images of cars still in the race. Despite the driving error, despite the wasted points, it was Villeneuve's appearance that remained etched in my memory. The intensity of my fandom for Jacques increased that day knowing that I was supporting the "cool" guy; the blond-haired, unshaven, baggy-clothed "maverick" World Champion.

Turning to an analysis of this spatial and temporal "moment," we can see that there are obvious banal dimensions embedded in the narrative, such as the depthless use of "cool" as an adjective and the seemingly inane enthrallment with Villeneuve's appearance. Equally, however, the narrative reveals how internal ruminations are processed and activated during such moments, with the intensity of deliberation inflected more by affect than reflexivity. Hence, while DS still equated performance with achievement and was frustrated at Villeneuve's crash, the seemingly vacuous fascination with his image was cementing an affective relationship and investment. Dual processes were at play in this particular naïve moment. First, as has been intimated, Villeneuve's mediated image was operating in the realm of a fatal strategy. Eschewing any consideration of self-conscious intent or agency on Villeneuve's part, as a media object his mediated image and appearance were seductive; deploying the rogue, rebel, and maverick traces (image/appearance, risk-taking, and dissent) as ruses, guises, lures, and strategies to captivate and corral F1 subjects. All seductive power resided with Villeneuve as the supreme object that infiltrated DS's quotidian fan existence. Such a process, while affective, is not necessarily about desire or the homoerotic and, strategically, Villeneuve the media object always evaded attempts at finding a "real" Villeneuve to care about (he is always already a media star) or possess (Villeneuve "disappears" at that very moment he circulates as a media object). Baudrillard asserts, "possession is the preoccupation and pride of the subject, but not of the object, which is totally indifferent to it, as to its liberation. The object wants only to seduce . . . the object always wins" (1990a, 124). DS's affective investment was grounded in its own fatal strategy of fascination and intrigue with an object that, while seductive, was illusory in its apparent coherence, and indifferent and unobtainable in its untouchable supremacy. Despite textual poaching, scavenging, reappropriating, and reproducing traces of Jacques across a fan career, Villeneuve's strategy as an object produced its own subterfuge while subverting any subjective attempts (real or veiled) at possession.

The second notable process is that the affective intensity of DS's reflexivity persisted in terms of the emotional investment in Villeneuve over the fan career (although of course, the intensities of affective energy always fluctuate in any form of fandom, such as an inevitable decrease due to his absence from F1 for much of 2004 and post-2006). Although DS's reflexive designs can be assumed to have become more critically informed as a result of both the intellectual rigor of a doctoral thesis and growing cultural capital and literacy, the affective dimension remained intact and stayed crystallized around Villeneuve. So, his mediated star image continued to fascinate and seduce despite the transition from a naïve to "insider" fan and gravitation toward a more serious academic *position*. In contradistinction to the first autoethnographic vignette, a second from 2006 anchors DS's fandom in the Formula One insider phase (relating to the status self-assumed by fans who are more highly knowledgeable in the minutiae of F1). This second narrative affords some insight into the increasing reflexivity of such deliberations, imparted via an external conversation which, nevertheless, demonstrates that such deliberations remain embedded in affect.

BMW Team Launch, January 2006

"Here he is honey, come look" I call across to Anna. "Do I have to?" she responds, reclining on the couch and engrossed in the film she is watching on television. "Go on, come see him for just a minute," I plead and stretch my arms out for an imaginary hug. Anna relents, pushing the pause button, and moves in to return my gesture. "Look there he is" I enthuse, motioning toward the computer as she approaches for a closer look. "Yes, very good" she proffers, patting my head and gesturing back toward her film. "And look, he didn't even shave . . . so cool," I continue. Anna is not so easily impressed and often grumbles at me when I can't be bothered to shave. "Yeah, well he looks a bit of mess—you shouldn't be proud Mister! And where's his hair gone, looking a bit old now!" she teases, scrutinizing his appearance and receding hairline. Anna is enjoying winding me up and I'm beginning to wonder why I did call for her attention after all. "Couldn't he have at least shaved?" she asks, raising her eyebrows in sarcastic disapproval. I pull Anna closer and kiss her on the forehead. "Exactly honey, how cool is this guy?" I ask rhetorically. Before she can disagree I press on, "that's the thing, this is the team launch, the big promotional day for BMW and its sponsors in front of Formula One and global media. Add to that, here is Jacques, the guy apparently lucky to still be in F1, not wanted by the team and all that. You would think that he would be happy just to have a drive and be bending over backwards for the team. But here he is, ever the maverick, doing his own thing, not performing to the corporate script," I gush proudly. "Yeah well, that's your thing but I still think that he should tidy himself up" Anna responds. "You know with his salary," she continues, "I'm sure he could afford a razor and comb." We both laugh but Anna is on a roll, "And what's with his glasses?" she asks, "they look more geek than chic." I can't help laughing with her as I focus on Villeneuve's thick black frames. "Yeah, I agree," I answer, "but that's what's so interesting about this guy, he always stands out. I mean look at him, the stubble, the thick glasses, the overalls that look two sizes too big for him. See, even in 2006, Jacques is still not conforming to the corporate cookie-cutter look for F1 drivers." "You and your warped idea of style," Anna grins in a friendly but also disapproving manner, "let's hope he actually finishes some races this year, buddy!" she mutters and heads back over to the couch to resume her film, leaving me to ponder Villeneuve's first public appearance with BMW.

It is these traces of "grit" within Villeneuve's media image that persistently resonated in an affective-reflexive manner for DS. The BMW narrative reveals a somewhat more critical component to his reflexive deliberations, evinced through the specificity of detail discussed with a partner in defense of Villeneuve's appearance as a stance against F1's corporate expectations. Of course, we should remind ourselves of Dyer's (1981) insight into popular entertainment, with the system producing dissatisfactions that the system then itself satisfies (Villeneuve's maverick look suiting BMW or sponsors on another level). Additionally, the narrative offers a concrete example of fandom integrated into gendered relationships where it remains clearly grounded in the to and fro movement of affect. The critical promise of reflexivity is subsumed by the intensity of affect in a nonreflexive manner (e.g., the attraction of "cool" persists to undermine any rational self-doubt occasioned by a partner's objectivity). As such, Villeneuve the media object still lures through represented "personality," while affording a nonreflexive pleasure in both the recognition and appropriation of these traces of supposed grit in the corporate machine. These traces are perceived as something exceptional and more profound than they might be permitted to be in any critical reflexive perspective. Nevertheless, it can be argued that the strategy-intensity field is fluid and dynamic, with reflexive deliberations seeping into parts of this "nonreflexive" nexus through the acquired academic and culturally literate forms of knowledge (e.g., knowing the marketing significance of a gritty image in counterbalancing a smoothly corporate reality). We will also see that affect can be married with these critical reflexive forms (and the strategically fatal with the banal) in the remaining trajectories, as the banal-reflexive nexus demonstrates.

Banal/Reflexive

Thus far, the vectors plotted onto the strategy-intensity field have been characterized by a strategically obedient, less critically informed reflexivity often steeped in routine (the banal/nonreflexive nexus) or the strategic supremacy of the object, again less critically informed but principally derived via intensities of affect rather than routinized practices (the fatal/nonreflexive nexus). Our attention now turns to the third location on the strategy-intensity field, the banal/reflexive nexus. This nexus, while strategically obedient, primarily moves away from habit, routine, or affect (although they may still have a degree of saliency) to more intense ways of traversing the concrete realities of one's quotidian existence. We can suggest that, within this nexus, individuals might have fewer of Archer's "similars and familiars" in their social contexts or they may feel less straightforwardly assimilated into those alliances and, hence, may rely on more intense reflexive deliberations to "mull over" their interests and to design (in)appropriate courses of action. This mode of reflexivity was introduced in the previous section as "autonomous." For these people, there will be a tendency to operate in a manner less dependent on interlocutors, relying instead on internal conversations that according to Archer are "going on 'all the time'" and that can be "prolonged and ubiquitous" (2007, 284). She suggests that these reflexive deliberations act as a mental resource and as a form of strategic mobility, although these practices never guarantee "upward" mobility. In summary, the autonomous reflexive mode is underpinned by ongoing evaluations and appraisals of such designs and is high in reflexive intensity.

Strategically, the banal/reflexive nexus appears to remain in a largely banal locus, with the subject *assuming* continuing supremacy over the object while providing some of what Baudrillard refers to as "fatal disobedience to the symbolic order" (1990a, 182). In other words, the banal is inflected by a knowing (reflexive) subject who now assumes there is depth, cunning, and a degree of Archer's autonomy to his/her own banal strategies. Given the high intensity of reflexivity bestowed on the subject in this nexus, they may be producing what Baudrillard refers to as *inhuman* strategies. As an example of an inhuman strategy, Baudrillard, in one of his typically provocative examples, suggests that people use their vacations as a means to locate a higher degree of boredom than they achieve in their daily lives, while having the foreknowledge that conventionalized elements, such as "happiness" and distraction, will confer legitimacy on this boredom. Baudrillard argues, "I'm not joking: people are not looking for amusement; instead they want to find a fatal distraction. Boredom is not the problem—the essential point is the increase of boredom; increase is salvation and ecstasy" (ibid., 184), which he also suggests is a hyper-banal strategy. In fact boredom in Formula One seems, if anything, to offer a more persuasive case for Baudrillard here than vacations! We will return to his evocation of the hyper-banal in due course. First, however, Formula One fan practices (or more precisely, reflexivities and strategies) need to be transposed onto the banal/reflexive nexus.

One central feature of the banal/reflexive nexus is the consumerist and consumptional practices of F1 fans. Operating within this given contemporary socioeconomic context, many fans will also to a degree be "critically" aware of their own duped or *determined* position. Through various degrees of reflexive deliberation, these fans will recognize their own consumptional practices as constitutive of contemporary fandom's being constructed for them, not something they originate, yet they see—or feel—a value or worth in enacting those practices anyway. Within F1 specifically, there are definite signs of the culturally literate Formula One insider finding affective satisfaction and a cultural worth or legitimacy in "playing the game." That is, the procurement and display of commercialized merchandise is modulated with symbolic value through the knowledgeable pursuit of F1-specific forms of cultural capital (functioning as symbolic capital and bestowing "status" on such fans). As a whole, these observations coalesce around the intensity of reflexive deliberations and designs as the reflexive capabilities vary for individuals and, additionally, can be refracted through or influenced by diverse intensities of affect. For DS, these goods and displays have been fundamental to fan performativity; a process that is high in affective investment and matched by an intensity of reflexive self-awareness that acknowledges and activates an affective pleasure in playing the game.

Strategically, consumption and performance remain banal by privileging the supposed supremacy of the subject in such relations although, arguably, these can often also become fatalistic in their design and implementation. For example, is DS's continued consumption of Villeneuve-specific merchandise at this point "knowingly" re-conferring supremacy to Villeneuve as media object? Forms of fan performativity constitute an assemblage of (and blur) banal/fatal strategies, as subject/object relations are manipulated through the fluidity of dynamic and reconstructed, recycled and reproduced displays of the fan performing as a fan while recognizing his/her own fandom. In DS's own (hyper)fandom practices, as we might now think of them, there is the concurrent fandom for Villeneuve as the media object, DS's (re)enactments of the fan subject position and an assemblage of both through performances that oscillate as banal and fatal strategies since the supremacy of the subject and/or object is never fixed. We can extrapolate these points to incorporate inhuman strategies and, especially, the hyper-banal. Re-invoking his assertion that subjects knowingly and strategically seek out boredom, Baudrillard notes that for subjects, "they'll make a destiny out of it: intensify it while seeming to do the opposite, plunge into it to the point of ecstasy, seal the monotony of it with an even greater monotony. This hyper-banality is the equivalent of fatality" (1990a, 184). The hyper-banal can be transposed onto fan practices through the regular, routinized repetition of fandom whereby the affective intensity most likely fluctuates across a continuum ranging from pleasure to monotony. If we pursue Baudrillard's line of thought then fandom, in its most hyper-banal form, is the simultaneous escalation and assuaging of monotony through the practices that fans "plunge into" to actualize their affective intensities in that very oscillation between escalating and assuaging. Problematically, however, such an assertion is also subject to the simplistic misinterpretation of fans "escaping" when, as Grossberg counters, it is these very affective investments and intensities that anchor individuals *in* a social reality.

DS's own trajectory as a fan also reworks the application of banal strategies found in the first nexus, the banal/nonreflexive. In the currently described nexus, the banal/reflexive, there is a shift away from routine and habit as F1 fandom is forged along a different path. For a New Zealander, the gravitation toward the global sport of Formula One disrupts the "similar and familiar" of national allegiances and the purported significance of certain other sports in accordance with a more broadly defined *habitus*—be it location or class-bound (Bourdieu 1977, 1984, 1991). The selection of F1 reveals an intensity of reflexive design by rejecting the socio-cultural elevation of rugby as "national game" in favor of a sport that problematizes links to the nation for a New Zealander. Moreover, by aligning with an individual French-Canadian, nationalistic processes of hailing and interpellation are thoroughly confounded. DS's reaction to New Zealand press coverage in May 2004 reveals a specific reading high in reflexive intensity. An article derived from Reuters international newswire but reproduced for a regional audience in *The Waikato Times*, reported that both Villeneuve and New Zealander Scott Dixon were in contention for a Williams F1 seat in 2005 ("Williams owner ducks question over Dixon" 2004). The substance of the story was team boss Frank Williams declining to comment on whether Dixon had a possible future with his team while also confirming that they had been in discussions with Villeneuve. Such a representation was hailing the assumed New Zealand reader and was geared toward a nationalistic reading through its heading (referring only to Dixon), layout (two columns, with one and a half dedicated to Dixon), content (the story focused on Dixon's future, Villeneuve was presented as secondary), and politics of identity (e.g., Scott Dixon versus "the Canadian"). Despite overtures which clearly engaged his national identity, these routine or habitual processes of interpellation were jettisoned through the reflexive intensity of DS's inevitably rapid analytical grasp of the article's rhetoric. By contrast, the longer-established pull of wanting Villeneuve to get a race-seat ahead of *any* other driver, regardless of their nationality, demonstrated an attachment high in affect and therefore quite resistant to other kinds of appeal.

DS's internal ruminations increasingly required reflexive negotiation to justify, legitimize, and sustain an affective attachment to a global sport and a transnational sporting star. DS notes that, concurrently, a banal/nonreflexive approach always remained intact via sustained low-level affective investments in New Zealand teams (e.g., cricket, rugby league, and soccer—especially at the 2010 Football World Cup). However, and this is a key point, located in the banal/reflexive nexus, his reflexive deliberations also recognized that, in relation to F1, what was happening was an atomized temporal/spatial construction of a solitary (noncommunal) and isolated form of fandom within the broader New Zealand sociocultural context. This is most apparent with the live televising of European races translating to a midnight start time on Sunday nights in New Zealand (or Monday morning 5:00 a.m./6:00 a.m. starts for races in Brazil, Canada and America) which generally are not conducive to live communal viewing. DS's deliberations about doing this facilitated the banal strategy of obedience to a new set of imperatives but these also navigated him toward isolation as its own strategy, one that produces an exclusive if not absolutely asocial domain for oneself as subject. Such an explanation is supported by Archer's observation that the "autonomous" reflexive individual tends to carve out "the space for the lone pursuit of his leisure pursuits" (2007, 297). The reflexively strategic aura of isolation is informed by an affectively "personalized" payoff as F1 affords an intense space for both reflexive internal deliberation (it has complexity) and the affective anchoring in temporal and spatial moments of everyday life through the manner in which it is delivered.

Filtered through Villeneuve, F1 also provides a "private" space to license isolated and individualized reflexive temporal/spatial moments (e.g., Villeneuve-specific perspectives when playing video games or often solitary television viewing habits). This even operated when attending the 2005 Canadian Grand Prix which was a symbolic "home" race for DS but, despite a shared object in Villeneuve, the Canadian and/or Quebecois attendees most likely drew upon habits of parochial, regional, or nationalistic allegiance that were less likely to be shaped by reflexively and strategically "chosen" intensities of attachment. This is reflected in DS's everyday social relations where he can be perceived as the "F1 guy." Such a "status" imparts, in turn, fluctuating levels of symbolic capital, acknowledging "insider" insight but also including suspicions of the duped consumer (e.g., the branded BAR team shirt within university environs), and re-isolates DS in specific spatial/temporal moments (exclusion from rugby-related interactions in his New Zealand setting). These observations bring us inexorably to the final trajectory on the strategy-intensity field.

Fatal/Reflexive

In the fatal/reflexive nexus, there is a continuation of the intense reflexivity characterizing the previous nexus, as well as an oscillating intensity in how individuals strategically navigate and anchor themselves within a broader social reality. More broadly, the fatal/reflexive nexus constructs positions for those who, through the activation of their own fatal strategies, are *simulating* their surrender to the supremacy of the object. These fans deploy a diverse array of strategic devices, such as the banal, hyperbanal, and inhuman as previously described, to facilitate this simulated enactment in their everyday lives. The link between boredom and leisure activity has already been noted but, in terms of broader subject/object relations, it is within the "ecstatic deepening of anything" (Baudrillard 1990a, 184) that the subject can assume a simulated and ultimately fatal logic beyond boredom. Baudrillard argues that "there is no liberation but this one: in the deepening of negative conditions. All forms that tend to project a dazzling and miraculous liberty are only revolutionary homilies . . . essentially it is a fatal logic that wins out" (ibid., 184–5). In the fatal/reflexive nexus it is the fatal logic and inhuman strategy of plunging into the object through excess that comes to matter. This "ecstatic deepening" acknowledges the object as supreme while remaining infused with both the banal (through the still convinced cunning and ruses of the subject) and the fatal (performing a simulated subservience) in its strategic deployment and blurring of subject/object relations. We will return to some final concrete examples of the actualization of this fatal strategy in fandom shortly.

Underscoring this simulative, fatalistic strategy is the high intensity of reflexivity that such a fan utilizes to frame and "know" such relationships. As with the banal/reflexive nexus, individuals draw on reflexive deliberations, relying on internal conversations to discern what matters to them, what they value, and to design courses of action (whether any of this is in the best interests of the person concerned is beyond the remit we have set ourselves here). Such fans correspond first to the previously discussed "autonomous" reflexives who tend to privilege their ruminations over external conversations as a resource for devising forms of strategic mobility across the field. But Archer's third mode of reflexivity, the "meta-reflexive," may be especially pertinent to the fatal/reflexive nexus. Like the autonomous, meta-reflexives are characterized by a high intensity in and privileging of their own deliberations, although meta-reflexives are also considered to be more value-orientated rather than task-orientated. Archer suggests that "by not sharing many of their (most important) inner deliberations with others, the meta-reflexive is insulated from the running commentaries of those surrounding her [*sic*] and their pressures to conformity" (2007, 301), using value orientations to shape their concerns and courses of action. The implementation of a fatal strategy and simulated adherence to the object despite what one knows, as it were, requires intensive reflexive deliberation to achieve its own actualization in specific contexts. Once more, F1 in this fan's trajectory provides the example.

Arguably, doing a doctoral thesis exploring one's own fandom provides a perfect example of the fatal/reflexive nexus enacted and realized meta-reflexively as a specific concrete practice (Sturm 2009). During the doctoral process DS was deploying a dense fatal strategy that recognized the supremacy of the object (F1 and Villeneuve), engaged with the rules, ruses, and strategies of these specific objects, embraced a banal strategy (the cunning subject) by assuming that he was knowingly "playing the game" of submission through the simulation of this submissive status while, simultaneously, folding the object's strategies back onto themselves to interrogate them meta-reflexively for academic scrutiny. Throughout the thesis work, F1 and Villeneuve remained marked as supreme in terms of this fandom, were used as objects for analysis while assumptions were made by DS that he was now in a privileged position to simulate his immersion within this fatal logic, through ongoing affective investments as a fan coupled with the initially banal strategy of an emerging scholar-fan. Outside of the thesis, these fatal/banal strategies were and are redeployed in DS's academic daily life. So, for example, the various thesis topics (e.g., fandom/audiences, stardom, cultural theory) or its fatal objects (Formula One and Villeneuve) are drawn upon to teach academic concepts and to apply these in other areas of cultural studies and to cowrite a book. Such a process generates its own oscillating fatal/banal strategy through elevating and reassembling these fatal objects in front of others, and publicly deploying the assumed symbolic capital of DS's scholar-fandom. This multilayered strategy in the academic workplace is also underpinned by an intensive reflexivity which overlaps with the meta-reflexive mode in terms of constant self-reflection and introspection operating more or less simultaneously on the planes of fandom and the concurrent academic "voice" of DS, as staged in the preceding chapter. Specifically, such ruminations first discerned what aspects were significant for shaping a doctoral thesis and required intense internal deliberations on how to actualize the project as a concrete reality (e.g., legitimization of topic, what to "reveal" and how to successfully complete) in terms of DS's own cluster of concerns, his appropriate courses of action and his scrutinizing of the depth and clarity of his own deliberations.

Through the combination of an oscillating fatal/banal strategy and the intensive reflexive processes, the affective investment in Villeneuve then unsurprisingly underwent its own fluctuations. At times, there was an increased affective intensity through being able to continue reveling, even in the workplace, in the pleasure derived from recognizing his elevated status for DS as the supreme object of fandom (the fatal strategy of Villeneuve the media object) while, conversely, the affective dimension/intensity could be diminished by the academic "requirements" of continual over-analysis, theorization, and rational sense-making—a process which also contributed to both the variations in reflexive intensities and the specific strategies deployed. Within the fatal/reflexive nexus, affect is still a salient feature, albeit as always via varying degrees of intensity embedded in specific temporal/spatial moments. For example, the affective intensity could be diminished when Villeneuve the media object was also "reduced" through rational critical theorization and cultural analysis; alternatively, affect could be enhanced by DS recalling and reactivating his affective investments in Villeneuve's "maverick" grit, to which DS remained attached and borrowed as an apprentice academic doing something "maverick." However, the role of routine and the habitual largely faded, with intensive deliberations and the oscillating fatalistic or banal strategic imperatives consigning routinization to a seemingly outgrown nonreflexive place in DS's Formula One fandom.

Reassembling fandom in the strategy-intensity field

By transposing DS's Formula One/Villeneuve fandom onto a strategy-intensity field, it would seem that the deployment of his own fatal strategy, aligned with the intensive deliberations characteristic of the trajectory of the (academic workplace reinforced) fatal/reflexive nexus, ultimately requires that DS step back and reassemble the fragmented spatial/temporal moments into a coherent narrative of the sociocultural significance of this fandom in relation to fandom generally, preferably by extricating himself from it. Indeed, a tidy conclusion to mapping this strategy-intensity field would repudiate the supremacy of the object (Formula One and Villeneuve), reject the fan practices as ultimately only scripted consumerist behaviors (the duped fan) and recognize the folly of the associated affective investments and intensities that have shaped DS's journey through fandom. In other words, the fatal/reflexive position ultimately extricates the subject from the entire field. However, this symbolic bonfire onto which all vestiges of a once foolhardy fandom are thrown will not be lit here. Equally, the effigy of Villeneuve, the apparent fallen "idol" will not be burnt; nor will DS discard Damion, the beguiled fan-self, who is expected to transcend to enlightened "scholar-self" by fanning those flames. For such an ending itself becomes a vector within the banal/nonreflexive nexus. That is, this extricated theory position undercuts its own intensive and critically informed reflexivity by falling back on the habits and routines of good scholarship (e.g., as could be written via a properly articulated academic position *in theory* and a disembodied scholarly voice expressing it), leaving the messy personal fragments around DS's fandom still secretly there. This strategically banal assumption of the supremacy of DS the no longer apprenticed scholar but the real thing, and the disavowal of fandom as a spatial/temporal phase that simply fades or passes, betrays the relative indestructibility of affect in the career of fandom. More simply, affective investments continue to permit forms of what Grossberg terms structured mobility that anchor individuals in the lived, concrete moments of social reality which have been theorized here as trajectories on a strategy-intensity field. It is the notion of maintained mobility that matters, when contrasted with the fixity of the endpoint (the bonfire) pictured above.

Operating within the fatal/reflexive nexus, maintaining any fandom within the academic requires a clever balancing of intensive reflexivity and oscillating degrees of strategic manipulation. In the "insider" phase of fandom, field-specific capital (cultural and symbolic) and cultural literacy are primarily registered in the domain of affect—acquired knowledge or capital that reveals that the insider is "passionate" or "cares" about his/her sport immensely. However, in the academic phase, these forms of capital and literacy are recognized as an example of Archer's "enablements" that are reflexively conceived and pursued, while being *differently* actualized in the social arenas of fandom and academia more broadly. These forms of capital and literacy facilitate (or are intended to facilitate) advancement in the academic workplace, for example, by legitimizing the larger object as something for future research and career progression. As an early career scholar, fandom as object in this sense grants DS entrance into and, to an extent, defines his initial route across the cultural studies field as his area of potential "expertise." Affect seems to have less to do with it.

Therefore, any contextual continuity to DS's academic F1 "fandom" is now invested with a reflexive intensity and oscillating fatal/banal strategies of cultural currency; ensuring the fan insider status and its associated literacy and forms of capital remain accessible, pertinent and deployable but as transferable knowledge and forms of empirical evidence for one of his areas of expertise in the workplace. Although the intensity of the affective investment in Villeneuve has to a large extent dissipated (especially without his regular presence in Formula One or other forms of motorsport), the fandom afforded the beginnings of an academic career that recontextualizes the strategically fatal and reflexively intensive investment in F1. In fact, what has also become plain in this academic phase of fandom is how much of the affective intensity and investment was specifically anchored in Villeneuve directly, and less orientated toward Formula One. Seduction, then, proffers a means for framing a final response to Villeneuve's personal significance as the locus for DS's fandom. Baudrillard, for once succinctly, observes, "surface and appearance, that is the space of seduction" (1988, 62), for an excessive plunging into objects within what we have identified as the fatal/reflexive nexus. Baudrillard also cautions that "challenge, and not desire, lies at the heart of seduction. Challenge is that to which one cannot avoid responding, while one can choose not to respond to desire" (ibid., 57). Seductions "no longer partake in the order of desire but in the order of the frenzy of the image" (ibid., 35). Moreover, for Baudrillard, appearances and disappearances are a crucial aspect of seduction, as the disappearance of the object vitalizes the seductive moment: "all that has been produced must be seduced (initiated into disappearance after having been initiated into existence)" (1990a, 133). So the challenge is now simple: how, after the disappearance, to maintain . . . but what is it that survives to be maintained? What residue remains from the order of the frenzy of the image? What is it that remains from an excessive plunging into objects, as the final definition of fandom's fatal strategy? What, in short survives the fatality? Surely affect itself, rather than its investment in particular representations, including the representation of a seductive Baudrillard as "object" trying to have the last word here (letters slip and JV becomes JB)?

*   *   *

This chapter operates within the seemingly incompatible theories of agency advanced by the sociologists Pierre Bourdieu and Margaret Archer. The "field" here, as an abstract space of position-takings where agents and their actions are organized, is a device indebted to the ways in which Bourdieu theorizes the *habitus* (the mediation of social structure within habitual formations of subjectivity) as intersecting with both agents' "capital" (economic, social, and cultural) and a field's particular rules (Bourdieu 1996). But the specific notion of structured mobility argued for here (the capacity to follow or devise trajectories across a field) depends on the kinds of reflexivity theorized by Margaret Archer, which would appear to be incompatible with Bourdieu's theory of agency. Bourdieu's view of agency does not include any capacity for planning, for strategies informed by deliberation, even if this takes "soft" form (ruminations, reveries) rather than "hard" form (planning). Any hard-line reading of the account in this chapter that was based on this reading of Bourdieu would want to redescribe the traced mobility as merely scripted moves within the interaction of *habitus*, agent, and field-specific rules. The deliberative vocabulary used throughout would then become a matter of retrospective reinterpretation interested in maintaining the illusion of reflexive agency.

So a field for Bourdieu consists of "position-takings which can only be understood in terms of relationships, as a system of differential variations" (1996, 205), whereas for Archer position-takings involve reflexivity as well. In one view, the fan (as an initially banal but usefully definable agent for theoretical purposes) deploys capital (money to buy fan stuff, distinction within a fan community), is positioned by the consumption field's rules and, as a result, is constructed subjectively within and around the habits and routines of a particular form of consumption that mediate an existing social regime (e.g., one that is Toyotist rather than Fordist). In the other view, much the same may be going on but the particular position-takings are nonetheless subject to a degree of agential choice based on reflexivity (Bourdieu puts scare quotes round the word 'choices' (ibid.)).

This question of "space for human choices," which is also a question about the internalization of externality and vice versa, has been explored by Dave Elder-Vass (2007, 325) as precisely an encounter between Bourdieu and Archer. It is not the aim here to engage directly in this theoretical debate (this book as a whole is an indirect engagement instead) but we should point out Elder-Vass's very helpful conclusion, which is that experiences "are a cause of the particular configurations of neurons and synapses that are the emergence base of our mental states" (ibid., 337) and that, therefore, Bourdieu has not extended his "system of differential variations" into the body of the subject where the determining relationships will then also include those embodied mental states. At that level, reflexivity is part of an "emergentist" theory of action, including mobile position-taking as conceived here, where reflexivity may start out as no more than "simple plans" embedded in reflexes (the former a term used by cognitive scientist Daniel Dennett). Elder-Vass uses the image of a tennis player to illustrate this:

> The "simple plan" here consists of a set of consciously chosen strategies, the precise strategy to be adopted being conditional on what type of serve is received, and the "reflexes" consist of the ability of our brain and body not only to execute predetermined strategies but also, when they have already been suitably trained by previous experience, to determine *how* to execute them (e.g., just how high and how wide to swing the racquet head) independently of any further conscious decision making. (338)

Expanding on this image, we might say that a social regime "serves" to the subject in a specific way, triggering a "simple plan" at any one moment which is then executed more or less automatically (even if accompanied by the comfortable and banal illusion of ongoing subjective control). The reflexivity consists of the choice of strategy in the moment of "simple" planning; thereafter the external system of differential variations (fatally) takes over and things play out accordingly.

Chapter 5

Containment 2:
The Companionship of Things

Maybe it's a guy thing. For years, my most meaningful relationship was with my car. I'd like to think that those were my teen years, but even into my 30s (oh, let's be honest, even now), my vehicle has held a very special place in my life. If one day it had kicked some butt and talked to me, I might have had to marry it.

—Josef Steiff 2009, 55

The vehicle that kicked butt and talked is of course one of the Transformers, since 1985 a taken-for-granted fact of boys' popular culture. Across toy ranges, television animation series, comics, computer games, and Hollywood movies, catalogs of cars, trucks, and other everyday machines have revealed themselves as aliens in disguise. Accidental arrivals on Earth, their story defies most science fiction and scientific speculation about first contact with aliens: we did not seek them out, nor did they seek us out—they just ended up here and hid themselves where they most readily could, among our machines. For more than 25 years, their incarnations across a range of interlinked media—and always the toy ranges—have carried on the story of their relationships with each other and, as their presence made itself known, their relationships with us.

Fleming (1996) sets out three interlinked theories about toys and popular culture. The first is that a very particular semiotic space is generated around the narrativization of toys by popular culture more generally (especially television and comics). The second is that toys reveal a process theorized as "object relational interpellation." The earlier book explores the interaction of these first two theoretical perspectives: so that the specific positioning of a toy within the semiotic space determines its precise function in terms of object relational interpellation, while the latter determines the broad positioning that a toy has in that space, in a self-reinforcing feedback loop. The third theory concerns the idea (derived from Jean-François Lyotard) that an "inhuman" always inhabits the human and, in this instance, can be detected in both the child before it is "interpellated," or processed as a social being, and in contemporary technoculture, before human beings project their own images into it, so when toys and technoculture come together something interesting happens. It will not be surprising, then, that the popular quarter-century-long Transformers phenomenon is considered worthy of some attention here. First, though, the terms being used require an initial clarification.

Narrativization refers to the ways in which the narratives of a popular culture get attached to things such as toys: for example, most obviously when a toy is also a character in a television series or comic. When an adult asks about some (to them) bizarrely nonfunctional toy, "but what does it do?", the answer is likely to be that it carries this narrativization as its main reason for being. A semiotic space, in the sense intended here, is a precisely structured significatory system that can be literally mapped out for interpretive convenience, in which a meaningful item does not carry meaning as some inherent quality that it has but as a function of its position in the overall system. Object relational interpellation is theorized as a parallel but distinct process in relation to the more familiar notion of ideological interpellation, the "hailing" or calling of persons into a fixed social identity by the ideological apparatuses of their society (such as law, schooling, religion, etc.), as theorized so influentially by Louis Althusser. Object relational interpellation, it is argued, calls people into place via their relations with objects, with things, but is a looser process than the Althusserian one, especially in the lives of children and the residual traces of that for adults. In other words there is parallelism but also the possibility of a nonalignment in the two modes of interpellation. Georg Simmel, who saw "objective" culture becoming the master of subjectivity, came close to recognizing a parallelism between the society of things and the society of persons as he looked at the objects gathered for the 1896 Berlin Trade Exhibition and there is a "Simmelian" perspective at work in Fleming (1996), as there is in the present book.

Commenting on that earlier book, Bignell (2000) takes up the notion of the inhuman and the way in which this imbues the semiotic space in which toys operate with a particular emphasis, an ongoing concern for the relation between human and nonhuman. Hills (2002) takes up the theory of object relational interpellation and pushes it further along the lines of a psychoanalytically informed explanation. Geraghty (2008) takes up the theory of narrativization, specifically in relation to Transformers, discussed in the original work but, a decade later, a considerably more busy popular franchise. Lash and Lury (2007) situate this kind of work in a larger shift from representation to objects in the production of meaning that characterizes contemporary culture. Beyond the objects, Rutter identifies the perspective on play that is also at work here: "Toys, as Dan Fleming reads them, function 'as a kind of cultural construction kit', equipping children to order the 'overheard' world of adults. They should be seen 'not as objects, or not only as objects' but as 'events' generating 'traffic'—called 'play'" (75, quoting Fleming 1996, 11, 35). Banks (1998 para 5) also picks up on this perspective, especially in relation to computer games: "an analysis of the symbolic content of games tells us very little about what it is actually like to play them. He [Fleming] takes the step of shifting our attention from the meanings of cultural objects to their status as events" (referring to Fleming 1996, 11–16). This shift from representations to objects and objects-as-events is, of course, very much reflected in the present book, which may be seen as a further contribution to, and a development of, these perspectives.

More specifically, this book picks out one aspect of the semiotic space explored in the earlier work—a machinic dimension organized around terms such as rigid, mechanical, and not-orgiastic—and focuses much more closely on this. Again some clarification of terms may be needed. The semiotic space in question (or the space of interacting semiotic constraints, to be more precise), takes its cue from the term "ascetic" as a way of identifying the self-denial at the heart of historical social constructions of the child: the good child is the self-denying child who is not dirty, troublesome, noisy, unruly, and so on. Historical liberalization around this semiotic fulcrum has not removed it from its position as that which more liberal conceptions define their differences in relation to. Semiotically, this implies the presence of its opposite or contrary—the "orgiastic," or the opposite of self-denial, that is, the animalistic rather than the self-controlled. Logically, there is then also a contradictory term to the "orgiastic" in the overall significatory system being mapped, and it will be the "not-orgiastic," which is where the machinic takes its place, except that a semiotic system does not pin things in place so much as put them into play within a system of constraints on what they can possibly mean. So the machinic exists in a state of significatory tension, and potential slippage, in relation to other dimensions of the space. Nonetheless, it is not our intention this time to pay much attention to the other dimensions in themselves. Instead, what we want to do here is to concentrate on the tensions and slippages that happen specifically around the machinic dimension (see Fleming 1996, 159). It has been necessary to sketch this bit of background simply in order to situate this work in relation to a more wide-ranging analysis of toys as sociocultural objects. It has been noted, for example, by Bignell (2000), how many toys and associated things can be organized according to the system of semiotic constraints just sketched (from construction toys to furry animals, "ascetic" Victorian dolls to "orgiastic" plastic fantasy creatures). Here, though, the coming together of toys and technoculture makes specific sorts of object of special interest, among them conspicuously Transformers. So we will look in some detail at the various commentaries on the original work in order to pick out their particular implications with regard to this singular interest.

Jonathan Bignell is interested in the ways in which a toy such as the Barbie doll functions "to subsume difference under the sign of Barbie" but at the same time it has registered, perhaps grudgingly, a growing social "anxiety about the mastery over such differences." He goes on to say, with reference to the various "multicultural" Barbies,

> The extension and fragmentation of the brand resonates with the extension and fragmentation of the toy market, of gender identities and of cultural hegemony. [. . .] However, Barbie's status as a set of objects processing versions of the feminine for the child must be read in relation to versions of the masculine, and I agree with Dan Fleming that masculinity is the central term around which various kinds of toy body and identity are constellated, a "structure of meanings within which toys appear to 'test' the nature of male identity by pulling it first in one direction, then in another . . .". (2000, 122, quoting Fleming 1996, 50–1)

Bignell then usefully illustrates this "pulling" by elaborating on some examples from contemporary popular culture; the kinds of example which "suggest for Fleming that a masculine scopophilic look has been replaced by an ambiguously gendered one directed at machines" (124). This ambiguously gendered look directed at machines is clearly an important object of inquiry for the present work, and something that Chapter 6 will trace out into the wider culture of gadgetry and fast machines. So one way in which we need to develop our account of the machinic dimension, where it functions within the semiotic constraints on what toys as objects and objects-as-events can mean, is to look at how it is embedded in the sort of "pulling" Bignell elaborates on, bearing in mind perhaps the discussion of force in Paul Souriau's 1889 book

L'esthétique du movement, which might help us not to rush toward representations (and what we will be referring to as semiotizations) in order to detect, or give content to, this "pulling."

Along similar lines to Bignell's examples, Lincoln Geraghty analyzes an episode of the early Transformers animated television series, with its self-evident function as advertisements for the toys, its assembly line churning out of stories, its often shaky early animation-on-the-cheap production values, and yet its widespread appeal to children. Focusing on how such an episode contributes to narrativizing the toys as objects, Geraghty carefully unpacks the implications of an episode called "Child's Play" (Sunbow Productions 1985). This episode can also serve here as a quick introduction to the world of Transformers, machines brought to life by a mysterious long-lost cube called the AllSpark, and to the backstory that underpins this world.

Smokescreen: A rocket ship!

Inferno: A toy rocket ship.

Perceptor: Well, anything's worth a try.

The characters speaking here are three Autobots, one of the two warring races of Transformers in the main backstory, the other being the Decepticons. In this episode, a group of Autobots has been sucked into a "space bridge" or portal forced open during a violent encounter with Decepticons and they awake from unconsciousness to find themselves in the bedroom of a gargantuan alien child called Aron (or Erin in Geraghty's transcription). Unfortunately, a group of Decepticons has been transported across the "space bridge" with them. Aron first hides the Transformers in a drawer but is compelled to show them to his parents, following which they are taken to a laboratory for dissection. But Aron, realizing that they are on the side of good, saves the Autobots, despite being pursued by the authorities. The Decepticons manage to free themselves and also come in pursuit of Aron and the Autobots. But the Autobots succeed in converting Aron's toy rocket ship for space travel and they escape. Where they escape back to is Earth, for it is on our planet that the Autobots have already taken up residence, and where they are the gargantuan ones. Shook and Swan, editors of a collection of "philosophical" essays about Transformers, summarize this larger backstory thus:

> While many traditional alien stories involve the good humans versus evil aliens dichotomy, Transformers are unique in having their own

dichotomy to deal with—evil Decepticons and good Autobots. Humans immediately get caught in between, on a moral plane as well as a physical plane. [. . .] The fact that the Autobots remain on Earth to protect the planet and its people from the evil Decepticons makes them immediately endearing to us. They had an independent reason for coming to Earth, namely to recover the AllSpark and restore peace on their home planet of Cybertron. Yet they are now determined to protect the human inhabitants of the planet throughout their mission on Earth. In the 2007 movie we see the Autobots develop deep and moving relationships with a few humans and begin to witness in them a new transformation: from mere machines or robots to more thoughtful, compassionate, humanlike subjects. Transformers bear little resemblance to the little green men of the horror-scifi genre that wanted to harvest the human race for food or make us their slaves; they are instead an admirable race of beings in their own right, with their own history and future, concerns and motives, one of which includes the protection of the young and weak human race from the tyranny of the evil Decepticons. (2009, viii)

Lincoln Geraghty dwells informatively on the details of the "Child's Play" episode, which is from Season Two of the first television animation series and, therefore, represents an early point in the evolution of the franchise across multiple media and several decades. It is unusual in one sense—through the device of the giant alien child this episode explicitly narrativizes the dual status of Transformers object as both toy (Aron plays with them and puts them in his bedroom drawer) and fictional character (Aron befriends and assists them):

After he [Aron] rescues the Transformers from the scientist's laboratory he runs into the school bully who has been teasing him about the "childish" toys he plays with. Thanks to a renewed faith in himself, brought about by the Transformers he has befriended, Erin [*sic*] is able to counter the bully's jibes and proudly shows off his new toys, only now they are not toys to him. (Geraghty 2008, 188)

Lincoln Geraghty makes two very good points about this. First, the toy/character becomes in an especially striking way a symbolic "object of resilience" (189), thematized in this particular episode as standing up to the mocking bully, but generalizable as a symbolic resilience in the face of other challenges too. Second (and here he is drawing on Engelhardt), an ideological interpellation is also being effected in the context of the United States in the 1980s, when an emerging fascination with imagining a "victory culture" (Geraghty 2008, 189) was detectable in response to the national trauma of the Vietnam War. Stories like this one called its young subjects to that imagined "victory culture" (and ultimately, in some instances, to militarized visions for achieving it). Whether this was a product of the New Right's political ascendancy or something that the latter took ideological advantage of is a complex question. Kapell and Lawrence (2006, 213–14), discussing Fleming's treatment of the Star Wars franchise, which set the standard for successful cross-media formats and related merchandising, note that it also largely inaugurated this "victory culture" fascination in American popular media. So it is unsurprising to find this in Transformers too, as its roots are in the same period.

Matt Hills (2002) focuses less, however, on that sort of direct ideological interpellation and more on the theory of object relational interpellation, which complicates somewhat the former's tendency to encourage a reading-off of ideological "messages" from cultural phenomena. Hills points out an absolutely key issue in all of this: the question of whether affect can also be read-off from cultural phenomena, as distinct from a view of affect that places it antecedently, as underpinning or preceding particular cultural formations, in short the view that affect can "create" culture in addition to being produced by it. In Geraghty's example, Aron's literal possession of the Transformers might symbolize a banal delusion at the very heart of fandom and compliant young Aron might become the very prototype of an obsessive fan, carrying his "toys" around in his pocket while imagining, even in the face of mockery, that they are much more than that, his "affective" attachment wholly constructed for him as delusional dupe. It is also possible, however, that Aron is not this prototype, that an early Transformers television episode cannot "know" these things after all, much less reveal them to us, and that affect materializes in cultural objects in a different manner. Hills notes: "For Fleming, 'ideological interpellation' implies a fixing of the subject from the 'outside'; it is a matter of compliance. 'Object relational interpellation', on the other hand, reserves greater space for the subject in terms of this positioning being navigated from the 'inside'" (2002, 94). A simplistic way of expressing this might be to note that Aron in "Child's Play" does not know what he is doing when he "collects" the Transformers—they just arrive in his bedroom unsought, not beckoned, not actively wanted, indeed literally from outer space—so his relationship with them lacks that quality of potential reflexivity, or even strategy, on which any further potential for his "positioning being navigated" (see Chapter 4) would depend. Affective investments in particular objects may be highly constructed processes within the structures of ideological interpellation but affect may nonetheless take antecedence. Hills notes, "Grossberg's model of affect has perhaps been most usefully extended in Dan Fleming's (1996) study" (94) but, in fact, that extension hid a seriously unresolved question and it is to this that we now turn our attention.

The extension at stake here is precisely the notion of antecedent affect, where Larry Grossberg's work on affect stops short in this regard. Grossberg's hugely useful contribution in getting us to this point (1992a, 1992b) has been in persuasively clarifying a constructionist view of affect and of affect's role in audience attachments and, therefore, in fandom, where affect blurs constantly into discernible emotion. But in the end that constructionist view can leave no room for anything more than the delusional explanation of the fan's attachments, no matter how empathetic or un-mocking we might want to be about such attachments. The social construction of the very feeling and color of one's affect, once recognized, prevents us from slipping into any of the many variants of subjectivism to which we might be prone, but it also closes down, if theorized too tightly, too unyieldingly, the possibility of affective play that Fleming and Hills both want to recognize. The mattering maps that, as Grossberg shows us, structure and direct affective investments, matter then only to subjects whose very sense of mattering is itself so socially constructed that we risk concluding things do not really matter to anybody in any meaningfully subjective sense; they are just constructed as mattering and then the question of "to whom" is dealt with by inserting a constructed subject into the picture in the right place. Superimposing on this some common sense notions, such as the fan's love of the object, floats a somewhat looser vocabulary on top of an unresolved theoretical conundrum (as Henry Jenkins tends to prefer to do on occasion), though this is of course a tempting and entirely understandable move in the interests of actually describing some observable behaviors of fandom (which Jenkins does so excellently).

Three ways forward suggest themselves: first, there is the possibility of developing the semiotic perspective introduced above, which is what Matt Briggs (2007) does; second, Matt Hills (2002) develops a psychoanalytic interpretation of fan cultures; third, an approach to affect and its materializing in things is being developed here. Matt Briggs' broadly semiotic approach to affective play needs to be considered first. But as a signpost to where we will be going with the larger argument, we should note that our conceptualization of affect is being proposed, in several ways, as an alternative to some features of both the semiotically and the psychoanalytically conceived ones: as a way of thinking about object relational interpellation that emphasizes the object as other than a production of semiosis or psychoanalytically described processes, as something more solid in itself, at which point the machinic (underlying F1, Transformers, etc.) takes on a particular character as forces, efforts, events, and materializations.

Matt Briggs focuses on "the semiotic productivity of . . . intertextual connections" (2007, 505), but also on the sorts of connection and "recontextualization processes" that Anne Haas Dyson (2003) emphasizes in her descriptions of "textual toys" and "the processes of transporting and transforming material across symbolic and social borders" (10), processes unconfined to the worlds of childhood as our examples in Chapter 1 suggest. However, where Haas Dyson goes the whole way with this and tends to collapse the actual toy object, the thing, into its larger textual network, as it were, and to redraw the boundary defining a toy in ways that are unconstrained by the physical object, Briggs still pays very close attention to the things themselves, in this instance the soft toys and linked objects that populate the lives of two children:

> A Disney film, a favorite book, a much loved toy, a child at play, a parent caring for her child: this is by no means a new phenomenon. It is of the "everyday". But we need to unpack the everyday, to see how the meanings of children's media culture are realized through practice, practices that are both *global* in their economic scope and *singular* in their concreteness. (504)

In a model piece of autoethnographic writing, Matt Briggs offers detailed observational accounts of Jessica and Isaac in situ, in their everyday contexts, engaging in activities with their parents (Matt and his partner in the case of Isaac) that are broadly typical but no less singular in their detailed particulars, while shifting his analytical framework in ways that progressively reveal the presence of the "global" in the singular (not just in the "typical"). It becomes very easy to see in this material how no other method than autoethnography would have had access to the level of detail needed. Briggs' overall method here is to combine acute autoethnographic observation with an analysis of how "meaning potentials" existing at the level of Haas Dyson's "textual toys" (where intertextual networks link toys, story books, television cartoons, other merchandizing, etc., including Jessica's t-shirt) get "drawn into semiosis" (504) in specific contexts and therefore organize the singular in particular ways at the level of observable detail. That the singular details are organized by- rather than wholly produced or predicted by—the systems of *meaning potential* Briggs identifies, is especially important since acknowledging this also recognizes that the globalized industries producing children's cul- ture via so many interacting channels do not produce every singular aspect of—every event constituting—the particular child's "everyday" contact with objects.

The phrase "drawn into semiosis" is derived from the work of Kress and Van Leeuwen who use it, for example, in arguing that the material under- pinning forms of artistic production (say the paint in a brushstroke) should itself be attended to because when "unsemioticized materiality is drawn into semiosis" something at the material level remains "less subject to the various forms of semiotic policing than are other regions of the semiotic landscape" (2006, 217). When analysis of artistic production assumes instead, as it so often does, that all the material used gets drawn into semiosis with nothing left over that is worth attending to, materiali- ty's potentially loose relationship with semiotic policing goes unacknowl- edged. Briggs does not trace the phrase's background in this way, but he implies the same kind of partially "unpoliced" quality in Jessica's young life, or Isaac's, where the material things that populate their everyday existence then get drawn into semiosis where they meet the "meaning potentials" deposited there (or drawn into semiosis from outside as it were) by the intertextual networks that are produced in turn by the global industries engaged in manufacturing contemporary children's culture.

Condensing our summary of Matt Briggs' piece in this way does not do justice to its supple articulations of observation and analysis. These are achieved using a distinction, derived from Volosinov, between the "upper" and "lower" limits of the meaning potentials referred to (for Volosinov, respectively, these are the words used in a concretely situated utterance and the more abstractly systemic contexts of a word within language, a distinction widely deployed within the literature of semiotics influenced by Volosinov), where Volosinov suggests that investigation of meaning has to choose which direction it is going in because it cannot do both simultaneously:

> while I refuse the either/or distinction suggested by Volosinov, this literature can be read alongside accounts such as those of Stephen Kline or of Dan Fleming, for example, which recognize the creativity

of children's play with textual toys but also raise quite legitimate concerns over its "modeling" by the products of the media and toy industries. (Briggs, 506)

Where Matt Briggs' most detailed account is based on infant Isaac's interactions with *Teletubbies*, a British television series for young children with spin-off manifestations in other forms, we want to extract his method to some degree and ask how it might be applied to exploring something like Transformers instead. Briggs' approach:

places emphasis on the *practice*-based ways in which textual boundaries are destabilized, and thus the location of the analysis. Typically, this will include the television program or film, a range of DVDs, website materials and the books they are either based on or generate, theme songs, comics, plush toys or other figurines, various other themed toys (such as vehicles from the books or programs), clothes, foodstuffs. Other merchandizing material will include items such as cereal packaging, stickers and pull-out posters. In such a field of intertextuality it is meaningless to try and identify the "primary" text, for this is not how children encounter them. (Briggs 2007, 513)

This surrendering of the primary text is a hard thing for the academic writer or reader to achieve, so accustomed are we to finding and concentrating on a primary text and consigning everything related to it to secondary or marginal status, if not to invisibility. So the term "Transformers" has probably already here conjured up one or other of the possibly "primary" texts (TV series, films?) and the expectation that we will soon shift to analyzing that. This is especially ironic in the case of Transformers, which started out and remains "primarily" a toy range. The brief discussion above of the "Child's Play" episode already flirted with this temptation. But for 2-year-old Jessica her Winnie the Pooh soft toy or even her t-shirt may be the "primary" text for her, the thing around which the rest of her Pooh universe orbits, no matter how much we might want to believe that A. A. Milne's book should be considered unassailably primary; though it is more likely that this status will circulate through her various things for Jessica as her interests shift, the things come and go and she changes (as DS did in the fan's career of affect documented in Chapter 4). So too with Transformers: we need to refuse any temptation to focus on a "primary" manifestation or at least to recognize that what is primary for a fan may change over time. Charting a trajectory across a strategy-intensity field, as we did in the previous chapter, may be one effective way of achieving this.

Briggs describes detailed sequences of interaction among child, parents, television, toys, books, and other objects in the room. Things that objectively assessed on their own might seem "disappointing," in Briggs' words, can take on a more interesting life interactively and dynamically in these contexts and at its fullest ". . . meaning potential is only realized—as the upper level of significance—as it connects to other media, play and parenting practices" (516). The processes through which these daily practices and discourses get interactively "drawn into semiosis" are neither accessible in any adequate sense to textual analysis on its own, nor is there some sort of abstract "inter-text" that can be extrapolated from them for separate analysis. "Methodologically, this is the most difficult aspect of semiosis to render in analysis as the nature of such a dynamic resists textualization" (519). Briggs' own solution is to look for those gravitational *moments* when the circulating stuff, whatever its provenance (a toy, a story, a belief about good parenting, "fantasies of our own childhoods, as well as culturally shaped imaging of Isaac's future" (519)) gets drawn into semiosis, because that process makes the moment, gives it its affective charge, makes it feel significant, organizes it. Alert, sensitive autoethnographic description should be able to recognize these moments as no other method can, because the "drawing into" deposits its own tracks and traces in what it is organizing and in what is autoethnographically describable, including trails that run back into the participants' own pasts (in Briggs' example their own childhoods). This is a long way away from any more self-indulgent autoethnography that merely exposes the self and its singular settings in the interests of subjective revelation. And its strength, methodologically, is that it recognizes how simultaneously being drawn into semiosis, organizing the very same moments from the outside, will be the "industrial" practices (the lower level of organization) that manufacture, package and sell the things, stories, beliefs, fantasies, and imagings. That these two levels of organization parallel each other and will always be at least loosely synchronized does not mean that they are identical, that one totally determines the other, as clearly the dynamic interactions in situ, in an everyday setting, though "modeled" from outside, afford too much inherent potential for dynamic, spontaneous, *playful* reorganization for them to be considered simply scripted actions. Determined textualists have often tried to find this kind of play within freestanding texts but this can seem a punishingly self-defeating task sometimes, so tight is the lower limit's grip on what is manufactured. In the spaces where texts go into play (form nesting loops) with other things, however, it can be a different story.

One of Matt Briggs' autoethnographic descriptions of interacting with Isaac (and with *Teletubbies* on television) is especially interesting for us:

> To get my attention, he empties out his cardboard brick bucket and puts it on his head. Discarding my pen and paper I kneel down and speak into it. We have played this before and it echoes like the talking periscope that constantly announces the teletubbies' comings and goings. My voice echoes: "time for tubby by-byes, time for tubby bye-byes". Laughing he takes it off, it's my turn now, "put it on your head daddy." As soon as *Teletubbies* finishes, Isaac quickly lost all interest in the television. (515)

Briggs is interested in unpacking this moment in the context of a larger flow of interaction, in which participants and objects are transported to and fro across Haas Dyson's symbolic and social borders, as textual boundaries are transgressed, television worlds merge with other worlds, and roles are modeled, reenacted and improvised, including fictional roles and parent/child roles understood in specific historically and culturally contingent ways (as well as the role that has daddy holding a pen and paper). The remainder of the present book could be given over to such unpackings and still not exhaust the multiple ways in which "drawing into semiosis" from the two limits of significance informs just this one moment. But instead we want to think about the bucket.

The little boy with the bucket over his head serves as a useful reminder of Kress and Van Leeuwen's very important point about "unsemiotized" materiality, even though the bucket and the body of the boy get instantly (re)organized by whatever is being drawn into semiosis in the moment. The image could also serve as a mocking indictment of the present book's seemingly banal objects of inquiry, its two authors mere reenactments of the boy with the bucket over his head. This might seem especially tempting when we make the point that it is very easy indeed to imagine the bucket as a racing helmet or Transformers "costume," not just a *Teletubbies* periscope: that those things could so readily be drawn into semiosis in slightly different circumstances (a different domestic setting, a child of a different age, something else on the television, etc.) This is not just to make an obvious point about the use of props in play. Rather, what we want to glimpse here is a "substrate" that is other than semiotic but more than brute matter and, in addition, is where the machinic is staged by father and son prior to its semiotization as peri-scope, helmet, or robot head. The little boy with the bucket over his head becomes prototypically android in the instant. The technology of the bucket with the body momentarily attached to it achieves a material-izing of affect that is not yet fully semiotized in specific ways.

At this point, having suggested that objects can be momentarily other than a production of semiosis, we need to turn to Matt Hill's offering of a psychoanalytic perspective on object relational interpellation as in some sense the most obvious way to explain that otherness, especially in the context of fan attachments (the boy with the bucket over his head also serving as a prototype "fan," in this instance of *Teletubbies*). We can see the move from a semiotic to a psychoanalytic perspective after Hills (2002) summarizes the exchange at the center of the object-relational perspective: "This ongoing process of exchange between 'inner' and 'outer' is what characterizes any broadly object-relations perspective: the self is always related to, and realized in, a particular environment" (97). Up to this point, the description could apply to Briggs' semiotic perspec-tive with its inner and outer limits on semiosis. But Hills goes on: "These exchanges of self and environment occur, however, at the level of uncon-scious fantasy: we are not aware of their dynamics" (97). This is a seem-ingly small but hugely important step, should it be taken. The processes of "unconscious fantasy" might be called upon to explain the boy's attachment to the bucket. The remainder of the present book could be given over to unpacking the inner workings of such unconscious fantasy and still not exhaust the multiple ways in which "drawing into fantasy," as we might now refer to it, informs just this one moment. But instead we still want to think about that bucket.

What Matt Hills is doing here, and quite persuasively, is wholly identify-ing object relational interpellation with the object relations school of psychoanalysis, from which much of the vocabulary about "objects" in this sense may be derived. But an "object" for this school of thought is for the most part another person, or a part of a person, rather than some-thing like our bucket. Good and bad objects, for example, in the life of the child, are used to split off and project parts of the self. Perhaps a feel-ing that one does not want to admit to being one's own or some other kind of stress or anxiety begin to threaten a "good" part of oneself so the latter is projected out onto an object where it is safe from compromise or damage but can also be identified with, so it remains unabandoned. A celebrity figure as object of fandom in this sense becomes a repository (whether deserving or not) for something that the fan needs or values, recognizes as "good," but fails to keep coherently integrated into the self. The drawing into fantasy of these others then becomes a characteristic of fandom where it is observed at its most apparently obsessive. But this also comes close to installing a stereotype of the "obsessed" fan as the norm in fandom and, where psychoanalysis in a clinical setting is typically concerned more with the unusual or aberrant case, a failure to "contain" psychoanalysis within such settings therefore poses its own risks, as Hills fully recognizes:

> This "containment" is important because it should strive to prevent a form of psychoanalytic "authority" from writing its "knowledge" over common sense categories. Just as I have observed that narrative and "common sense" closures in autoethnographies are narcissistic, so too are all types of psychoanalytic closure which are achieved by surreptitiously filtering psychoanalytic expertise through "common sense". (97)

Thus, "the theory concerned is projected onto the object (fan culture), blanketing it without remainder or resistance" (97). Hills "mischievously" suggests that the theorist is, in this case, allowing no creative object-relationship between themselves and the object of study, just as they are allowing no playful object-relationship between fan and object of attachment, merely a playing out of the theory time and again and in every situation, observed by the objectively detached theorist. Far from being mischievous, this is a vital admonition. As a counterbalance, we might recall Matt Briggs setting down his pencil and pen in order to crawl around on the floor saying "time for tubby by-byes!"

Notwithstanding, though, this careful refusal of an ultimate psychoanalytic authority over everyday things, Matt Hills goes on to propose that Winnicottian "little madnesses" may explain a lot about everyday fandom. Winnicott was a key figure in the British object relations school (along with Klein and Fairbairn, the latter the originator of the term "object relations theory"). Winnicott's descriptions of what he termed transitional objects in a third space or "no-man's land" between the "inner" and "outer" worlds help explain what he called (1988, 107) the little madnesses characteristic of the cultural enthusiasms he saw around him. For Winnicott, the child is indulged when inhabiting that no-man's-land but the adult attempting to do so is frequently seen as deranged: "Someone claiming indulgence in this respect at a later age is called mad" (107). But in cultural attachments, "we see the claim socialized so that the individual is not called mad and can enjoy . . . the rest that human beings need from absolute and never-failing discrimination between fact and fantasy" (107). An editorial footnote tells us that these lines are from a paragraph found separately typed from Winnicott's post-humously published manuscript for *Human Nature*, accompanied by a note that the paragraph should be added, so what for us is an important point about culture as a domain of affective play was for Winnicott some-thing of an afterthought. Were we to have found Matt Briggs crawling around on the floor saying "time for tubby by-byes" in the absence of any child, we might have had a candidate for labeling deranged. Were we to find Matt watching *Teletubbies* on television on his own because he likes them, we just might though have a candidate for Winnicottian indul-gence (although noticing a pen and paper by his side would definitively save him from any potential embarrassment). The point is that Winnicott's little madnesses are not too difficult to indulge within the cultural domain these days; the claim for indulgence has been quite thoroughly socialized, as Winnicott puts it. So that third space is itself indulged and, therefore, becomes available for psychoanalytically inclined theorizing without implying any aberrance, but at the same time (this is Hills' key point) can then be rationalized away as just the site of more of these little madnesses. The latter start to lose any specificity as a consequence. Any "transitional" objects will do if all that is happening is another variant of the person hanging on to their teddy bear a bit longer than one might have expected, a harmlessly failed discrimination between Winnicott's "fact and fantasy" that can be indulged, especially in the guise of fandom (where curiously the collector of teddy bears hardly needs any "indul-gence" compared with the adult person who is significantly attached to only one, such are the paradoxes of socialized indulgence).

What is at stake here is what we mean by "inner," if we continue to use that term. The Winnicottian identification of "inner" with "fantasy" and "outer" with "fact," implied in his note above, is of course simplistic (and in Winnicott's defense he was only using the terms casually in this instance in order to make a more general point), but there is a risk of retrospec-tively misreading Briggs' use of the terms "upper" and "lower" limits of significance to imply some sort of "outer" and "inner" as well. In fact, using Volosinov, Briggs was positing a flatter but potentially vast semiotic landscape, extending through and beyond the room in which he was playing with his son, with no particular sense of there being an "inside" and an "outside" to it (other than the merely architectural with its public/private zone distinction); its "lower" limit defined instead by a systemic production of meanings, in this case by the global manufacturing of children's culture, its "upper" limit defined by the intertextual play thus supported in specific instances. So it is tempting to build a composite picture by inserting the object-relational psychoanalytic approach into that semiotic landscape in order to give the moments of play there some more depth. But we need at exactly this point to step back and ask what a psychoanalytic conception of depth, of an "inside," really entails. In his introduction to Ronald Fairbairn's (1952) *Psychoanalytic Studies of the Personality*, Ernest Jones (Freud's official biographer) nails this for us with lucid precision:

> Instead of starting, as Freud did, from stimulation of the nervous system proceeding from excitation of various erotogenous zones and internal tension arising from gonadic activity, Dr Fairbairn starts at the center of the personality, the ego, and depicts its strivings and difficulties in its endeavor to reach an object where it may find support. (Fairbairn 1952, v)

Fairbairn, a key figure in the development of the object-relations perspective, was interested primarily in the self's orientation toward its "outer" environment, its strategies for survival there, its attachments less to fantasized "inner" objects than to things in that environment, where the kinds of "excitation" that so interested Freud attach themselves to objects as signs of the latter's significance to the self, rather than the objects being sought out in order then to release pent up "inner" excitation—in the form of pleasures—channeled through them. Jones' vocabulary also reminds us forcefully that we are listening here to the words of late nineteenth and early twentieth century medical men, for the most part; doctors whose ideas about what goes on "inside" the person were largely determined by their own times and situations. Jacques Lacan's subsequent updating of psychoanalytic theory for a flatter world, a time at which it was more feasible to articulate psychoanalytic interests in terms of language structures, released a torrent of new ideas but few of them returned to any robust notion of an "inside," in part because that terrain was being taken over by neuroscientists and, in particular, by what would subsequently come to be thought of as the "affect revolution" (Eakin 2003).

Antonio Damasio has been at the forefront in explaining the turn to affect in neuroscience. Damasio (2004) includes an intriguing discussion of a remark by Fred Astaire about the dancer Cyd Charisse, with whom Astaire was cinematically partnered so often: "'She came at me in sections; she had more curves than a scenic highway' said Fred Astaire . . . Very stirring, indeed, and very mappable in the body-sensing and cognitive support brain regions" (94). Far from reducing the magic of the (very object-relational) moment to brain and body maps that leave no room for feelings, Damasio describes more or less the opposite based on today's neuroscientific research. He summarizes the growing body of evidence for "the idea that we are privy to a sense of the body's interior, an *interoceptive* sense" (106), a sense not delivered to us cognitively but affectively because:

> the peripheral nerve fibers and neural pathways dedicated to convey-ing information from the body's interior to the brain do not termi-nate, as once thought, in the cortex that receives signals related to touch . . . Instead, those pathways terminate in their own dedicated region . . . precisely the same region whose activity patterns are per-turbed by feelings of emotion. [. . .] From a variety of perspectives, then, the somatosensing regions appear to be a critical substrate for feelings. (106)

So rather than being like touch, delivered from "outside" for cognitive processing, a sense of the body's "inside" is delivered by different neural pathways for affective processing. Counterintuitive though this may be, the neuroscientific evidence suggests that Fred is stirred by Cyd not because affect generated from "outside" stirs the body's internal systems but because those systems stir the affect that then attaches itself to the object. Just as Damasio's "somatosensing" or body-interior-sensing pro-vides a "critical substrate" for affect (by "feelings of emotion" Damasio means affect), so affect provides a critical substrate for object relations.

Which brings us back again to the boy with his head in the bucket. What Matt Briggs' autoethnographic account allows us to see is bodies:

> Sara and I are watching *Teletubbies* with Isaac one Sunday morning. Tinky Winky, Dipsy, La La and Po are dancing and stretching just as the children had been. Standing up to demonstrate, Sara joins in this dialogue and asks Isaac if he can jump. I join in as Isaac laughs by pick-ing him up. All three of us dance and stretch along with the Teletub-bies on the screen. After a few moments I launch Isaac up into the air. When I put him back down he jumps himself, with bended knees launching himself upwards giggling gleefully. A little later Isaac takes my pen as I write my notes; he seems to say "daddy, we're watching

Teletubbies with mummy—put that down and play". There is little doubt about this; he is insistent as only a toddler can be and actions speak louder than words. To get my attention, he empties out his cardboard brick bucket and puts it on his head. Discarding my pen and paper I kneel down and speak into it. (2007, 515)

The bucket then becomes the Teletubbies' "periscope" because that is available in the moment for semiotic appropriation, is available for affect to attach itself to, having already attached itself to the bucket, at which point the affective substrate tends to disappear from view, as it were, under the weight of all the things getting drawn into semiosis in the moment. So there is an "inside" here but it is not particularly helpful to theorize it in any specific psychoanalytical terms, because it is the affective substrate with its neural links to the body's interior, the body so clearly engaged in the scene described. Isaac and his parents have generated an affective state that is almost palpable from Matt's vivid description (his pen and notes were after all to hand) and what we witness is affect reaching out for objects delivered to it from both the upper and the lower limits of significance.

If we retain, then, something of Fairbairn's notion that there is in such instances of attachment to things an "endeavor to reach an object where [the subject] may find support," then we are also returned to the idea of "interpellation" in the theory of object relational interpellation: of a possible calling into place via attachments to objects. If we are to understand Transformers in these terms, it may be useful to step up from the bucket through a series of progressively more complex objects, culminating in Transformers.

A place to start is the School Boot—a big, colorful plastic toy that is simultaneously a friendly old boot and a miniature schoolhouse. Aimed at children who are beginning to negotiate that tricky boundary between home and school for the first time, the boot has windows and doors and a clock above its chunky green laces. The child can open it up to reveal an idyllic schoolroom within, with removable plastic desks, blackboard, teacher and pupils, the latter all smiling happily. At a moment in their lives when mastery of such things becomes important, children can learn to tell the time from the School Boot's clock or to tie shoelaces with its big green strings. Described thus, it may sound like a rather bizarre object but it isn't. Somehow it all works together, even to the adult eye, because—we would suggest—it is so affectively satisfying and symbolically functional. Where the boundary between home and school is experienced as hard and even threatening to the child at first, the School Boot softens that boundary, blurs the categories, and offers symbolic mastery and reassurance. It functions in many other ways (there are pleasures in the required dexterity, the colors, the scope for taking the little figures in and out, in that familiar Freudian fort-da game) but centrally it functions as a symbolic resolution of things in the environment that would otherwise be in an unsettling state of tension and contradiction for the child. We would argue that many toys function in this way—indeed that toys that are embedded in today's complex media marketing matrix probably always work in this way, because this is how popular culture tends to function in general. A persistent, informing satisfaction of media-generated popular culture in the late industrial societies has been the cultural resolution of social contradictions. Where social life in industrial and postindustrial nations has been fraught with increasing tensions and contradictions, the television, the popular music, the multiplex cinema entertainment, the popular bestseller have all found successful formulas for engaging with those tensions just deeply enough to then effect a symbolic sleight of hand, magically finding time and again the narrative resolutions, the generic archetypes, the emotional conventions, the closures, that "make it better," like a mother rubbing the child's grazed elbow. Of course, in order to achieve this effect, the cultural has to admit the contradictions and consequent tensions in the first place, so there is always the risk that the most simplistic resolutions will not work, will not contain all the leaky affect. Therein resides some radical potential, but that is a point to be returned to toward the end of this book.

To shift our attention from the School Boot to a more complex object— the Terminator 2 Bio-Regenerator toy—is only to move to a more complex, more clearly contemporary instance of the same process of symbolic resolution. With the Bio-Regenerator toy the child pours plastic into a mold to form a human-looking skin round a little robot skeleton, creating a Terminator-style android from which the skin can then be peeled off in any number of imaginative scenarios (derived loosely from James Cameron's Terminator films). It is not the boundary between home and school at issue here but that between the human and the machine, our theme here, one of the great themes of late twentieth century culture and a source of very real ideological tensions as we have suggested. The point here is not, however, to pursue further examples (which are everywhere when one starts looking for them), but to develop some of the implications that arise from this interest in symbolic resolutions. (For other examples see Fleming 2008.) Having recognized the importance

of symbolic resolutions in the function of toys as popular cultural arti-
facts, we can see that these resolutions are ways of managing anxiety,
whether personal (going to school for the first time) or social (the tension between the human and the machine). It may be useful, consequently, to raid some of the existing research on the management of
anxiety in order to see if there is anything we can adapt to our specific
interest in toys and, ultimately, to relate back to the hypothesized affective substrate. We are thinking, in particular, of Csikszentmihalyi's work
on "flow" in relation to happiness. Children are usually happy when playing with toys and happiness is more than an accumulation of little pleasures (or "little madnesses"). The summary form of Csikszentmihalyi's
long-term research on happiness is the notion, which he himself has
popularized, of the "flow channel" between anxiety-inducing challenges
and the exercise of anxiety-reducing skills. In that flow channel, athletes
perform at their best, surgeons save most lives, musicians reach the sublime and, if we are lucky, we all do our best work—and our best play. If we
examine Csikszentmihalyi's (1992, 74) visual representation of this flow
channel (Figure 5.1), we will find that it raises some interesting questions
about toys and object-relational symbolic resolutions. It also suggests how
the affective component in affective play may be operating.

Position A1 here is where somebody starts doing something fairly
simple for the first time (the standard example is a child hitting a tennis ball over a net). There is a brief interlude of flow occasioned by the

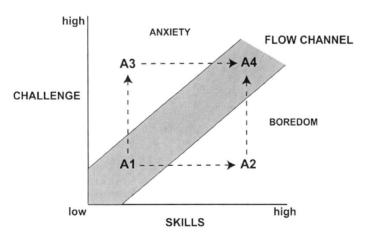

FIGURE 5.1 The flow channel for "optimal experience" (Csikszentmihalyi
1992, 74).

newness of the activity and the simple satisfaction of doing it but this does not last long. Two things can happen quickly to shift the experience out of the flow channel: to either A2 where the activity simply becomes boring (the skill is greater than the challenge) or A3, where a greater challenge is posed but the available skill is insufficient and anxiety results (in the example, a more skilled opponent starts returning the ball). To become happy with the situation once more, to have affect reach out satisfactorily to its objects, our player has to find some way of reaching position A4. From being bored, the way back is to take on more challenges. From being anxious, the way back is to develop more skill. In fact, in reality, both routes are likely to be taken because the person is likely to oscillate between anxiety and boredom at different times (though Baudrillard has reminded us that boredom often seems to be an end in itself, perhaps as the ultimate evasion of anxiety). Oscillating without ever settling in the flow channel is a reliable recipe for unhappiness (in many areas of life, of course, not just when "playing"). Now, what happens if we further apply this simple model to playing with the kinds of toy that offer symbolic resolutions of the sort evoked above?

Figure 5.2 represents such an adaptation. Here the zone of "anxiety" is identified with unresolved social and cultural contradictions. "Boredom" remains an adequate way of describing the other zone, although at this more generalized level "affective apathy" might be more accurate. Effective play in the flow channel will reduce the challenges of the social zone

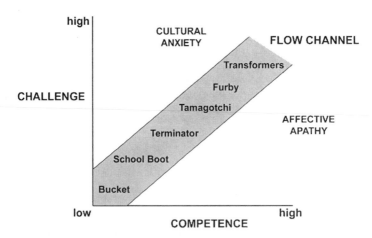

FIGURE 5.2   The flow channel "populated."

to more manageable demands, compatible with the potential skill levels of the child. The School Boot can be located fairly low on the flow channel—its symbolic reductionism is considerable and the required skills fairly basic but this is not incompatible with the target age range of 3–5 year olds. The Terminator 2 Bio Flesh Regenerator is higher on the flow channel, not least because of the sophistication required to "read" the toy in terms of its filmic reference points. It is also more complicated to use and captures a more challenging site of social contradiction—the deeply ambiguous love-hate relationship between human beings and their increasingly powerful machines in the late twentieth and early twenty-first centuries (although we will shortly challenge such vocabulary for expressing only a "weak" version of the kinds of contradiction we need to identify). Before we consider the other examples that have been entered in the flow channel in Figure 5.2, it remains to emphasize in more general terms the value of this appropriation of Csikszentmihalyi's model.

By hypothesizing a flow channel located between, on the one hand, the "tensions" of the real or the "challenges" of the social world and, on the other, the child's descent into affective apathy in relation to those tensions and challenges, we may have identified where and why certain toys have proved to be particularly successful. What happens in this flow channel may be that play actively manages the anxiety-producing material of the social world, given the right resources from the toy manufacturers. The sometimes unholy alliance between toy manufacturers and popular media has given the former access to a larger proving ground for imaginative concepts capable of effecting those symbolic resolutions—the television series, comics, movies, computer games, and so on—a Darwinian arena where only the most symbolically resilient concepts survive and prosper. It has to be noted, though, that this approach has very little to say directly about the manipulative marketing now so characteristic of that alliance. We can take as given the fact that the media marketing matrix now entraps children and parents in one vicious cycle after another where fads are invented and promoted and the "I want" is rendered almost irresistible by combined marketing and peer pressure, until today's fad is dropped and the cycle moves on to another one. But that is a matter of the sorts of society we want and the sorts of economies we require in order to have them—the toy industry cannot necessarily be faulted for behaving like the industry it is, especially in a period when media have become central to the global economy (itself virtually in so many respects an "entertainment economy," as some would now have it) and toys are an integral part of media-sustained popular culture generally. But central to this economy is the realization that people consume meanings that attach to things, that have been drawn into semiosis around things, and that such meanings have to mean something to people before they will consume them as happily as the marketers intend. One major function of the most happily consumed meanings—in our selective sample, from those of the School Boot to the Transformers 2 Bio-Regenerator toy and on through various early manifestations of the android *imaginaire* to Transformers—is to offer symbolic resolutions of "outside" stuff that would otherwise be experienced as splintered by contradictions and anxieties. So we—and more importantly our children—can find the productive resources required by affective play's flow channel amidst the marketing pressures exerted by those who themselves may have no idea how play works in these terms, or at this level, but who can recognize something that is working (selling) when they see it.

That is an appropriate introduction to the other toys located in Figure 5.2, the Tamagotchi, Furby, and Transformers; the first two from early in Transformers' quarter-century career. High on play's flow channel in recent years we find these examples of "artificial life." Growing interest in species of "cyberpet" conceived and nurtured online as well as in computers and portable devices extended this list for a while. Why else should this be, if not because the issue of machine intelligence was among the most challenging scientific, technological and social conundrums at the turn of the millennium. As microprocessor-driven machines outpaced their human creators in many areas of information handling, a great cultural theme became the difference (if there is one) between human and machine intelligence. Unsurprisingly then, toys have emerged that put that theme into the hands of children. The Tamagotchi introduced the notion of cyberpets to children. Its eight iconic manifestations of "life" delimited a narrow but engaging range of interaction around food, light, play, health, medicine, toilet, discipline, and attention (the eight kinds of interaction which could be selected on the first Tamagotchi's tiny controls). But subsequent developments of the cyberpet concept reached into the realm of computer-based simulations of life processes to offer children a much more complex range of interactions with artificial life-forms. The "classic" Tamagotchi from Bandai was in essence a tiny, highly portable computer game. FinFin was a PC-based pet from Fujitsu, where the eponymous creature (half bird, half dolphin) lived in a represented natural environment which the owner could view through an on-screen window, with basic navigation controls that allowed different locations to be visited and for FinFin to be tracked and observed like a wild animal. Creatures, a computer game from Mindscape Entertainment, elaborated this idea into an even more complex world where one became parentally responsible for raising little creatures called Norns. The Norns developed different personalities and interacted both with each other and with the "player," who appeared in their world as a large disembodied hand that could lift and move objects and even slap them for being naughty. These examples spanned the range from the minimalist, one-dimensional "pet" to the realistic computer-based environment where artificial life-forms can be hatched, nurtured, bred, and mourned when they die. What, then, is really going on in sociocultural terms with this still comparatively recent trend? Clearly it was first and foremost precisely that—a trend. These things have their own momentum, driven by the marketing tendency to pursue a winning formula. Beyond this, however, we want to argue that we see here another large-scale symbolic resolution. The question of whether smart machines are like us (or we are like them) has been one of the hot contemporary topics in cognitive science. It is also a topic that has broken out of scientific debate into popular culture—the androids of more recent cinematic and televisual science fiction have had the symbolic resonance that robots had in an earlier period. Transformers, however, stepped up the game yet again.

It is necessary, though, to admit that this way of describing "tensions" and "contradictions" around the techno-machinic is a form of weak description. We are writing in generalizations in order to evoke some generalized "anxiety" at this level that can be mapped onto Csikszentmihalyi's highly situation-specific use of that term (e.g., the specific anxiety of facing a much better opponent on the other side of the tennis net). What would a *strong* description look like?

For this we can usefully return to 1984, the year of the Transformers' birth, and to a strong description from that same moment of the "tensions" and "contradictions" posed by a simmering crisis in "What We Believe Ourselves To Be," a chapter title from Derek Parfit's *Reasons and Persons* (and where the Orwellian aura that still hangs around that date contributes to a sense of appropriateness in doing so). Derek Parfit, in a book of sometimes mind-bending step-by-step philosophical logic, leads us toward some profound conclusions that still resonate a quarter century later, one of which bears directly on our more mundane concerns here, as well as tapping into the zeitgeist and explaining something fundamental about these toys. Parfit begins this particular chapter with an invocation of something like Star Trek's transporter, the omnipresent device in the various Star Trek television series that instantly disassembled people, transported them elsewhere ("beam me up Scotty!") and reassembled them, in casually confident disregard of any nonmaterial component of the person. Parfit imagines himself getting teletransported to Mars: "Though I believe that this is what will happen, I still hesitate. But then I remember seeing my wife grin when, at breakfast today, I revealed my nervousness. As she reminded me, she has often been teletransported, and there is nothing wrong with *her*" (Parfit 1984, 199). Now here is a real anxiety. Despite our utter familiarity with, and suspension of disbelief in, the concept from Star Trek, who among us would not share Derek Parfit's hesitation if confronted by the real opportunity? Would we not worry about something integral to our self being lost despite replication of "the exact states of all my cells" (199), and this even if we did not have some faith in a nonmaterial element such as personality or soul? As Parfit goes on to demonstrate, this nervousness is a sign of a much larger and pervasive anxiety about what it means to be a person in the face of such potential powers. We might suggest that the person stepping into the transporter is accepting their own gadgetization, as we shall be calling it in the next chapter. Parfit notes Quine's objection to taking the imaginary cases of science fiction too seriously (Quine said, "The method of science fiction has its uses in philosophy" but suggested that it clouded the clarity of philosophical logic and language): "This criticism might be justified if, when considering such imagined cases, we had no reactions. But these cases arouse in most of us strong beliefs. And these are beliefs, not about our words, but about ourselves" (200). This is Parfit the philosopher speaking, of course, while his imaginary piece of autoethnography also nicely suggests the affective substrate that is additionally involved in this arousal of beliefs, the immediate nervousness antecedent to any expression of belief.

Where Star Trek's technology conveniently destroyed the original in the act of replicating it, Parfit imagines himself being recreated on Mars without this destruction of the first self taking place and therefore himself existing in two places and in two instantly diverging lives that cannot then be the same (what he terms the Non-Identity Problem): the beginning of a fascinating philosophical excursus that we need to truncate a good deal in order to get to the key points for our present purpose. The first point is that we share with the philosopher a nervousness about "what we believe ourselves to be" in the context of techno-machinic powers that seem to usurp us in so many ways and ever-increasingly so given the pace of technological advance (some of it, such as in the areas of military progress, driven by what Parfit would term Risky Policy). Parfit is offering a strong description of this anxiety—not some generalized sociocultural "nervousness" (though we may readily feel we see the signs of that) but a highly specific anxiety that he goes on to articulate in this way:

> Because we can easily affect the identities of future people, we face the Non-Identity Problem. To solve this problem we need a new theory about beneficence. [. . .] Since I have not yet found this theory, these conclusions are unwelcome. They undermine our beliefs about our obligations to future generations. [. . .] In the meanwhile, we should conceal this problem from those who will decide whether we increase our use of nuclear energy. These people know that the Risky Policy might cause catastrophes in the further future. It will be better if these people believe, falsely, that the choice of the Risky Policy would be against the interests of the people killed by such a catastrophe. If they have this false belief, they will be more likely to reach the right decision. (ibid., 451–2)

Here we have, not a weak description of a contradiction, but a very strong one.

To grasp Derek Parfit's extension of the Non-Identity Problem from sci-fi transporter to future generations, we can take one of his own examples, an example that also illustrates how such contradictions are affectively charged:

> Some years ago, a British politician welcomed the fact that, in the previous year, there had been fewer teenage pregnancies. A middle-aged man wrote in anger to *The Times.* He had been born when his mother was only 14. He admitted that, because his mother was so young, his early years had been hard for both of them. But his life was now well worth living. Was the politician suggesting that it would have been better if he had never been born? This suggestion seemed to him outrageous. (ibid., 364)

The politician was suggesting that this man's life (and his mother's) would have been better had his mother not become pregnant until several years later. But the Non-Identity Problem tells us that this would not then have been the same man (right down to the level of different cells combining at the moment of conception even in the unlikely event of the father being the same). The Non-Identity Problem tells us that, in fact, this particular man's outrage is not unjustified because it is some-one else we are imagining in his mother's future and basing our benefi-cence on, if we agree with the politician. We and the politician, however, are following a false belief in order to reach a right decision: we are allowing ourselves to think that this man might have been born later, in effect we are "transporting" him forward in order beneficently to secure his imagined better life. So too with the interests of future people killed by a nuclear catastrophe. We are transporting generations forward with-out thinking about them in the terms suggested by Outraged in *The Times*: as people whose lives would not only be well worth living but might well be so much better were the pressing problems of energy supply to be solved for them by increased use of nuclear energy. In fact we are showing beneficence, not to those people, but to some other people who are better off without that increased use of nuclear energy. In Parfit's persuasive argument they really are different people, because the scale and density of systems and interconnections in our modern world changes everything when one such change is effected and so the people born into a world with high-risk nuclear proliferation are going to be different from the people born into a world free of those risks, even if they have the same names and look the same. It is the same difference as distinguishes Outraged of *The Times* from "himself" born 10 years later. We choose to ignore that difference and to think that our beneficence is directed at the same people, because there is at the moment no other theory about beneficence that works so well for us. Parfit's example of nuclear technology is only a representative example of the powerful technologies in question and of our deep-seated anxieties about how to distinguish the good from the bad ways forward. What the contempo-rary technologized lifeworld does is to force this contradiction time and again into the cultural domain where it gets picked up and symbolically resolved in all sorts of little ways, from Star Trek's transporter to Transformers.

Not only does Transformers embody—literally—the idea of persistent selfhood across the massive changes wrought by technological transfor-mation, but it also affords its own theory of beneficence. The machine world imagined here is dominated by technology that has forked in both "good" and "bad" directions (Autobot and Decepticon) and it is in the technology itself (the Autobots) that beneficence is now located, not in us. We are largely absolved of that responsibility. As a symbolic resolution of very real anxieties and contradictions, for which there is a strong description, this is several steps up in its scale and effectiveness from Star Trek's transporter. Our weaker description, of a lifeworld in which the blurrings of the categories "human" and "machine" increasingly confuse us, still pertains. Both descriptions place Transformers squarely at a high point in the "flow channel" schematized here. It needs to be emphasized, for the sake of the book's larger argument, that this is so when we look at Transformers as objects, as objects in which affect materializes, and as objects around which meanings get drawn into semiosis, rather than looking at Transformers as texts to be read and analyzed in much detail. Transformers is academically disappointing in that regard, which may explain a good deal about academia's relative lack of interest, if not comparative disdain, for it.

The following exercise in autoethnographies involved three participants in making short-form digital stories: first-person narrations accompanied by video collages of imagery and produced out of a "story circle" process in which they talked together about their narrations before producing them. Overseen by a graduate student of ours, the three participants were identified to us as A, B, and C. So we will call them Alex, Ben, and Colin. Their narrations follow. We will discuss the imagery after we listen to their voices, as it were. Often digital storytelling is more tightly scripted but these narrations retained some conversational qualities.

Alex (21 years old): My earliest memories would probably be when I was about 5 years old I guess, when I would have been watching the cartoons and the toys came out. I was massively into them, definitely one of the more defining toys of childhood: trying to get them all and the set ones that joined together to make the giant ones. I had a lot of them, a lot of them. I had Optimus Prime, I had Megatron, I had all the big ones. It was a robust collection. Back then it was generally parents that would buy most of them, Christmas presents, birthday presents, that sort of thing. Whatever money we could get together as kids, just go out and buy Transformers. That was pretty much the deal. I remember them very well. I remember watching the cartoons on a Saturday morning but I don't remember them in much detail. After childhood ended I would say that the connection stopped right there. There were a few reincarnations in the form of new cartoons. I remember *Beast*

Wars. And then once again the new movies—the Michael Bay ones—came out and I was interested in that, in the spectacle. And probably a nostalgic sense had a lot to do with why I enjoyed it. Being one of the defining toys we grew up with, it's always got the memories thing going for it. Optimus Prime, he was awesome. He was iconic for a lot of people my age. But when I was little it was one of the toys I had, one of the Dinobots, this golden stegosaurus—I was pretty big into him. Everyone usually says Optimus Prime because he's really the pop culture icon, the icon of the Transformers franchise. But I was pretty big into dinosaurs when I was a kid. When I was really little and Transformers was the cool toy, from the library all I'd get was these same dinosaur books out over and over again. So there was some connection with that. Put them together and you have a winning formula. That probably had a lot to do with it. When we were kids, story arcs don't mean a lot to you. These are just robots that change into dinosaurs and planes and cars. That's just awesome. I think any implications of what they change into, as a character thing, would be more from what people read into it, rather than what the creators put in there. Let's put it that way. They might have put a little bit of an idea in there but people see what they want to see in some ways.

Alex's story establishes 3 things for us: (1) He remains very keenly aware of the lower limit of significance—of the "system" manufacturing things for him through television animation series, collectable toys, movies, a "winning formula"; (2) he expresses the intensity involved (spending all of one's pocket money on Transformers, the volume of toys involved, "obsessively" looking at the same dinosaur books over and over again and connecting these intertextually with a favorite Dinobot); and (3) his memory latches on to that favorite Transformer where "system" and "intensity" intersect in a precarious point of personal attachment ("I was pretty big into him"), an affective attachment expressed in genuine terms despite the simultaneous admission of a "winning formula" systematically at work. High in sporadic intensity, but relatively low in terms of strategy (on this evidence), Alex's attachment to Transformers comes across here as reactively synchronized to the availability of stimuli from the franchise—triggered again by the Hollywood movies in young adulthood—rather than as somewhere that he personally went to "read into" the toys something he was bringing to them. Except that, that little stegosaurus Dinobot will not quite go away. That Transformer, called Snarl, first made an appearance in the mid-1980s as a rescuer of Optimus Prime from the Decepticons called Slag, Sludge, and Grimlock who had captured the Autobot leader. Alex's description of his early childhood memory, however, is of "this golden stegosaurus," more of a physically attractive thing in his hand than a character or representation. Is there not also something fleetingly revealing in Alex's phrase, "Everyone usually says Optimus Prime because he's really the pop culture icon"—an implied claim to not being quite like "everyone," to have found his own special relationship?

Ben (30 years old): I think for my generation the cartoon series and the toys are the things that, I mean, we have discussions with my mates about how we are the privileged age group—we've got that real connection from growing up with that stuff. They are all your basic goodies and baddies, real basic story structure that they had. Good versus evil, save the planet, friends of the humans, we hate the humans, get the [AllSpark] cube. The characters are just timeless characters. I don't think they've had to develop them for a new audience at all. I think that's why they're all coming back in. That's a tried and true kind of formula they haven't had to do much work with to make it appealing to a new audience. I was always going to this guy's house down the road who had the meanest collection of Transformers. I remember going to his house and I remember being left in the bedroom by myself, playing with his Transformers while he was doing whatever. I went to visit him for his Transformers. I had the Dinobots but this guy had his whole room just full of Transformers. I'd say to have an interest in the toys—I mean looking back at it now—it probably came from watching the cartoons. I mean, playing with the toys I knew all the guy's names, who were the goodies and who were the baddies, what were their special kinds of personalities and all that, which is information that I would have had to get from the TV programs. The reason I always liked the "balls to the wall" action guys—like Tyrannosaurus Rex from the Dinobots—I don't know if it's necessarily looking up to that character or wanting to be that character but I think that character was just more entertaining. I mean when I was young I always used to, in theory, think the baddies were cooler but when it came to playing with the toys or running around and saying I'm this guy or I'm this guy, I'd always go toward the good guys: Optimus Prime, kind of like this sturdy, reliable, dependable leader, transforms into the big, kind of, sturdy reliable truck. Megatron, the ruthless destroyer, transforms into a gun. Starscream, the runaway kind of character, turns into a jet. I think their personalities totally come from what they turn into. Like Bumblebee, which seems to be everyone's favorite these days just was never on my radar back then, whereas Optimus Prime was this big truck, you know, and Megatron was this gun and you had tank guys and space jets and all of that but I think there's probably more appeal to Bumblebee now because he's a fast, hot Camaro. I mean, if you look at it back then, the VW—maybe it was a cool car in some circles but also it was the personality that came with being a VW, not the out there, full-on personality. It's that kind of reinforcing of the characters and their personalities and the background story and everything made the toys more exciting, and it made them more kind of real. Younger guys that are maybe my age that I was back then when I was watching the original stuff, they still think it's cool now to watch the new version of Transformers, but it's kind of like you've got history with it so I think it means more to us.

Ben's story adds 2 things to Alex's: (4) the intensity of engagement is still invoked but Ben extends it very explicitly into the notion of "entertaining" and "exciting" aspects that he describes in terms of "personalities"— for Ben not necessarily characters to identify with within remembered narratives so much as "personalities" to be affectively engaged by; (5) the personal memory here centers around the confession of a strategically planned "friendship" with the boy down the street in whose more extensive Transformers collection Ben was really interested—that bedroom populated by all the "personalities" that Ben knew from the television series. So the television series was where narratives and characters established the objects' "personalities" but the other boy's bedroom, when left alone there, was where Ben could find their companionship.

Colin (22 years old): I remember watching the cartoon, the original generation one cartoon, when I was a little kid. I remember all of that imagery, I remember the style of the cartoon—it was that separation from the Looney Tunes. For me it was the first time I saw a cartoon that had an overarching storyline, like there was something bigger going on. I think the really big thing with Transformers that hadn't really been done before or that I wasn't aware of having been done before was the extended universe. You had the sense that there was so much more to what was going on and you were seeing just a snippet of it. There was nothing like it, there was nothing else that transformed. One thing became another. One thing that was so alien became so normal, in an instant. It was cool that they transformed but for me it was always the process of the transformation that I found fascinating, the ability to do it. I hung out with the trucks waiting for them to transform back into the robots just because I loved that—of when they transformed, when they became something else, not what it was that necessarily they were becoming. You know, what it meant by them transforming—that it was time to act, it was time to do something, that they could actively choose to become something greater, they could actively choose to become something bigger than themselves and make a real change, make a real difference, and do it so visually. I always loved having the toys and watching the show. They had so much more meaning because you knew these characters and you were holding these characters in your hand. I guess you could come up with quite complicated—mimicking but quite complicated—storylines. In some way you were reducing the amount of thought that went into it, you were no longer having to build these characters in your mind, no longer having to fill roles and things but in some ways it was more like the template was already there for you, you already had those characters to play with. I remember the original Transformers, the original Optimus Prime with the hands that came off. I remember how badly I wanted that toy, but . . . I guess my parents didn't really understand it. All they knew was that I was into Transformers. They didn't understand what it was. You weren't just playing with the toys but you were joining their fight. And I remember opening this toy one Christmas day and it was Starscream and he was notorious for always starting a fight and running away. He didn't have much morals, he didn't have much strength in him. I always despised that character. I just remember the disgust and the guilt when I opened that toy—that I had to play with it. Of course you didn't want to go back to your parents and say, Oh I don't want this one. But I just hated that toy.

Colin reinforces what Alex and Ben had to say about the intensity of attachment, but he adds some insight into how important the very idea of transformation is. Made meaningful by, but sustaining improvisation around, the given template, these things in the hand (6) came to mean "transformation," one thing becoming another and yet retaining the same personality. In fact, the transforming was itself key to the personality, rather than the "before" and "after" states, and in those transformations Colin sees a choice being enacted, a choice of selfhood rather than acceptance of the given limitations: in short he empathetically recognizes strategy in action. The attachment to particular, and persistent, personalities was so strong for a younger Colin that his distaste for the personality of a specific toy comes across, all these years later, with quite striking intensity.

Although all of these stories, with their six revealing insights, were illustrated with collaged images, predominantly from television series, comics and toy ranges, three images in particular were placed alongside the stories' three most reflective moments: Alex's little golden object, Ben's Camaro, and Colin's Optimus Prime. In Alex's story it is a photograph of Snarl (whose name Alex in fact could not recall, despite his vivid recollection of the toy object itself): a small "gold" armored dinosaur-like creature that transformed by unpacking its compact form into a more expansive humanoid robot. In Ben's story it is a racy yellow Chevrolet Camaro (GM actually, in 2009, produced a Transformers customization package of accessories for Camaro buyers, with Autobot badges, wheel caps, etc., after the car's appearance in one of the movies): for Ben, who was not especially interested in this particular character/personality, it nonetheless makes an important point about the notion of persistent personality invested in machines. In Colin's story it is a photograph of a regular trailer truck: more precisely a sturdy big red Freightliner FL-86 flat-nose cab-over semi truck. This is placed in his story where he is talking about Optimus Prime, contrasted with the toy he "hated," and the effect is to suggest that, for Colin, Optimus Prime and the other Transformers ultimately reconnect strongly with the place where he "hung out with the trucks"—in other words not, for Colin, in his external reality but where he went in his imagination for the affective satisfaction of hanging out there. For all three men, what becomes entirely clear here is the object-relational basis of their past and, to some degree, present attachments to Transformers, as well as "personality" as the locus of that attachment, but also the inner places of *autonomous reflexivity*, to use Margaret Archer's terminology, where affect settled.

What is quite striking about these accounts is how individualistic they are. There are no "similars and familiars," as Margaret Archer calls them, except for that other boy in the neighborhood whose toys were coveted. These are very much internal conversations, of which play of a certain kind is itself some sort of prototype (despite our widespread valorization of the more social forms of play). Our depiction of a flow channel places such internal conversations within an external system of variations and offers them only one trajectory, from a banal nonreflexive ground zero as it were (where the axes of skill and challenge converge at point zero) through to a banal-reflexive attachment to objects of considerable symbolic power. Were anything to shift out of this trajectory, what would it be that effected the shift? Perhaps affect reaching out for objects in a way less attached to what they represent. However, immersion in the object world *contains* any such "reaching out" in other ways, as we shall see.

Chapter 6

Containment 3: Boys' Toys

Stuff sexologist: What's the one thing that really turns you on?

Brooke: Universalize my remote and I'll be yours forever.

—*Stuff* magazine, April 2002, 162

Stuff magazine, aimed at males in their late teens and twenties, was very much a sign of its times. The US edition folded in 2007, but the UK edition continued with a stronger focus on consumer gadgets. Before its closure, the US edition positioned the gadgets very obviously as accessories of a "new laddism," with the latter's irreverent, throwback prefeminist attitudes and imagery explicitly foregrounded alongside sport, cars, and alcohol. This had all been something of a journalistic invention of the 1990s, although it has never been too difficult to find examples of young people at the lower end of that age range in particular whose behavior furnished the required stereotype, including plenty of female "ladettes," but this is more because the late teens and early twenties have always been thus for some, not because the label genuinely identified a social change or trend. On the other hand, *Stuff* did provide the forum for one revealing form of advertising around new "stuff," which is to say the new generation of consumer gadget driven by digital technologies. In a typical example, a digital portable CD player might be advertised by a captioned image of a stereotypically "glamorous" young woman, her body parts, or scant clothing labeled "detachable front," "head unit remembers thirty positions," or "coaxial 2-way with injection molded polypropylene cones." This kind of thing became such a repeated device in advertisements appearing in *Stuff* that it started to seem more revealing of an affective trend in relations with these technological objects than merely a throwback to prefeminist imagery of women. It was not so much that the women in the advertisements were being objectified (the old story) as that the objects in the advertisements were being affectively charged, not by mere association but in virtually (auto) eroticized ways.

In mid-2010, British television's *The Gadget Show* (Channel 5) jumped on the bandwagon for "augmented reality" advertising and put presenter Suzi Perry (a motor sports correspondent on British television) in a body-hugging black leather jumpsuit for an innovative campaign to promote a new season of the show. In a print ad carried by gadget magazine *T3* in August that year (and printable off the show's own website) Perry was draped over a large version of the show's stylized G logo. With the right plug-in installed in a web browser, the viewer could hold the ad in front of their computer's webcam and, triggered by programmed recognition of the logo, Perry's figure, in a video window fed from webcam to browser, sprang into life off the page. Tipping and tilting the page and moving it backwards or forwards from the screen saw the pint-sized Perry balance on the moving paper surface beside the viewer as she announced the new series: "Look where I am, right in the palm of your hands—well, if you want to see more of me and my gadgets . . ." The particular "gadget" behind this little trick involved a piece of software called D'Fusion from the company Total Immersion that had hit its stride in 2009 with over 250 commercial and promotional projects for major clients including Coca-Cola, McDonald's, CNN, Boeing, Sony Ericsson, BMW, as well as Hollywood studios and toy companies. These had begun to establish a kind of faux-hologram augmented reality (AR) as the next big thing in hybrid print/web/TV advertising at a moment when commercial cinema was being reenergized by digital 3D's own take on the idea of immersion. Total Immersion's working definition of AR was: "an interactive experience where virtual components are dynamically merged into a video stream in real time" (according to their corporate website).

The Gadget Show, along with the longer established magazines *Stuff* and *T3* (originally *Tomorrow's Technology Today*) and the globally franchised television motoring show *Top Gear*, represent an interlinked media environment of content and modes of address aimed predominantly at gadget-interested men who like cars, computers, and other "stuff" and have an appetite for continuous coverage of that sort. These and similar formats carve up that broad audience and readership in overlapping ways: *Stuff* specifically targeting 18- to 30- year-old men for whom the "stuff" prominently includes so-called glamor photography and other male "lifestyle" interests, *T3* retaining more of its "geek" beginnings while drifting into Stuff's terrain (especially with its covers), programs like *The Gadget Show* maintaining some links back to the older television format of the consumer affairs program, while *Top Gear* reaches a more diverse global audience in terms of gender and age but retains an unabashedly materialist ethos with its own brand of (rather aging) laddish derring-do and unconcern for anything politically correct (no green consciousness here). It is not our intention to collapse the differences between these examples or among their many emulators—the media environment is based on formats that get adapted and modified to fit well defined subsections of any such "audience"—but at the same time it will be useful to generalize about a media-fueled culture of consumerist gadgetry that self-evidently informs all of these instances at one level or another, in which the car is as much of a gadget as the smart phone, irrespective of the level of "new" (i.e., advanced digital) technology on display. Moreover, all of this begins to seem more deeply interrelated from the perspective provocatively developed by iconoclastic and contrarian technological guru Jaron Lanier in his book *You Are Not a Gadget*.

Lanier argues, from within the very heart of the actual technological development process, that a culture of gadgetry based on what he terms cybernetic totalism has led people (we might suppose especially men on this sort of evidence) to self-identify increasingly as gadgets, as "parts" rather than persons. Overstated for rhetorical effect, this is a version of what we have called the android *imaginaire*. It also resonates perturbingly when set alongside *The Gadget Show*'s little piece of AR theater.

A key thing to note about that experience of being able to "see Suzi come to life" (the ad's punch line), is that it unsettlingly replicates, at least on reflection, the scene between cyborg queen and passive android male from *Star Trek: First Contact* that we discussed in Chapter 1. The male holding the print ad up to his webcam to trigger Suzi's appearance becomes very much a component part in a gadgetry circuit, completing the loop that links devices and software together and maintaining that connection by continuing to "balance" the figure of Suzi on the page (tip it too far and she disappears back into the paper g-spot on the flat surface). Held somewhat tensely in place in this way, in order to maintain the illusion, the male (for we are assuming that it is predominantly if not exclusively males here) has to watch the webcam's feed in the browser window and so gets physically framed and restrained by the whole experience, while the video image of Suzi bounces around energetically in her animated manner. Lanier's cybernetic totalism—where everything is understood in terms of machinic parts operating in controlled synchronization—seems deeply characteristic of the AR experience offered by these advertising innovations. The participating human being is "gadgetized" in the very act of taking part.

There are a lot of disposable and replaceable gadgets being reviewed, written, and spoken about these days, in magazines, in television technology and consumer programs, and on websites. The concept of "reviewing," a putative rationale for all of this, seems fairly straightforward. Gadgets are reviewed in order to assess whether they offer some benefit in relation to other already available gadgets; whether they conflict in any way with the existing world of gadgets (e.g., introduce incompatibilities or make something else unnecessarily redundant, where the emphasis is on the word "unnecessarily" and how that is understood in a world in which redundancy is not at all unacceptable and "necessity" is a complicated thing); whether they are so difficult to use that any proffered advantage in theory is nullified in practice; and whether they appear to be trustworthy, robust, likely to last without breaking. These aspects may get cloaked in various kinds of razzamatazz, in dramatic tests or trials or in-depth technological explanations, but at root surely those are the four things justifying, in any *practical* sense, the attention that any gadget might be getting? But then there is style. Gadgets also get endlessly talked about in terms of their supposed style, where those four aspects of utility become insufficient on their own to make a gadget "cool." It has to look and feel right as well. We will return to the question of how this look and feel gets recognized, because it is clearly not as simple as adhering to some universal standard of attractiveness defined by any general design aesthetic.

The examples with which we began this chapter are all concerned, on one level, with the arrival of new gadgets and gadget-generating technologies, their reception and their dissemination or penetration into society at large. According to one useful way of looking at these things, the attributes of an innovation in technology that determine its rate of adoption (or "diffusion") are organized into five clusters. The first four, matching our 4 features of gadget "reviewing," would be (1) attributes associated with its relative advantage, (2) attributes associated with its compatibility, (3) attributes associated with its complexity/simplicity balance, and (4) attributes associated with its reliability. The "it" in question may be any new item of technology, a gadget, a thing. Slightly modified, these categories are derived from the work of Everett Rogers (1995) and (along with a fifth factor, of which more below) they constitute what has come to be known as "diffusion theory"—a helpful way of analyzing the adoption pattern of new technologies. In fact Rogers' original schema identified "trialability" instead of reliability, though the latter is a component of the former. We have extracted the reliability component here because we want to argue that "trialability" has become public: not that the original testing and trialing of a technology in the development and manufacturing process is any more public than it ever was but that a kind of pseudo-trialability stage is now embedded in the larger culture of gadgetry, where magazines, television shows, and websites stage a specific mode of trialability in public, rationalized as "reviewing," integrated into the marketing of products, but also in fact functioning as an important part of a fifth diffusion factor.

Those first four clusters of attribute are clearly concerned with the sociotechnical. They map out a set of issues around such questions as whether people perceive a technology to be too "hard" to deal with satisfactorily, whether it interconnects with existing technologies, whether it has a reputation for being trustworthy, and so on. These sociotechnical questions range across both the purely technological and the less predictable areas such as word-of-mouth, perceptions, expectations, and fears. Indeed each of Rogers' clusters invites us always to consider the technical as inseparable from the social. This chapter will extricate a fifth cluster of attributes and suggest that it constitutes, in effect, a different dimension from the sociotechnical. Before reaching that point, however, it is necessary to consider in more detail the first four clusters. As an example, in each case, we will consider a simpler technology—the Swiss Army Knife—as well as instances of more complex gadgets.

Relative advantage is easy enough to grasp. The Swiss Army Knife we are looking at as we write has an integral screwdriver, can opener, and scissors. This offers unmistakable relative advantage over carrying those separate implements around in a pocket. Marketing campaigns may work hard to imply that some new technology offers equally persuasive advantages but, in fact, it is often much more difficult to assess the claim. When Digital Versatile Disc first came on the scene was it clearly offering "versatile" advantages over existing alternatives? A then nonrecordable medium for the distribution of movies was offering some advantages over VHS tape— improved audiovisual quality being the greatest—while removing others, such as home recording capability. In other words, there is a frequent precariousness in such cases around any judgment of relative advantage (unless the advantage is to the producer, of which more in due course).

Compatibility looks equally straightforward at first. The Swiss Army Knife fits in the pocket nicely, will open any can (if a little messily on occasions) and renders nothing else obsolete. But while an early adopter's new CD player simply replaced their turntable without rendering their amplifier obsolete, it could not (prior to the more widespread implementation of the Universal Serial Bus for connecting things) be plugged into their computer—whereas their computer's CD-ROM drive could play their audio CDs. In short, there are often compatibility "niches" into which such technologies have to fit where they are compatible enough for most common practices of usage. Incompatibilities are commonplace but seem to be socially acceptable so long as they do not prevent the occupation of such a niche. The arrival of digital television was held back by incompatibilities between set-top boxes, where the niche was too specific to be fought over without casualties and delays (as the old videotape wars proved, before VHS emerged as the technologically inferior victor).

The complexity/simplicity balance is another delicate equation. Something has to be complex enough to deliver its technological promise but simple enough to be readily used in everyday life. The VCR (for recording video on tape) was long bedeviled by the old adage "it's too difficult to program." This commonplace got so well established as a "fact" about VCRs that even the simplest programming systems tended to go unappreciated as working solutions—in most people's minds VCRs remained difficult to program. The Swiss Army Knife has just enough tools folded away inside for the user to remember what is where—any more and it would become too frustrating to find the right implement. Moreover, what is simple enough in one setting becomes overly complex in another. Computer-style menus that presented no difficulty on a personal computer seemed overly complex in the 1990s prototype VoD systems when viewers were relaxing in a soft chair and pointing a remote control instead of sitting at a desk with keyboard and mouse, as many of the telecommunications companies discovered when they ran their first VoD trials.

Even reliability proves to be less straightforward than it first seems. The genuine Swiss Army Knife is built to last—a small piece of precision engineering. But it performs no new function. Its value is merely in the portable integration of long established functions. A user would be entitled to disappointment if it ever failed to open a can or tighten a screw. On the other hand, there seems to be a fair degree of tolerance toward unreliability where new ground is clearly being broken. If something is perceived to be at the cutting edge of technological advances it can apparently be forgiven for some unreliability. Had this not been so, the Windows operating system would never have achieved its hegemony (as it took some years to reach a point where "crashes" were not a grudgingly accepted fact of life).

Even if these four clusters of attribute hide some ambiguities, trade-offs, or contradictions, of the sorts evoked by these few examples, they constitute nonetheless a fairly straightforward way of understanding basic aspects of how new technologies find their way in the world. We want to suggest, though, that they are only one part of what is going on; that there is a further dimension to the whole matter of technological diffusion, and that this dimension is especially significant in relation to the broader topics pursued by this book. Relative advantage, compatibility, the complexity/simplicity balance, and reliability mark out a sort of flat "diffusion space" for new technologies. To add some depth to this space we need to consider diffusion theory's fifth cluster of attributes—observability.

Observability is conventionally taken to be of the same order as the others. Any new technology progressively becomes more observable in patchy and unpredictable ways. Early adopters may give it its first visibility and, as it spreads more widely, potential users become more aware of existing users, this observability generating its own marketing momentum, buoyed further by any media coverage. After a while, potential but hesitant users of personal stereos were observing enough users around them for the wearing of the devices (such as the Sony Walkman) to seem no longer obtrusive or unusual. Later the iPod almost instantaneously took over that niche.

The central hypothesis here, though, is that "observability" is not in fact of the same order as the first four factors, because it cannot usefully be limited to the visibility of users in any market. The first four factors were concerned with the sociotechnical but observability raises the fundamental matter of the cultural. Technological advances have a visibility in a culture as well as in the hands of actual users. They get written about, represented fictionally, exchanged as media images, evoked as utopian signs, demonized as dehumanizing, and so on. Consequently, we have here a different dimension of diffusion—one not well captured by the original theory. The internet as new technology provided especially good raw material for the construction of cultural observability—from the rhetoric and imagery of a supposed information revolution to the mythology of hackers and viruses or the metaphors of giant artificial brains and cyborg creatures. So a case can be made for extending each of the first four factors into what we might term the symbolic realm in order to find there their cultural reflections, so to speak (Figure 6.1). So, relative advantage becomes symbolic value. When they are honest about it, many possessors hardly ever use their Swiss Army Knife. The idea of its usefulness is enough. This symbolic value endows the object with meaning, even if a possessor seldom actually uses the thing. How many other

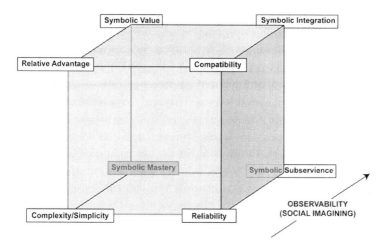

FIGURE 6.1 Adaptation of diffusion field to include a symbolic dimension.

objects in the contemporary world have more symbolic value than actual utility? A moment's reflection suggests that very many things fall into this category. A make of automobile often relies on symbolic value more than on any special or unique advantage in getting from A to B, so too, perhaps, with the internet in its early stages. The idea of its power may initially have been even more important than any practical realization of that power for most people who "got" the idea.

Compatibility becomes symbolic integration. The Sony Walkman's central message was not necessarily that it offered a better way of listening to music but that it integrated listening into almost any other activity that could be achieved while wearing the device. In practice, we may not have often tested the limits of its practicality in diverse situations but, again, the idea that it could be used in all those situations carried its own inherent appeal, an appeal that Apple then appropriated so successfully for their stable of portable gadgetry. The internet long promised such symbolic integration—with personal digital assistants, domestic appliances, even "body nets"—but it proved to be convergence with the mobile phone that delivered it. Whether such integration becomes actual rather than symbolic is perhaps less important than that the integration should be convincingly promised in the "image" of the technology, as it was with the Sony Walkman, then the iPod, then the smart phone.

The complexity/simplicity balance becomes symbolic mastery. Early adopters and many ongoing users derive real pleasure from coming to grips with the technically complex. In social and domestic situations it is easy to find those people—often men according to the stereotype—who grab the remote control or keyboard or smart phone to show others "how easy it is." Make the technology too easy and these users are cheated out of a special satisfaction. Videogames trade in this symbolic mastery. In many games, the mastery of "levels," puzzles, and challenges is where the ultimate pleasure lies, rather than in the more immediate satisfactions of sensory stimulation. The PC industry and computing publishers know that they serve this urge to mastery and cater for it with endless "utilities" and how-to books. Reliability becomes symbolic subservience, the corollary of symbolic mastery. To be reliably subservient—for example, to be fixable with a little tinkering—is often more important than reliability per se, especially to those practical men of our Foreword.

Positioned within this extended diffusion space, where the symbolic dimension extends each of the sociotechnical factors into the cultural realm, technologies become susceptible to a complex process where cultural representations interact with sociotechnical attributes. A simpler way of expressing this is to suggest that we have mapped out the three-dimensional space of social imagining, within which our hypothesized android *imaginaire* must then necessarily find its place.

To recapitulate, "observability" in diffusion theory introduces a symbolic dimension and this dimension is organized as an analogon of the sociotechnical. New technologies and the gadgets that embody them are repositories of symbolic value which have to find niches for integrating themselves into people's lives, while the grand themes of subservience and mastery play themselves out in our hopes and fears. At an abstract level, this sometimes fuels fictions in which the technologies run out of control. In the previous century we saw robots, the nuclear bomb, space travel, the computer, and genetic engineering all spawn their own subindustries of fictional utopianism or dystopianism. Similarly, the internet quickly spawned representations in popular culture, from literary science fiction to television drama and movies. For Hollywood, the fantasized internet, before the latter became omnipresent and familiar, was for a while a virtual realm of mysterious and mischievous playing with identities and hidden powers—from accidentally triggering a nuclear launch to losing one's identity. In literary science fiction, particularly cyberpunk, that "net" has often taken a more imaginative form—as a virtual world of data and projected identities where new social norms can be explored, and with which online social networking is only now starting to catch up. In television drama, at least in Britain, the "net" tended to be demonized early on as the haunt of manipulative criminals and deviants. In the British television serial drama *Killer Net*, for example (1998, written and produced by Lynda la Plante and directed by Geoff Sax for Channel 4), an impressionable young male student gets drawn into a bizarre online game of stalking and murder that turns out to have ramifications in the real world. But the point to be made about any such examples is that they rapidly populated, in often contradictory ways, the space of social imagining that opened up for the diffusion of the internet as an actual complex of technologies. If this space of social imagining is as significant in diffusion as the sociotechnical factors, then it matters profoundly what ways of imagining these things are available to us. The cultural realm, where such things find their images endlessly reconstructed, becomes more than just an epiphenomenon of a sociotechnical "reality" where all the important things happen.

Diffusion theory needs to recognize this symbolic dimension—the space of social imagining through cultural representations—if it is to stand any chance of grasping the process through which technology grips affect as much as it stimulates rational assessments of its usefulness. It is within this space of social imagining that a particular way of imagining— an *imaginaire*—develops.

So the virtual Suzi with which we began this chapter clearly inhabits the symbolic dimension, but we can now understand that dimension as an analogon, or a projected image so to speak, of the sociotechnical domain that is structured around four diffusion-determining sets of attribute against which actual gadgets are judged. The symbolic projection of these remains similarly structured but at a greater level of abstraction (symbolic value, integration, subservience, mastery) where gadgets endlessly succeed each other as they are cycled through the symbolic space (Figure 6.1).

We can, therefore, trace the layers constituting the "virtual Suzi" example with which we began this chapter. *The Gadget Show* on British television has, as its rationale, the weekly reviewing of gadgets. The show is part of a larger brand devised by Channel 5 called FiveFWD (Cars and Gadgets from Five) that represents the channel's overall presence for the larger audience we evoked at the outset (their *Fifth Gear* cousin of the BBC's phenomenally successful *Top Gear* grounding itself more in traditional reviewing of new vehicles). FiveFWD and *The Gadget Show* make an implicit claim to be operating on the flat front surface of our figure, as it were, and indeed this is where much of their content comes from, week after week—the presentation and discussion of things according to the fairly predictable formulas involved in examining those things' diffusion-determining attributes, combined with some judgments of "style." But of course it is on the symbolic dimensions that this gains some real traction in terms of engaging deeper forms of audience allegiance, beyond consumerist information and buyers' advice.

"Virtual Suzi" functions almost entirely on the symbolic dimensions, or, to push the visualization of this in our figure, the symbolic plane constituted by the projection along symbolic dimensions of the factors making up the sociotechnical plane. She is promoting the show's more mundane sociotechnical interests but doing so in a way that is largely abstracted from them. So what the little piece of interesting AR theater does is to dramatize symbolic value, integration, subservience, and mastery. The clever technical integration of this simple bit of AR, with its circuit of printed advertisement, webcam, browser plug-in, and a user who manipulates the components to trigger the faux-hologram, momentarily dramatizes the symbolic integration of gadgetry into gadget-filled (male?) lives, at the same time dramatizing the subservience/mastery dimensions in a staged visualization of apparent mastery by user over subservient technology as embodied by "Suzi." The symbolic value encapsulated by this moment appears to be in its promise of empowerment and release: mastering subservient gadgetry releases something more than the sum of the parts. But in fact, as we have suggested, the user is "gadgetized" rather than empowered, drawn into the circuit of devices and restrained there. So what is actually being staged is a moment of potential self-recognition for the android *imaginaire* on the underpinning "observability" dimension that is in fact nothing else than the dimension of projection from sociotechnical to symbolic planes. The cyborg Queen's promise of empowerment and release to the physically restrained android Data in our Star Trek scene from Chapter 1 is brought to mind yet again here, and not coincidentally.

The final layer in this example is that of a gender performativity (performativity being somewhat different from performance per se, where something is being intentionally and explicitly performed as such and where a calculated self-presentation is knowingly offered as a performance). This piece of AR theater puts a lively, glamorous, pseudo-holographic woman into the hands of an awkwardly restrained, "gadgetized" male. The seeming mastery/subservience relation gets turned on its head, as the man (android fashion) is made machinic while (cyborg fashion) the woman lives "in" and through the technology. She does not look at the image of the man sharing her video space but out at where he exists in reality, so the on-screen image of himself becomes, in peripheral vision or occasional glance, an awkward presence, a third party interrupting his otherwise potentially invisible voyeuristic pleasure and reminding him that he is structured into the circuit as slave rather than master (Suzi's leather jumpsuit even toying with the sadomasochistic connotations of that). The existence of what we have termed an android *imaginaire* in the symbolic space has increased the chances of it recognizing itself in this way (whereas the classic era of cinematic voyeurism afforded considerably less potential for such self-recognition—there was no filmic equivalent of this self in the video stream). The DVD release of the second *Transformers* film included a similar AR artifact—an Optimus Prime that could be activated on the desktop off the DVD package.

If we shift outwards from this specific example to the whole culture of gadgetry represented by these television shows, magazines, and so on, a persuasive case might be made for the same gender performativity characterizing it all in large measure. In other words, the android *imaginaire*, with its gendered implications, is the specific form of social imagining characterizing the entire symbolic space projected from the contemporary sociotechnical field of gadgetry, and organized around an ambiguously gendered "look" directed at the machine.

It is possible to think of gender performativity in progressive terms: to think that, because there is no fixed gender identity biologically underpinning gender, the "performance" of gendered identities is relatively free to experiment with the traditional configurations, even though it may not know this most of the time. However, our example strongly suggests the restraining power of cultural representations on such performativity; in short, the ways in which performativity is always being staged for us, is taking place in highly structured stagings that allow scant opportunity, if any, for troubling the way things are, unless one takes the big leap and really queers the traditional configurations. Caught within un-queered configurations of heterosexuality, though, one's staging in a small show like Suzi's replicates the larger stagings of heterosexuality to which one remains subject.

So we want to look at aspects of the *Top Gear* phenomenon on television as a staging in these terms, beginning with a cover feature on the show that appeared in the British listings magazine *Radio Times* in June 2010, with the cover tagline "How Jeremy Clarkson's schoolboy gang conquered the world" (Clarkson being the main presenter since the show's 2002 relaunch by the BBC with its distinctive new format). NBC (America's National Broadcasting Company) included this optimistically worded summary in 2008–2009 mid-season promotional material when they had an American version of *Top Gear* under consideration for their schedule:

> REV YOUR ENGINES . . . This Emmy award-winning television phenomenon follows three friends as they attempt to perform outrageous challenges and stunts through the crazy transformations they make to their cars. Full of high-octane adventure and extreme comedy, *Top Gear* has been an international success for over 30 years. Whether you're a car fan or not, the drama, horsepower and tricked-out hot rods are sure to drive you back to this series again and again.

This did not quite capture the series' roots in, and its still maintained links with, television-studio based magazine-style programming that tends not to be where most "high-octane adventure and extreme comedy" happen on television. But it did neatly flag the motorsport connection ("gentlemen/drivers start your engines" is a NASCAR and IndyCar racing catchphrase in the US) while at the same time underscoring the content's broader interest "whether you're a car fan or not." NBC ran a pilot but did not adopt the show itself, a subsequent deal by the BBC moving the US version to The History Channel in the United States instead from late 2010, where it closely followed the format of the BBC original. NBC executives seem not to have grasped the necessary adjective that *Top Gear* in effect requires antecedently to any use of terms such as adventure and comedy—the adjective being "schoolboy"—which is a key to understanding both its appeal and its place within the symbolic space we have been mapping.

As we consider *Top Gear* we need to keep one enduring aspect of the show's format in mind, since it will in due course link this discussion back to F1. It should not have escaped attention either that NBC's marketing description included the prominent word "transformations" which, as we have already suggested, cannot be used in this context altogether innocently of any association with Transformers as an idea. But the aspect that links to F1 is the show's deliberately mysterious character called The Stig, an anonymous always-helmeted racing driver who tested high-performance cars earlier in the show's run but mostly assists celebrity guest drivers to perform a fast lap round a race track, their lap times being recorded on a scoreboard that features in the *Top Gear* studio where they are subsequently interviewed. Not in fact one person, The Stig has been "played" on occasion by several drivers, including a stuntman who raced in American speedway (and doubled for actor Daniel Craig in a Bond film) as well as F1 drivers Perry McCarthy (whose foray into F1 in 1992 was short lived) and, on at least one occasion, current Lotus F1 racer Heikki Kovalainen. The show enjoys persistent speculation that this or that F1 driver may be The Stig, capitalizing on F1's aura of glamor, though in actuality the regular Stig is much more likely to be a jobbing driver or stuntman given the demands of television production scheduling and filming. The name "Stig" is English public school patois, new boys at Jeremy Clarkson's old boarding school being called "stigs."

It is this schoolboy quality that English motoring journalist Paul Horrell focuses on in his extended feature in *Radio Times*, which is both an advertorial for *Top Gear* and at the same time a surprisingly insightful piece of writing about the makers' ethos and values (probably because Horrell has also worked for the show as a blogging reviewer of cars on its website and clearly knows it from the inside). The cover of that issue also bears closer scrutiny. It shows Clarkson and his two copresenters dressed in schoolboy blazers and shorts, complete with invented "TG" school badge on their breast pockets, striped ties at half mast, woolen kneesocks round their hairy ankles, riding a rickety nailed-together wooden go-kart that Clarkson is steering with string bound to its front axle. The three hunch together on the kart, half-smiling with a restrained knowingness, the tableau Photoshopped onto a stylized green hillock, the kart lifting off the ground as its wheels spin against a picture-book blue sky. It is a strikingly self-deflating cover in one sense, undercutting any notion that their "high-octane adventure and extreme comedy" is anything more than pranks and larks. It is also probably the single best self-conscious evocation ever of the phrase *boys' toys* that is so often used (and so often deprecatingly) to describe the whole culture of gadgetry and cars. In addition to connecting back playfully and knowingly to a tradition of English children's fiction (Richmal Crompton's *Just William* books from the 1920s to the 1970s come particularly to mind, with the *Top Gear* crew here in the role of William's prankster gang The Outlaws), the image also suggests a gender performativity that is a good deal cleverer than any notion of men who have simply never grown up.

Rather, what is suggested is somewhat more akin to a moment from Joseph O'Neill's brilliant post 9/11 novel *Netherland*, where the protagonist Hans notes,

For those under the age of forty-five it seemed that world events had finally contrived a meaningful test of their capacity for conscientious political thought. Many of my acquaintances, I realized, had passed the last decade or two in a state of intellectual and psychical yearning for such a moment . . . . I , however, was almost completely caught out. (2009, 130)

Jeremy Clarkson and his pals here, co-presenters James May and Richard Hammond, all when *Top Gear* started in 2002 approximately the right age to be included in Hans' observation, do look caught out. (We introduced May in the Foreword.) Like schoolboys caught in the act, they look unprepared for contemporary life's big questions, and like school dropouts they look like they have given up on ever being entirely prepared in the sense suggested by O'Neill's characters, who have conscientiously developed well rehearsed, revised, and road-tested answers for the examination in contemporary life's complexities, when current events have upped the stakes so considerably. This is not about refusing to grow up so much as about the bravado of refusing to be prepared in that sense, like partying the night before an examination.

Cast that *Radio Times* magazine cover as an iconic piece of gender performativity at a time of challenging sociopolitical complexity and these men look pitiably caught out, which becomes part of their unexpected honesty and charm. Their recourse to the culture of gadgetry and cars becomes, then, less a matter of straightforward regression or even escapism and more like Hans' recourse to cricket (in the West Indian communities of Manhattan's nether regions), while he learns to drive; a recourse to the microcosms where things make some kind of sense. These are clearly well-tuned television roles for the presenters: James May, for example, is a pianist and flautist with a proven interest in doing much more "serious" documentary work but his *Top Gear* persona is something rather more bumbling and deliberately unknowing.

The contrast between this iteration of *Top Gear* and its BBC predecessor is revealing. An utterly traditional studio magazine format, with inoffensively middle-of-the-road presenters, focused on straightforward motoring news, road tests, and bland studio chat, the pre-2001 *Top Gear* was a schedule filler on British television with a moderately sized audience that had little hint of fandom about it. The post-2002 *Top Gear*, with its global distribution (over a hundred countries) and localized versions in Russia, Australia, and the United States, raked back over US$3 million in profit in 2009 for parent company Bedder 6 alone (the name of a boys' dormitory at the school attended by company cofounders Clarkson and series producer Andy Wilman). It fosters an enthusiastic fan community as well as its own subindustry of related merchandising, and has made multimillionaires out of Wilman and Clarkson. James May describes the constant patter in which the copresenters engage as centrally characterized by "bitchiness" (Horrell, 15) while Hammond emphasizes that the show's appeal depends in some measure on its refusal to overidentify with "petrolheads," men who live for cars, whether rolling up their sleeves to get stuck into repairing an engine or spectating at the sub-F1 levels of motorsport where there is often more of a mechanic's ethos in evidence than a sportsperson's. The way in which both *Top Gear* and F1 lift themselves to a notable degree out of the "petrolhead" universe is an interesting and quite subtle aspect of their phenomenal global reach and appeal. Both operate on a level where people do not so conspicuously get their hands dirty working with cars, which is part of the particular gender performativity (with its decidedly middle-class overtones) that *Top Gear* stages.

Journalist Paul Horrel offhandedly employs the phrase "weak-smiles" to describe the presenters on the current show's predecessor (Horrell, 12). In fact that is a very useful observation indeed, for it suggests that two entirely different levels of presenter engagement have been involved: from the routinely recognizable television professional's pseudo-involvement, masked not just by those discernibly contrived weak-smiles but by a palpable lack of much real enthusiasm, to the Clarkson gang's schoolboyish excitement that always seems genuine when it occurs. Not that *Top Gear* maintains a steady state of excitement—far from it. The show's tone is a cool, wry, often cynical one, interrupted by outbreaks of enthusiasm on the part of the presenters (e.g., when test-driving a car), that frequently ratchets up the intensity in a way entirely foreign to its predecessor or, indeed, to most other television gadget and car shows. (A popular US-originated series called *Mythbusters* has a similar quality in the dynamic shifts and peaks of its presenters' engagement with the material but the context is rather different—using technologies to test "myths" such as whether mobile phone use can threaten an aircraft's systems or whether nitroglycerin heart patches, worn by patients with angina, can explode, the presenters typically hitting a spike of convincingly genuine excitement when something works or they destroy something.)

Top Gear's segment format for test-driving high-performance cars emphasizes this. Typically the stationary vehicles are shot from low and high angles to emphasize their shapes and aerodynamic features, with wide-angle close-ups of detailing; then the presenter is seen in-car commenting in what seems like an unscripted way on how it feels to be driving it at speed (intercut with moving crane shots or road-level angles at tire-smoking bends or weaving camera-car shots or diagonally tilted camera angles or static frames through which the car speeds); then, if such a moment is to be found at all with the car in question, the presenter bursts into one of the *Top Gear* distinguishing expressions of delight, surprise, or boyish excitement, before explaining it in briefly more technical terms (usually in voiceover) and coming to a summary conclusion (usually when the vehicle has stopped again). Endlessly replicated, this basic pattern is kept fresh by the change of vehicle being test driven and the spontaneous, improvised quality of the presenter's always slightly different in-car reaction. So although there is always the necessary element of what we have termed "reviewing" ("actually, that's the sound of two turbos"), perhaps superimposed in cool-toned postproduction voiceover commentary, the key moment in each segment is always where the presenter in-car reaches for a greater intensity of spontaneous response (e.g., Clarkson mimicking *Star Wars*' Darth Vader's voice to capture the growl subsequently explained as "two turbos"), then encapsulating the moment either in laughter, sheerly delighted body language, some exaggerated pouting or smirking, an expressive remark ("Oh, I like that!") or just an outburst of nonverbal sound of the sort that a child might make.

On occasion, this segment format is structured even more self-consciously—a piece of sedate, even classical background music accompanying a slow lead-in by the presenter, before a sudden pedal-flooring interruption, a change to high-energy synthesized pop or heavy metal, fast iris wipes and rapid cutting, setting up the anticipated moment of excitement. This deliberate and repetitive staging of a graph against an intensity scale, with its plateaus and peaks, is absolutely central to *Top Gear*'s successful format.

The *Top Gear* studio audience is made up of members of the public who have applied for free tickets to the weekend 5-hour studio recording sessions. The BBC's advice to ticket applicants warns that there is no audience seating in the studio, under-18s are not admitted and groups attending together should have a gender balance, asking, with the pointed jocularity typical of the show, "that groups of people coming to the recordings have a roughly 50/50 male/female split, so we don't end up with a bunch of ugly male car geeks." As a consequence, the studio staging of *Top Gear* has some distinctive features, including its careful avoidance of the "petrolhead" image. A typically large and quite diverse audience stands around somewhat passively, often semicircled tightly round the presenters, with none of the audience-stoking frenzy generated by warm-up staffers on many US studio shows. If anything, they look like aging clubbers waiting for the music to start. This initially curious way of handling the studio audience works well for *Top Gear* because it protects the show's real moments of intensity from any phony excitement. The feeling of a subdued audience, interested and responsive but not intensely so (many will have been standing in the studio for hours by the time they make a screen appearance in the background) helps the program achieve its distinctive graph of intensity, which is very different from the sustained pseudo-intensity that many studio shows aspire to achieve by manipulating the audience response with cues and prompts. On-set audiences have been used before on television but probably never quite so successfully. They generate here a palpable feeling of expectancy that is only satisfied when the show's magazine format breaks out of the studio for one of its segments.

In addition to its track test segments, *Top Gear* depends on location-based segments where a vehicle is put through its paces in an appropriate setting, sometimes with guest drivers. Production versions of rally cars get taken on a mountain road, a sleek sports-car gets treated to an exotic seaside venue, a grunty 4-wheel drive goes to a quarry, and so on. Other high-performance or advanced machines or technologies, from a jet aircraft to a high-tech suspension bridge, often play bit parts in these segments, underscoring the way in which cars are being located within a bigger technologized culture. The deliberate faux-pas ("there's a flock of cows") is used from time to time to suggest that any excursions into nonurban landscapes are to places that remain foreign to the show's determinedly techno-urban worldview.

Two examples of these other segments, and not atypical ones at that, reveal a great deal about how *Top Gear* operates so successfully in the symbolic space we have diagrammed. In the first, copresenter Richard Hammond, with the help of a specialist driving instructor, introduced a group of elderly women (referred to as "the grannies") to the technique of pulling a smoking "donut," rotating the rear of a car around the front wheels by locking the steering wheel hard to one side while over-revving, leaving a "donut" of skid marks amidst a pall of white tire smoke. Several of the "grannies" (in their 70s and 80s) turned out to be extraordinarily adept at this, after a bit of encouragement and instruction, and their outbursts of glee made for a great television moment. This could have been done patronizingly and at the elderly ladies' expense as a piece of cheap entertainment, but it was not. Richard Hammond comes across on such occasions as every granny's favorite grandson and the segment staged and celebrated a small moment of genuine stereotype-busting adventure for the elderly participants (one to another: "Did you bring your incontinence pants Sadie?"). In such moments *Top Gear* very successfully transcends the "petrolhead" stereotype to which it is itself susceptible and underscores its wider reach. The "donut" is something that the winning drivers from NASCAR and Indy racing do as an almost obligatory postrace celebration (a few, less corporately disciplined F1 drivers also do so on occasion but risk sanctions from the sport's governing body on safety grounds as well as potentially damaging the finely engineered superexpensive vehicle). The tire burnouts are also associated with "antisocial" teenage male drivers having dangerous street fun, rev-heads showing off, including even British F1 ex-champion Lewis Hamilton, who was fined under Australian law in 2010 for performing a "burnout" and "fishtail" in a street car after leaving the race track in Melbourne. The unexpected appropriation of this act and its image by a group of elderly women very effectively emphasized where *Top Gear's* center of gravity is in the symbolic domain: it is all about these promised moments of machine-mediated *intensity* and the moments are perhaps anybody's for the having. (Another segment suited up a representative group of churchmen, including a rabbi and an Anglican bishop, taking them onto the racetrack to find out which was the fastest religion!)

"Let's talk to the man who's driving the Ferrari." Our second example, however, complicates this picture somewhat, as it seems to be about restraining, or limiting the accessibility of, the promised intensity. To road test a Ferrari 575 and Aston Martin's then flagship "Vanquish" (James Bond's car in *Die Another Day*), two evenly matched high-end two-seater "grand tourers" (luxury cars designed for high-speed long-distance driving), *Top Gear* enlisted ex F1 world champion Damon Hill. He and presenter Clarkson swapped seats in the two cars to compare them on the open road, starting with Hill in the Ferrari. Unlike the carefully staged excitement of the show's test-track segments, this was shot in a notably cool style, with slower cutting, fewer camera pyrotechnics and a deferential emphasis on the two cars' pedigrees and on Hill's own emotionally restrained professionalism. In short, it lifted this topic well out of the reach of the grandmother or the bishop. Looking more like a slick commercial for the cars (which of course it was, given the likely deals done with vehicle suppliers who support the show), the item exposed especially clearly the ultimate logic at work in *Top Gear's* successful occupancy of the symbolic space we have described. Delivering his in-car "review" Damon Hill makes the point that "after a Formula One car" it is difficult to use especially emotive language about even these exotic high-end grand tourers, so he comments respectfully on their performance without any of the schoolboyish glee that is *Top Gear's* more normal trademark. Hill on the Ferrari, referring to its world-famous brand: "You have to pay it some respect, it's a prancing horse. You don't actually feel completely comfortable in the car—you enjoy driving it but at the same time you're very wary of losing concentration." His flatly matter-of-fact conclusion about the Ferrari: "This is a very very impressive piece." Piece of machinery, we probably finish the thought for him. The absent presence here is the true intensity implied at the next level, where F1 affords something that ordinary drivers (or even sub-F1 racing drivers) will never ever experience, an experience of course that the Ferrari name is historically so associated with (having been and remaining to this day, despite inevitable ups and downs, F1's most successful constructor's team). When Clarkson and Hill step back at the end to deliver, over two pints of beer, their judgment on the Ferrari, its "style" is remarked on not in any objective aesthetic terms but as an embodiment of its "Ferrari" identity. Style becomes inseparable from the personality of things.

So what is going on here? *Top Gear's* endless restaging, segment after segment, of a machine-mediated "intensity" is about the promise of something not only ultimately inaccessible to its viewers (all consumer culture depends of course on the unfulfilled promise) but something that properly belongs in the end, we are being told, in Damon Hill's world, not in yours or mine. In the instance described, when Hill gets out of the Ferrari (which is to say enters our world) he looks awkward and uncomfortable, so the segment keeps those moments brief. In the space of symbolic value, integration, subservience, and mastery, a mythologized true intensity at a steering wheel, where driver, android fashion, becomes integrated with the machine (and the driver's life becomes integrated with that lifeworld) is something that belongs to special people. This is where the show's clever device of The Stig, the anonymous, latterly white-clad driver with the special skill is so revealing: he embodies on a regular basis the supposed essence, the specialness, shared by the F1 driver. What Casanova was to the art of seduction, The Stig becomes to the art of the machine, the soul-in-the-elbow (with ordinary people occasionally being privileged to have him at their elbow), at which point *Top Gear's* ultimate banality comes especially clearly into view.

Returning to our diagram, it becomes possible to say that *Top Gear*'s extension of the format along the symbolic dimensions never gets beyond representing "intensity" as distinct from affording intensity. This, of course, is what keeps the whole mediated culture of gadgets and cars going, with its endlessly repetitive formulas based around putative reviewing of things on the sociotechnical plane, while projecting along the symbolic dimensions a representation of "intense" engagement with these things which is not in itself affording the sort of intensity we have described earlier in these pages. Which leaves us here with one key question: where, in that case, does the intensity go? The answer, we have argued, is that it goes into the phenomenon we call fandom as a vehicle of affect.

Andy Wilman, *Top Gear*'s producer, in an interview during the Edinburgh Television Festival in 2009, offered the thought that women like *Top Gear* (making up just under half of its average eight million audience in the United Kingdom) because it takes them inside the male mind where they find two things reassuring: it is not as sexist there as they might have feared and there is a boyish naïvete in evidence where the fascination with fast machines is not loutishly threatening but an unexpectedly endearing enthusiasm. Indeed at that level it is an enthusiasm shared by many women themselves. As a consequence, couples and their families find the Sunday evening slot that the show has on British television a time when dad's interests can be the whole family's for a change. The much publicized lack of political correctness is actually cleverly judged to come over as a throwaway irreverence (just more of dad's bad jokes) while also often recognizably a tongue-in-cheek pastiche of stereotypical English xenophobia dating back at least to World War II: on an under-performing French car, "I think the problem is it's French— it's a surrender monkey"; or about two cars getting a review for build quality, "These cars are both as reliable as a Swiss bus-driver's Austrian pacemaker." The series' digital colorist often takes the wishy-washy English light and pale skies and adds deep contrast and exaggerated hues or coppered filtering that also bring out the metallic color of painted bodywork on the cars, rendering the whole carefully worked effect often dreamlike in a way that is seldom remarked upon. The sum effect is of a fantasy of accessible male thinking and feeling.

Where some men go to turn this into a more strategically developed intensity for themselves is into their own fandom, undoubtedly a place that is less comfortably accessible to others. Formula One is a site for fantastic gadgetry and fandom. F1 has the allure of the hi-tech with its ultrafast racing machines as four-wheeled computers in many ways;

however, while it offers itself as a popular public sport, it operates technically in an elitist, insular, and secretive manner. It keeps its best gadgetry to itself. This is reflected in F1's publicly accessible gadgetry or "geek" culture being distinctly trivial (technically super-detailed radio-controlled model cars, etc.), compared with the sophistication of the machines F1 actually uses, and not just on the track. As much of Formula One's revenue is derived from selling television rights, digital technologies have primarily provided new ways either to access or to complement the existing televised content. So new applications facilitate sending race updates to mobile phones, provide "live timing" on the internet (plotting of cars on the circuit) or, trackside, spectators holding "kangaroo TV" handsets to view a combination of televised footage and live timing while having the track in front of them, and offering more personalized control (they can focus on only one driver for the entire race if they so wish). There are also increasingly sophisticated simulators and video game versions, as well as an array of inventive television graphics (g-force monitors) or camera placements (especially point-of-view shots mounted on the cars) but, by and large, Formula One gadgetry for consumers is either replicating or reproducing the television footage through applications and across platforms or is operating at the level of toys. In its representational links to the broader contemporary male gadget culture, Formula One seems to be trapped in *Stuff* magazine territory or an early James Bond film franchise time bubble of gendered relations and technology. Outside of the racing spectacle, even in 2010 the predominantly male audience is addressed through imagery of pit babes or grid girls whose skimpy outfits (replete with corporate logos of course), passive roles (holding grid position number boards for cars) and spray-on smiles associate "glamor" images with hi-tech race-cars and bravado-exhibiting male racing drivers in a fashion that is cartoonish in its perpetuation of old stereotypes. The actual expensive, cutting edge technology of Formula One (often behind the scenes as much as in the sophisticated cars) is communicated to the public journalistically but remains, at present, relatively remote from the real gadget worlds of fans, certainly from ordinary drivers. It is on the symbolic plane that F1's hi-tech machinery is most present over and above the sociotechnical plane of actuality.

"Let's talk to the man wearing the Ferrari." Damon Hill's unexcited appraisal (on *Top Gear*) of the ordinary capabilities of even a high-performance Ferrari road-car compared with an F1 racing car comes laden with symbolic implications, not least given Ferrari's own dominance there. With a long history that dates back to the origins of Formula

One in 1950 and a fervent following, Ferrari is *the* F1 brand among brands. The symbolism of Ferrari generally, despite its less glamorous (and underplayed) Fiat ownership, transfers into F1 far more readily and successfully than for most other manufacturer teams—as Honda's and Toyota's forays into F1 as constructors attest. Of course, both Ferrari and F1 at large operate as commercialized entities, with aggressive branding and lucrative merchandising central to their well-oiled corporate machines. But also creating an aura has been vital to Ferrari and Formula One (and to their aura-less parent companies, Fiat and Bernie Ecclestone's Formula One Administration). Toyota failed to achieve this during their Formula One campaign (2002–2009). On the back of a rumored US$2 billion launch, Toyota's bland corporate imagery, workmanlike personalities, lack of success despite talent (no F1 race wins), and meager fan base failed to produce a "passion for prestige or charisma" (Baudrillard 2002, 169). By contrast, the Ferrari name itself evokes precisely this on the symbolic dimension. So despite controversies or periods of poor performance, Ferrari has always been part of F1, its prestige derived in part from being the only original team still competing and the most successful with 16 Constructors' Championships. Its occasional follies are even recast in terms of "personality" (passionate or fiery Latin temperament), while the "charisma" is mythically associated with the late Enzo Ferrari himself in order to sustain and substantiate the Ferrari myth more generally.

The myth is furnished through, among other things, toys, collectors' models, and memorabilia (with personality-based or historical themes); most prevalently, winning cars, Enzo himself, and "legendary" F1 drivers such as Alberto Ascari, Juan Fangio, Nikki Lauda, and Gilles Villeneuve. More recent options allow one to "drive" most of their road and sports cars in the Ferrari video games (the *Ferrari Challenge* titles), there are online virtual simulators and, of course, the array of Formula One games (console, computer, mobile) that allow gamers to compete in Grands Prix, which always include a Ferrari driver. Various immersive cockpit simulators have already been constructed to give fans a taste of driving an F1 car (especially trackside at Formula One events), although these are not as advanced as the large data-crunching simulators that the real drivers regularly use at factories. From these generic precedents Ferrari is developing its own "multisensory experience" with the "Ferrari World" theme park opened in 2010, providing themed roller coasters, simulators, 3-D screenings, scaled race tracks, and other F1-related attractions all housed within a 1-kilometer site in Abu Dhabi. Ferrari regalia (e.g., on branded clothing) puts the symbolic in all of this onto the bodies of fans in a more accessible form, where the complexly engineered machinery of F1 will never translate fully into consumer gadgetry beyond the examples cited. So, F1 is in fact where Ferrari regularly, and in front of a large public, seeks to transcend the sociotechnical plane of machinery and gadgetry (on which of course it actually depends) by projecting from it a carefully nurtured prestige and charisma symbolized by its "prancing horse" logo as the linchpin of its social observability, as well as its compensatory sign for unobtainable things.

To be absolutely clear about what we are suggesting here, it may be useful to offer the metaphor of a pressure cooker. The space we have diagrammed—the projection of a sociotechnical domain of gadgets and cars into symbolic dimensions—is where the seemingly endless cycling of things and representations of things generates a particular sort of pressure. The filling and refilling of this space with so much "stuff" is, of course, driven by economic logic, but the cultural process we have diagrammed is organized around its own logic, which is the promise of an intensity in one's relationships with things. Something like *Top Gear* struck just the right note at the right time by finding a formulaic treatment of this promise, literally a staging of it, that contributes, along with all the other popular media coverage of gadgets, cars, and technological things, to a constant buildup of pressure around the sought-for intensity of relationship with things. Some of these things will be more genuinely attainable than others and this will vary across social categories. But like all the key processes and practices of consumerism, leaving the "sought-for" ultimately unsatisfied is where the cultural logic intersects with the economic, driving consumption to new heights. Fandom, however, is where the pressure escapes to, the place where intensity becomes livable rather than endlessly promisable. To be overly literal in interpreting our own diagram, we might suggest that the latter represents a container for the buildup of pressure around the promised intensity, while fandom operates as a sort of escape valve on this container.

The delivery of new stuff into the realm of a public trialability of things in the popular culture of gadgetry and hi-tech machines (fed by magazines and television shows) just reflects an endlessly renewable sociotechnical base that sustains a more elaborate structure of social imagining organized around the logic of a promised intensity. We are promised an intense relationship with things. This promise is endlessly implied, staged, and reenacted. Fandom appropriates this promise and makes intensity its own, but (a key point) it does so in its own ways.

An intellectual debt must be acknowledged here to Georg Simmel's extraordinary summing up in his essay on the 1896 Berlin Trade Exhibition, quite possibly the first piece of academic writing about things and material culture to evoke the sorts of relation we have been describing, albeit in our case in a considerably extended way in comparison with Simmel's limpid if unsystematic summary. Looking at an array of objects in the exhibition, Simmel sees their relations structured as society's are:

> Indeed it strikes one as curious that the separate objects in an exhibition show the same relationships and modifications that are made by the individual within society. On the one side, the depreciation of an otherwise qualified neighbor, on the other, accentuation at the expense of the same; on the one side, the leveling and uniformity due to an environment of the same, on the other, the individual is even more accentuated through the summation of many impressions; on the one side, the individual is only an element of the whole, only a member of a higher unity, on the other, the claim that the same individual is a whole and a unity. Thus the objective relation between social elements is reflected in the impression of things in unison within a single frame yet composed of interactively excited forces, and of contradictions, yet also their confluence. (Frisby and Featherstone 1997, 257–8)

There is an unintended but suggestive echo here of the discussion of "force" in Paul Souriau's 1889 book *L'esthétique du movement.* The society of things evoked here by Simmel, within a framework of those "interactively excited forces," powerfully expands what he described elsewhere as the absorption into life of "impersonal contents" (Simmel 2004, 467), placing before us an image in which it becomes tantalizingly difficult to know whether one is looking at people or their things, so rapidly do they seem to oscillate here. And Simmel even pointed out the peculiarly masculine aspect in these sedimenting things, or "solidified objectifications" as Habermas has called them (Habermas 1996, 414), that replicate the relationships of the "individual within society." But it is perhaps in an early piece of writing by Baudrillard (on the designed organization of objects in modern interiors) that we find an even more apt evocation of the self's dependency on culturally produced objects, Simmel's great theme here, though Baudrillard has a not unpredictable fatalism about this, which Simmel did not:

> First of all, man must stop mixing himself up with things and investing them with his own image; he will then be able, beyond the utility they have for him, to project onto them his game plan, his calculations, his discourse, and invest these maneuvers themselves with the sense of a message to others, and a message to oneself. (Baudrillard 2005, 24)

So out of a Simmelian society of things, out of its excited forces in particular, emerges a Baudrillardian game plan, a strategy. In our more mundane terms here, out of the culture of gadgetry and hi-tech machines with all its banal utility emerges the strategies of fandom in pursuit of intensity, rather than being satisfied with mere consumption of its promissory notes.

Chapter 7

Masculinities, Vitality, and the Machine

Deep inside every middle-managing . . . minivan-driving man lives a wide-eyed 9-year-old, one who reacts to the sight of a race car the exact same way.

—"Speed Thrills," undated *Men's Health Magazine* website article promoting a commercial "motor racing experience day"

The preceding three chapters have all been about containment of agency in the technologized lifeworld—in the object relations that pertain between machine and an android *imaginaire* (not necessarily an exclusively male preserve but a place where masculinities tend to go). There has been no "see-saw" model in any of this, with "resistant" meanings available on one end and the machine on the other. Instead we have sought, fairly forensically, though with only a very narrow section through that lifeworld, to diagram the forces of containment by modeling a field, a semiotic channel and a diffusion pattern amidst the stuff of everyday life (banal and seemingly unimportant though much of that stuff may be). We saw mobility in all three places of containment but it was, one might say, going nowhere. Throughout, however, we have also been building a case for an affective domain as the crucial location where mobility finds itself, but where representational appropriations of affect are in contest with a nonrepresentational stratum to affect. "Identity" is where the representational strategies become most visible.

It is relatively easy to think of identities today not just as more fluid than they once were under the sway of stronger traditions but also as projects of self-construction and self-narrativization resourced by a rich media and leisure environment that communicates many more options (the glossy magazine rack being perhaps the most conspicuous symbol of this). Working on one's identity, whether in close proximity to less insistent but still omnipresent traditions or more experimentally, can appear to be a principal purpose in much of contemporary social life, leisured activity, and cultural consumption in the richer economies, especially in the world of social media that encourages easy disjunctions between presented selves and whatever pre-presentational selves, if any, we might still want to believe in. We have not yet, perhaps, begun properly to explore the extent to which there are risks inherent in the rapidity of this shift toward what are often quite superficial projects of self-(re)invention and how this might relate, for example, to Ulrich Beck's larger invocation of the "risk society" in which we now live, a society built on all kinds of instabilities from financial and environmental to technological (Beck 1992). Generational cycles course through all of this, bringing with them, not so much an ongoing potential for intergenerational conflicts over traditions, though those still flare up sporadically, as the prospect of a "lifecycle" to our projects of self-(re)invention, with experimental phases tending to occur at particular points, which can include midlife crises or retirement these days just as readily as the late teens. Whenever and wherever one of these phases occurs it is likely to be well catered for by media resources offering narrative templates, role models to orientate around, and advice to consider, whether for relocating to a more exotic place, cooking more adventurously, treating oneself to a "motor racing experience" day in a fast single-seater car, or just making over one's wardrobe. Inevitably, it becomes not just feasible but necessary to wonder whether the media environment, having capitalized on the impulse toward self-(re)invention does not then merely box it off into safe categories of activity that are formulaic enough to become popular television formats and to stock the nonfiction bestseller shelves in the bookstores.

Gender, of course, deeply informs these heavily catered for categories, with gendered "lifestyle" material in the media celebrating supposed options while still circulating around a very small core of questions about the effective presentation of a gendered identity. The shift from assuming that the gendered aspects of identity are a given to the inclusion of gender in the self-making project has been a noticeable one, glossy magazines servicing that shift with maintenance advice and endless formulaic retellings of how fraught the process of effectively maintaining a presentable gendered identity can be these days, whether this is to be seen in celebrity scandals or in the faux pas of everyday relationships and self-presentation that might drive one to the advice pages. Ironically, the gravitational tendency for this wealth of material about self-making is to organize itself around fairly stable identity images so that the "maintenance" advice and examples become less about (re)inventing oneself experimentally and much more about how, in a world of fluid identities, it is all too easy for one's own to become leaky, untethered, to drift off unattended, to get insufficient maintenance, and to start looking both uncared for and uninteresting to others. So there is a corrective quality to much of this material, masquerading as resources for self-construction but in actuality pressuring the presentationally unreflexive self into compliance. Maybe I do need to think about what my cheaper Korean mp3 player says about me in an iPod dominated world and whether it would be a good idea to renovate an old cowshed in the Pyrenees, have a fun certificate on my wall saying I've driven a single-seater at the Silverstone F1 circuit in England, or learn Cambodian cooking. When, after buying the magazines and books and watching the television shows, some of that starts to look impractical at the moment, I will probably just buy the iPod.

Given the focus of the present book, the latter reaction is of particular interest. The gadgetized object world perhaps presents more specifically usable resources for masculine image self-maintenance than the more varied choices afforded to a popular feminism that so much more enthusiastically embraced the message "you can be anything you want to be" (although when in 1991 Freddie Mercury, England's first Asian pop star and already ill with AIDS, sang that line on the last album he recorded with Queen, his flamboyant vocal range helped momentarily give the phrase both a poignancy and the kind of edgy resonance it had lacked for many men). The waning of "new man" rhetoric seems on this evidence to have left a somewhat bemused or ambivalent man in its wake, defined in part by his awareness of the situation described above, so a sort of feigned reluctance to do the self-remaking thing is combined with a grudging curiosity about the possibilities. The so-called metrosexual—heterosexual urban men more enthusiastically concerned with body image in a way that was once supposedly the preserve of women (Brumberg 1997; Barber 2008), an early sign of which was the narcissistic mode of address adopted by Calvin Klein underwear advertisements for men from 1982 onwards—remains a revealing subcategory of masculinities in this regard. Within what Mort (1988) calls the "new bricolage of masculinity" detectable in "the noise coming from the fashion house, the market place and the street" (194) it is always possible to trace various subcategories, like the metrosexual or a "new laddishness" that may be less visible than it was in the 1990s but still persists in, for instance, young male windsurfing communities, around skateboarding and in other so-called new sports (Wheaton 2000). However, it has been *Men's Health Magazine*, with an estimated worldwide readership of fifteen million monthly and a correspondingly high-traffic web presence, that has emerged as a dominant force at the present time in satisfying this curiosity about remaking the self and proclaiming the message that the possibilities not only exist for men but are now essential to a "healthy" masculinity. One of the most recognizable and successful magazine brands in the world (with 38 international print editions and 25 regional or language-specific versions of the website), *Men's Health* may be more revealing about contemporary masculinities at this point in time (not just about "metrosexuals," though if they exist they probably constitute a significant core of readers) than much of the commentary that has tried to explain these shifts by developing typologies of masculinity. *Men's Health* also has a legitimate claim to representing a hegemonic masculinity and to having somewhat marginalized those competitors in the field that were more focused on "new laddishness," which has tended to become more concentrated in specialist publications (such as some "new sports" magazines with their own subcultures of gadgetry and constructions of "attitude"). Trawling *Men's Health* in print and on the web for material about childhood—especially about sons' relationships with their fathers—is especially revealing.

"How to Raise a Tough Guy" (undated *Men's Health* website article) is not untypical. A father worries about how he is less "tough" than his own father was, the father having escaped Nazi Germany as a child, lost one parent to cancer and the other to suicide, served in the Vietnam War, and then had difficulty understanding his son as a typical child of American suburban affluence, untroubled by any real hardship and absorbed by escapist popular culture such as fantasy role-playing games. That son in turn is worrying about his own son: "While his friends are off skateboarding, he's in his room looking at his ant farm." What these sorts of item have in common is an invoking of a particular ground on which responsibilities and continuities get established: "Life will kick your ass in ways that aren't physical, and you need to handle those moments with dignity" (ibid.). What Badcott (2003) identifies as emotional dignity is repeatedly, explicitly, and implicitly, invoked by *Men's Health* as that ground. Time and again in those pages, it is emotional dignity that a father wants his children to see in him, even if old-fashioned, physical toughness is inappropriate; that a son admires in his father as death approaches; that a man wants women to see in him; that a boy needs to show if bullied about his ant farm by his skateboarding peers. Grooming one's emotional dignity becomes part of the self-maintenance toolkit advocated by *Men's Health* but more than that, it is constructed as the very ground for defining "healthy" personality in a perhaps confoundingly fluid world.

David Badcott situates the notion of emotional dignity in relation to both social dignity (constructed on privilege, status, esteem, etc.) and the concept of a fundamental dignity accorded to the condition of being human. While the latter encounters the problem of essentialism (what is it that persists from embryo to dead body if indeed the concept is tenable?), the former encounters the problem of relativism (can someone be born into dignity as a result of inherited privilege, does the dignity in a role survive some less than dignified occupancy of that role?). The notion of emotional dignity, however, can be democratically applied in accessible everyday ways that are troubled less by either essentialism or relativism and when *Men's Health Magazine* enshrined it in its numerous practical examples of men's behavior it added a key component to the panoply of groomable and maintainable features (along with clothes, hair, or gadgets) that are this magazine's and its ilk's popular stock in trade. Badcott defines emotional dignity as the feeling of having or recognizing dignity: that is, as an *affective* dimension rather than a rights-based or socially constructed understanding. *Men's Health Magazine* does not so much define it as evoke its contribution to a hegemonic masculinity by implying its presence in all kinds of practical instances of male behavior and attitudes. But more than this, the notion of emotional dignity has a particular flexibility, it strategically reworks an earlier phase of masculinist thinking, and it affords a ground on which something can be "inherited" and "passed on" generationally. Its flexibility resides in the way that emotional dignity can characterize a grandfather's reactions to war and cancer but can also be demonstrated in how a son plays a game or a grandson reacts to grazing his knee after falling off a skateboard. In other words, emotional dignity scales. And it becomes recognizable especially when it is absent—as in this moment from *Men's Health Magazine*'s "How to Raise a Tough Guy" story:

> I was drunk and listless at a bar in Austin, Texas, four or five years ago, when I ran into a friend. He started giving me crap about something. My lizard brain stirred. I began to shriek, much like my son does when he's having a tantrum.

This kind of material makes it very clear what emotional dignity means in terms of the hegemonic masculinity being constructed: it means not having that tantrum. It also reworks an earlier masculinist idiom rather cleverly.

Connell (1995), in tracing the evolution of masculinist ideologies from within the framework of masculinity studies, identifies Warren Farrell,

Herb Goldberg, and Robert Bly (significant "men's movement" figures)
as representative of a larger reaction to feminism, one based often in
pop psychology and a call to male tribalism:

> Like Farrell and Goldberg, Bly thought men have been unjustly accused
> by feminism; that men should not accept blame; that they should acknowl-
> edge and celebrate their difference from women. Like Farrell and Gold-
> berg he rejected the politics of social equality and emphasized the arena
> of emotions. His blind spots—race, sexuality, cultural difference, class—
> are much the same. (209)

What the *Men's Health* version of emotional dignity does is both to reclaim
the terrain of emotion from this reactionary masculinist tendency and
obliquely to recognize those "blind spots" of race, sexuality, cultural difference, and class as constitutive elements of a challenging and perhaps
sometimes confounding social world where the nurturing of emotional
dignity in the face of uncertainties, paradoxes, and conflicts is constructed as an ultimate male value in itself, whatever one's "positions." By
this measure, one does not always have to fully understand or be in control of situations or to know the "right" answer or the "right" solution but
presenting a communicable emotional dignity is the "right" response.
Occasional exposures of the front that can be erected in this way, for
example, in relation to scandal mongering—as perhaps with the Tiger
Woods imbroglio of 2010—only serve to consolidate the hegemonic hold
that the notion of emotional dignity has on the world according to *Men's
Health Magazine*, something also deeply characteristic of, for example,
Lance Armstrong's self-presentation in his autobiography as we saw in
Chapter 3. There can therefore be a fairly robust confidence in the *Men's
Health* vision of the world because these men do not have to change the
world, they only need (among the other aspects of the self-care being
promoted) to groom their emotional dignity as a perfectly respectable
response to it. Where a reactionary populist "masculinity therapy" sought
a return to supposedly basic male archetypes and to emotional release—
including anger—as a response to being "blamed" (and this continues in
certain sometimes lucrative workshop practices for collective male confidence building), the now much more widespread and successful *Men's
Health* ideology has successfully—and even more lucratively—reclaimed
the question of emotion by making it into a groomable asset instead.
Incidentally, it is worth pointing out that ex-F1 driver Jacques Villeneuve's
once "maverick" style is now achievable by purchasing a Remington
PG410 High Precision Designer Stubble Kit, advertised in those pages.

Finally, emotional dignity in the world of *Men's Health* is also constructed as something that can be inherited and passed on by example.
Almost every article about fathers and sons touches on this in some way,
the communicable quantum that is emotional dignity passing wordlessly
between an aging father and his adult son as they walk in the woods and
contemplate the father's death or between a young stay-at-home father
and his toddler going to kindergarten and overcoming his initially
embarrassing moment of first-day panic. It is important to note that in
Men's Health these kinds of item are typically brief vignettes, fragments
glimpsed in the overall busyness of lifestyles filled with things, and self-
improvement activities. But their very haiku like brevity only serves to
underscore the way in which emotional dignity—and, beyond this, emotion more generally as a field of self-presentational opportunity—is being
presented as a resource among others in the richly resourced lives that
are being represented, where emotional dignity becomes a contemporary trope of personality in general and an affective zone of media
curiosity.

In order to bring these observations back to the main interests of the
present book, it will be useful first to consider the evolution of another
popular media format—television's *MasterChef*—as an arena for staging
the question of emotional dignity. Developed by the BBC in the United
Kingdom as a popular format of the 1990s, this was revamped in 2005,
then adapted as *MasterChef Australia* and from the Australian version a
US version was launched in 2010. Briefly tracing the remarkable way in
which the format evolved will reveal something more about the topic at
hand. The original somewhat austere BBC version was a television cookery program, with a strong focus on the detailed preparation and judgment of dishes. The revamp of this (by Shine TV, a company founded by
Elisabeth Murdoch, daughter of media mogul Rupert Murdoch) began
to put more emphasis on the personal dramas of those aspiring to
become top chefs, so the now familiar tension-building devices (the
pauses before delivery of judgment, the heavy use of reaction shots in
the cutting) began to get foregrounded, as did the time pressure on
contestants and the broad-brush judgments at the taste-tests rather than
detailed culinary feedback. The Australian spin-off version took these
elements to the next level by starting with a much larger pool of aspiring
chefs whose cooking was now "auditioned" more competitively in order
to ramp up the sense of cutthroat pressure. It also played up the ostensi-
bly life-changing nature of what was being aspired to, so the "life makeover" format merged with the competitive reality television and cookery

formats as participants with no professional cooking experience vied to win professional training and recognition (as well as cash). The US version took this adapted format and distilled it to its essential ingredients by elaborately staging the show in two linked spaces: a communal cooking studio and an adjacent judgment-delivery studio. While a television studio warm-up crew kept the level of collective emotion high in the contestants' space, the production picked out contestants to follow whose reactions were most visibly emotional and whose back stories underpinned those reactions with added "human interest" (e.g., the woman who was using recipes from her recently deceased mother's family cookbook). By the time these individuals presented their cooked dishes to the three judges in the adjacent "courtroom," emotion was already running high. All the contrived devices of timing, pregnant pauses, biting commentary, and cutaway reaction shots were then operatically deployed in order to stage these moments, the culinary details utterly marginalized in favor of constructing moments of high emotion in which judges and participants faced off in what had become self-presentational dramas where the food was merely an excuse. Closer scrutiny reveals that the editing process in postproduction clearly selected and reassembled sequences of reaction shots (looks, glances, expressions) that had little narrative continuity but hung together as emotion-amplifying assemblages. This evolution of the format toward the purely affective-representational dimension (even at the expense of narrative seamlessness) is deeply revealing. Emotional dignity for all the participants, not just the men, was being publicly tested by *MasterChef USA*, but the all-male judging panel emphasized that this was a largely masculinized arena, as did the de-domesticated studio set and the fact that one of the judges was the celebrity chef Gordon Ramsay whose media persona generally has been deliberately constructed as testosterone charged and confrontational. Any pseudo "feminizing" involved in the emphasis on emotion was overtaken by the masculinized logic of the format as a whole, leaving us to understand its emphasis on the affective-representational in another way.

What we are suggesting with this excursion into the relatively current examples of both *Men's Health* and *MasterChef* is that there has been a discernible shift toward the affective-representational in the domains of popular culture most concerned with "identities," that is with the ostensible fluidity of contemporary identities and the potential, therefore, for self-(re)invention or makeover; moreover, that this shift has manifested itself in particular ways in relation to masculinities, where emotional dignity is both erected as a self-presentational virtue and at the same time publicly tested in little "dramas" that demonstrate its importance by putting it under pressure. The contemporary media environment tends to be organized this way, with what is constructed in one site subjected, not just to repetition, but to reworking or even interrogation in another, so that maximum value gets extracted from any trend. (Other instances could be cited, including those more narrowly focused on metrosexuals or laddishness; see MTV's *Jackass*, *Jersey Shore* and their kind. But these merely shift things into less hegemonically secured representations of masculinity where emotional dignity often gets tested beyond its limits by the very premise of the shows.) By the term "affective-representational" we mean to distinguish this from the non-representational affective stratum that we have focused on elsewhere. In the former, the affective is immediately representationally projected into moments of micro-drama. Emotional dignity proves to be a good focus for these moments because it can be endlessly exposed, tested, and reinstated without elaborate narrativization, and so lends itself to being assembled into the lifestyle imagery of *Men's Health* or the melodramatic televisual staging of a cooking competition, both of which are merely examples of a much larger trend here. We are adapting the term "affective-representational" from the field of cognitive psychology, and specifically from Zavalloni (1986) where it identifies, within everyday life and what cognitive psychologists call "natural thinking," the projection of representations that are simultaneously cognitive and affective constructs. For us, this helpfully labels the process of taking the affective and projecting it representationally, so that affect becomes an emotional expression embedded in, for example, the moments of "personality"-revealing micro-drama that we have described here, whether an amateur chef having his cooking judged on television or a father in a glossy magazine trying to get his son onto a school bus for the first time or any of the other multitudinous instances.

This perspective now enables us to suggest that a different sort of affective attachment—something much closer to Walter Benjamin's notion, as filtered for us through Mark Hansen, of "a corporeal agency sensitive to the inhuman rhythms of the mechanosphere" (Hansen 2000, 243)—exists in a condition of tension with the affective-representational, and that the affective gets drawn then in two directions—outwards into these representational projections and inwards, as it were, as a defining aspect of this corporeal agency. Before tracing this dual movement in an emblematic scene from one of the Transformers films, and then coming back to F1, we can pause to note that it was present too in the "stories" told by our autoethnographic subjects talking about Transformers at the end of Chapter 5. In further analyzing those examples, we have recourse to the useful annotation framework developed by Wiebe, Wilson, and Cardie (2006). This framework is concerned with identifying private states in linguistic expression and achieves this by identifying what these authors call a "private state frame." These frames may be nested within each other in a layering of material and, in this analytical framework, are of two types: expressive subjective element frames and direct subjective frames, the former consisting of expressive subjective elements that imply the existence of a private state while the latter refers directly—for example, more reflexively—to the existence of such a private state. Unlike the analysis by Wiebe, Wilson, and Cardie of transcripts, we also have access via the participants' digital stories to their voices. We can, therefore, listen for the "anchors" indicating frames of these types in the actual voices—in how the words are spoken—not just in the words on the page after transcription. In doing so, we now want to be alert to the possibility that expressive subjective element frames may be more associated with what we are calling the affective-representational dimension, whereas direct subjective frames may be more indicative of a less representationally oriented affective dimension.

Alex, Ben, and Colin, our three adult autoethnographic informants, who expressed their attachments to Transformers through short audiovisual digital stories (transcribed at the end of Chapter 5), all display the same kinds of framing of private states. (We should emphasize that the transcripts are not the autoethnographies, which were audiovisual; merely extracted material.) The common expressive subjective element frame is constructed around the very notion of attachment itself—of having been "massively into" the toys and so on as boys, of "wanting" collections—and of adult recollections of "growing up with that stuff." This shared outer frame carries the expressions of attachment, both direct ones as boys and indirect ones as adults with still evidently fond memories of their boyhood enthusiasms: they are "attached" to the boys they were in this sense. The descriptive accounts they use to elaborate on this—to populate the frame as it were—are focused very much on the "personalities" of the toys (e.g., as television characters whose narrativized identities are mapped onto the toys) and it is when these descriptions touch on personally meaningful memories that "emotional" qualities are detectable in the delivery—in higher speech rates, wider pitch range, shorter inter-word silences, and increases in the rate at which they articulate their thoughts; in short, a clear impression of more emotionally driven intensity invested in those specific moments of the telling. These affective markers or "anchors" help us to pinpoint the inner frames which in these cases all turn out to be of the "direct subjective" order, that is, reflexively expressing the existence of specific private states (in the research by Wiebe, Wilson, and Cardie on a diverse corpus of language this is not an inevitable feature of the "nesting" they observed, where the two different types of frame may nest within each other in various ways). These private states are clearly a feature of what Margaret Archer terms autonomous reflexivity. In our material, Alex's private state concerns his particular boyhood "dinobot," a state which he does not try to "explain" (slipping instead into contextual representations—his associated habit of borrowing the same dinosaur books from the public library). Ben's private state concerns how he felt when left alone with a neighborhood boy's more extensive Transformers collection (a state Ben contrived by frequently visiting the other boy for that express purpose). Again, Ben does not "explain" this state, shifting instead back into general discussion of the "personalities" of various toys. Colin's private state concerns the emotion felt when his parents gave him the "wrong" Transformers toy but Colin also provides the beginnings of a nonrepresentational explanation when he says of his attachment that it was about "You know, what it meant by them transforming—that it was time to act, it was time to do something. . ." (the problem with the "wrong" toy being that it then acted badly, in terms of narrativized "personality," as we shift back out onto the affective-representational dimension).

Anchored by the detectable traces of emotion in their spoken language, these direct subjective frames are framing moments that our three informants evidently felt intensely but do not "explain" directly. They exist in a clearly evident state of tension with the representational accounts focused on the "personality of things" that form the content of the outer expressive subjective element frame for all three, and which has as its own outer limit as it were the general theme of attachment. Colin's "time to do something" as a reading of the very idea of Transformers is the closest we get here to an expression of an affective dimension to this attachment that is apprehended less representationally (the presence of a corporeal agency?), but Colin's remains an important moment of potentially generalizable insight.

As we take this insight forward into a consideration of the big-budget Hollywood movies that capped the Transformers' quarter-century run in 2007 and 2009 with massive box-office success and critical pannings, it is important to make the point that conventional textual analysis will tell us very little of interest about these films. Narratively unsophisticated with two-dimensional characters and shallowly predictable plotting, the Transformers films combine seductive production values with a worldview best described as John Hughes meets Tom Clancy, which is to say spoiled but oddly likeable suburban teens meet lovingly detailed American militarism. (Hughes made teen films such as *Ferris Bueller's Day Off*, Clancy wrote thrillers such as *The Sum of All Fears*.) What director Michael Bay brings to this mix is a music-video director's sensibility, capable of crafting and hooking together strings of memorable high-energy moments that may not have much holistic integrity or depth but nonetheless grab the viewer's attention at the time, not least through visually arresting if ultimately repetitive pyrotechnics. As Michael Ryan and Douglas Kellner (1988) have pointed out, "In American culture, film representations of military prowess seem inseparable from national self-esteem" (194) and, at a period when the United States' international role demands a projection of national self-esteem, Bay's virtually sycophantic recreations of military prowess depict complex, near-seamless networks of military technology and ground-level musculature in perfect communication, backed by command and control systems of awe-inspiring surveillance capability but also tinged with clichéd human concern ("Bring those boys home"). Other filmmakers, such as Tony Scott and Roland Emmerich, have on occasion tapped the same vein of aestheticized military-technological imagery using much the same music-video sensibility, but in the Transformers films Bay and his collaborators cleverly combine this with teen movie conventions that introduce some facetious undercutting of authority when the latter is at its most strutting and overblown. This latter quality allows Bay to split off the solid, reliable, professional military people from the shady, secretive, government-sanctioned men in black whose machinations may have contributed to the crises that the military are then left to clean up, with the help of a handful of kids.

The overall storyline is familiar from the Transformers franchise as a whole—alien robotic life-forms use Earth as their coincidental battleground and disguise themselves as our machinery, especially automobiles, transforming back into their original identities to do battle. The US military gets caught up in this conflict as do several teens and 20-somethings, the latter valuable for their specialist IT skills (and including various stereotypical nerds and video game players). Straying not at all in their representations of large-scale conflict and aggression from what Ryan and Kellner called "penis-brained militarism" (ibid., 297), the films also insinuate into this the facetious tone that knows it is all just one big game in the end. Again, Ryan and Kellner called this trend some time ago when they noted that, as the "rightist, militarist, patriarchal strain in US culture came to full realization" it would be "toppled into a mannerist period of almost ridiculous excess" (ibid., 298). So the Transformers films are evidence, if any were needed, of how long the long tail of this mannerist period has proven to be, and of how director Michael Bay has come single-handedly to represent this ridiculous excess. The films, however, must still draw for their unquestionably large-scale appeal on the Transformers franchise's general capacity to offer an imaginary resolution of anxieties around technology's ongoing infiltration of the category of the "human," as we saw in Chapter 5.

A key emblematic moment for our overall argument comes at the first act dénouement in the first Michael Bay *Transformers* film (2007). The presence on Earth of the "bad" Transformers, the Decepticons, has been established and they have had a couple of spectacular run-ins with the US military ("What is that thing?" encounters, long a familiar convention of the science-fiction genre). A local backstory has also been set up, with young Sam Witwicky, still working his way clumsily out of pubescence, identified as the grandson of an Arctic explorer who discovered the Transformers' AllSpark cube (source of all their energy) crashed and buried in ice along with Megatron, the leader of the Decepticons. These turn out to have been secretly extricated and hidden in a frozen state by a shadowy government sanctioned agency. Unknowingly, Sam possesses (digitally encoded on the lens of his grandfather's old spectacles, which he has been trying to sell on eBay) the location of the All-Spark cube. The "good" Transformers, the Autobots, having checked out eBay, are coming to Earth where they will disguise themselves as automobiles and so on in order to track it down. One has already hidden himself as the battered but grunty old yellow Camaro with racing stripes that Sam's father has just bought him as his first car (the General Motors product placement being hardly under-stated in this film). By the particular point in the film we are interested in here, Sam has discovered that his car is some sort of robot ("It's definitely Japanese") and the rest of the Autobot team have just arrived on Earth like a group of sentient meteors, plunging fierily through the atmosphere to converge on Sam and his "car." Director Bay brings a strong sense of pacing and structure to his first act setups (though thereafter things typically become frenetically overblown and shapeless), so this moment feels important as we go into it.

Up to this point we have glimpsed the Transformers in their robotic states but they have been largely impersonal hulks of battling animated machinery, objects of awe and terror, unknown things. As the Autobots disguised as vehicles converge around Sam, and his "car" unpacks itself into its robotic identity to join them, this scene for the first time in the film more fully endows them with their "personalities." Despite every-thing we have suggested above about the film's limitations, it is very dif-ficult not to be seduced by this particular moment. The seduction happens on two levels. First, each Transformer is introduced as its char-acter. For fans, especially young adults who grew up with the toys and television series, this is the payoff moment when the characters take on a "reality" so much more visually and physically present and convincing than the toys, the flatly drawn animation on television, or the comics ever achieved. The Transformers films used the best (and most expen-sive) special effects and CG animation techniques that Hollywood was capable of at the time, so the "realization" of these characters is undeni-ably impressive at that level. Each character is introduced in turn and the effects techniques give each its distinctive personality, evoked in body language as much as in named identity or synthesized voice (they some-times speak in snippets sampled from human popular culture). And it is in the body language that the scene finds its other, second level of seduc-tion. For even a viewer largely uninformed about the main Transformers backstory and unfamiliar with the toys/characters, the extraordinary sense of individual aliveness achieved in these machine bodies is quite striking.

This scene is deeply emblematic of something we have been progres-sively exposing as the book proceeded: the existence of an affective layer of fascinated attachment to technologies that carry the "grace" of human-like vitality (as we referred to it in Chapter 1) but that is almost immedi-ately projected representationally into what we identify as the personality of things. This representational projection (or particular drawing into semiosis) may well work across the entire field of contemporary techn-oculture, but at its most elaborate becomes something like the prolifer-ated Transformers franchise with its story arcs and character armies built around piles of toys, so this becomes an especially clear example of the process. However, a scene such as the one described here also momen-tarily collapses all of this back again onto that affective layer, where a certain irresistible seduction takes place in the affective moment when the machine shows grace, the moment when a felt vitality unites human and machine in their common materiality.

Each of these robotic figures started life as hundreds of actual car parts and other bits and pieces of machinery, photographed and remodeled as digital components and then hooked onto an animation "rig" in the computers at effects company Industrial Light and Magic (ILM), with programmed inbuilt rules determining how they interconnected, so that the CG animators could achieve frame-by-frame movements in which the various parts disarticulated and rearticulated themselves smoothly and convincingly around some 20,000 internal nodes per "model," with the programmed rules ensuring that moving parts did not interfere with each other during transformations. This quality of internal structural consistency gives the Transformer movements a mechanical believability, while obsessive attention to rendering the surfaces of various materials, complete with light effects and reflections, contributes a verisimilitude rooted in the very physicality of the objects. Even ensuring that the mass remains the same while the objects transform contributes to this striking verisimilitude, so a car and a robot do not lose or gain virtual mass as one transforms into the other. But the animators at ILM also brought an extraordinary believability to the "human" movements of the robotic figures, giving each its own physical distinctiveness. For the action sequences, of which of course there are many, video of kung-fu and "ninja" moves were studied and then replicated in the animation, without in this case much use of the motion-capture technique that is currently in vogue for capturing human movement using digitized data points recorded off a human figure in motion. This background information has been mostly gleaned, appropriately perhaps, from a 2007 press conference in Second Life. One reporter's account began:

> When I first arrived, I was on a street above the event . . . . A greeter advised me to take the stairs down, make a couple of turns, and then wait for the elevator to take all of us down. When we hit bottom, we were in a tunnel area that was quite expansive. This led us into the "press room", which consisted of chairs, a screen, a gigantic Megatron, and a couple of rooms you could go into. While we waited for the director, producer, and cast to appear, we had a chance to see the trailer for the new movie. I'm not much of an action fan, but Transformers is a throwback to my childhood, so it's a must see for me. *(Moo Money, who then worked full-time in Second Life as a virtual journalist and "machinimist" or maker of computer animations from hacked computer game parts)*

There is something deeply ironic about the fact that these Transformers characters feel almost more real on screen than did a press conference to launch the film in the virtual levels, tunnels, and rooms of the Second Life environment.

Now the point of reporting this background information is to underscore how important it evidently was to the ILM effects specialists to treat the Transformers as assemblages of material parts, the materiality of which was constantly emphasized. The discovery of grace within these material assemblages is then all the more seductive, where we intend the term "grace" to refer, in the manner proposed by Hans Ulrich Gumbrecht, to the dehumanized body that nonetheless displays the most intense vitality (not just a mere elegance in the eye of the beholder)—a state where the human body and the machine body find that their common vitalized materiality has the capacity to afford what the Olympic swimmer Pablo Morales called "focused intensity" and Gumbrecht calls transfiguration (Gumbrecht 2009). We will stage something of this in our Afterwords.

The representational projections of the Transformers' "personalities" from this point interweave with both the franchise's overall narrative arc and with this particular film's local version of that, which includes in particular the kids' negotiation of roles for themselves in the overall structure of authority organized around the "good" Transformers, the military professionals, the shadowy agency behind the scenes, and the world of their parents (as exemplified by the Witwicky family). There is nothing very sophisticated about the way this plays out in the film—and certainly no interpretive move that will reveal it as more than it is—but it is nonetheless important to note that, once again, the theme of emotional dignity provides a key "humanizing" factor in most of the nonaction scenes. Glen, one of the geeks enlisted for his code-breaking skills, talks tough to Maggie, the cool uber-geek, in an FBI interrogation room but cracks the moment the interrogators enter the room, screaming deliriously that he is innocent and it is all Maggie's fault, then blaming his outburst on a "sugar rush" from eating a plate of donuts. Glen is the most conspicuous example of how most of the young men in the film struggle to attain an emotional dignity, whether in front of women or the various authority figures. So too, in fact, with the Transformers themselves, which is one of the cleverer aspects of the "personalities" they are given. Stumbling clumsily through the Witwicky's suburban neighborhood they discover that shorting the power lines is "tingly" ("Yeah, that looks like fun"); after a confrontation with operatives of the secret agency one of them pops the cap off the oil tank in his groin and "lubricates" the head agent: in short, the Transformers tend to behave at times very much like the teens, a quality reinforced by their sampling of popular cultural soundtracks which has them speaking on occasion like Dirty Harry, rappers, or a bad impersonation of John Wayne. At the center of this as the always stabilizing influence is Optimus Prime, the Autobot leader, whose authority—the most convincing in the film—is based very much on the emotional dignity he displays in every situation, whether telling an overexcited Sam to calm down or controlling his own exuberant gang of Transformers. The film's most revealing scene in this regard is probably when Sam is frantically searching his room for his grandfather's spectacles, while the Autobots wait impatiently outside. Sam's suspicious parents think he has locked his door because he is masturbating—is there any greater threat to a teen's emotional dignity than to be discovered masturbating by his parents?—but the discovery in his room of Mikeala, object of his affections and tough daughter of a car-stealing greasemonkey father, deposited through his bedroom window by Optimus Prime, saves face all round (and Mikeala is played by Megan Fox, ranked second on the *Maxim* magazine "Hot 100 of 2009" list, so probably something of a fantasy for many teen boys caught red-handed in similar circumstances). So emotional dignity becomes a main trope of personality here, a thematically pertinent way for the projection of the "personality of things" to intersect narratively with the human world represented by the Witwicky family.

Shifting back to Formula One at this point may seem like a somewhat arbitrary move but we have two points to make about this: first, representational thinking tends to be generically bounded—to discourage the kinds of jump we are making (in the book, not just here) across genres and forms of contemporary popular culture—but the nonrepresentational affective layer we are looking to trace may significantly disrespect such boundaries; second, F1, as we shall demonstrate, not only sets up "personality" as a representational projection from that affective layer but then—uniquely—exposes the utter artifice involved by affording occasional and seemingly unavoidable moments when the illusion collapses and the object world reasserts itself brutally. In these moments, it is precisely emotional dignity that gets betrayed as a subjectivist illusion in the circumstances. These moments happen as a result of what in F1 are called "team orders," an enactment of the very logic of money and machinery; at this the highest level where the driver, the man, is exposed for what he always was—a thing among things, an object, a commodity-self, despite F1 being based so determinedly on projecting a core ambiguity around this for much of the time.

Not surprisingly then, Jean Baudrillard was interested in F1:

Formula One is a rather good example of the era of performance, in which the heights achieved are the work of man and machine simultaneously, each propelling the other to extremes without it being really clear which is the engine of this meteoric advance and which merely the other's double. (2002, 166)

Baudrillard evokes the complexity of F1's underpinning structural apparatuses, as well as the corresponding ambiguity around determining whether man or machine takes priority in the technologized performance that F1 celebrates. Behind the scenes, the driver is deeply technologized as a component in a finely tuned system. The nonpublic, inner workings of F1 systematically scrutinize and assess driver performance in relation to the machinery of the car and, by reducing this to data about interacting parts of a system, reconceptualize the driver/man as an integrated machine. Publicly, though, there is the projection of personality that underpins F1's popular myths and global mediations that focus audience attention on the man (DS's "Jacques Villeneuve" and his maverick personality), promote the human dimension of performance and emphasize the star system (e.g., to sell high-priced men's watches in the pages of international news magazines, as but one example). Of course, this outward projection in its own way packages the person as object, constructing mediated, globalized, and commercialized star images and personas, but on that representational level "personality" remains nonetheless available for imaginary recognition in a way that the unrelenting behind-the-scenes instrumentalism could not itself support.

Viewed in machine terms, Formula One looks like a pyramid: a pyramidal synthesis of the efforts of thousands of people which culminate in a single car, a single man, a single brief, dazzling moment. The condensation is extreme, and the mirror of the race refracts all the energies deployed—energies all working towards one goal—into the performance of a single man [. . .] The collective fascination with the race certainly owes much to this transformation of all into one. (Baudrillard 2002, 166–7)

F1's public narrative works hard to find its own version of what we have termed the personality of things and to install it at the top of this pyramid, in large measure of course to sustain audience fascination with—not the extensive underpinning systems—but the spectacle of a driver "manfully" manipulating the machine on race day; otherwise there would be a logical next technical step to having machines controlling these machines—a fully robotic F1? This also reflects how relatively easy it would be to view F1 drivers as corporate drones, PR functionaries of the corporations sponsoring them; so their conformity is deflected through a promotional mode of address to fans that, in the first instance, may be derived from familiar tropes such as national allegiance (support "your" home nation's driver). Paradoxically though, to perform consistently and then to excel in F1, these men have to become deeply robotic in their reliably metronomic driving capabilities, to come as close as possible to that wholly technologized vision of a *fully robotic F1*.

Enter Michael Schumacher. If F1's star system culminates in the Drivers' Championship as the mark of the man (as implied master of the machine), then German driver Michael Schumacher has in F1's recent era been the yard stick for all contemporary drivers to be measured against—akin to a Juan Manuel Fangio, Jim Clark, Jackie Stewart, or Ayrton Senna in their respective generations. Schumacher is literally the benchmark performative man-machine unit, having won a record seven world championships (including 91 Grand Prix wins) while establishing new levels of fitness, work ethic, and standards of car control throughout his "first" F1 racing career 1991–2006 (he subsequently embarked on a second, less successful foray into F1 with Mercedes in 2010). Schumacher was revered in this first career for his driving talent and attributes but ironically his near-perfect integration within the F1 machinery (in terms also of compliance with team and sponsor requirements outside the car) sometimes seemed too polished, too seamless, too close in fact to exposing the paradoxical logic described above. Such characterizations tended to reduce Schumacher to an uncharismatic and emotionless figure, Allen noting, for example, that "Schumacher is often accused of being more like a robot than a human being" (2000, 78). This came with obvious rewards though. Accompanying his seven world championships was phenomenal wealth, Schumacher being the highest paid driver and rumored to be earning approximately US$70–80 million annually post-2004 (over half of which was derived from commercial endorsements). As both a "streamlined product of sponsors and PR men" (Allen 2000, 84) and a robot in the car, Schumacher represents better than most the contradictions at the very heart of F1.

This is not to say that extraordinary personal skill was not involved. Schumacher clearly excelled in his personal ability to set up cars and adjust to their characteristics (including his much touted wet-weather car control), and he displayed an especially agile mind for adapting race tactics or making in-car setup alterations while racing at 200mph (the robotic mind computing extra data?). Gumbrecht suggests that the "tools" for the extension or complexification of the human body in this sort of doubled relationship are twofold: "First they make it possible to go beyond the limits of an exclusively human performance, by, for example, multiplying the maximum speed at which a body can move through space" (2006, 174). Baudrillard puts this more bluntly, noting that "car and driver are merely a living projectile" (2002, 167) and that "the car becomes a tactile, tactical extension of the human body" (168). However, Gumbrecht also identifies a second key component:

> Rather than emphasizing the ability of tools to enhance human abilities, this second aspect emphasizes the ability of a human to adapt his body to the form, movements, or function of the tool. [. . .] Success depends on an inherent paradox: the more perfectly an athlete manages to adapt his body to the form and movements of a horse or car, the better he will control them and the more he will maximize his body's effectiveness. (2006, 175)

Not only adroit at this adaptive effectiveness-maximizing process, during his Ferrari team years (1996–2006) Schumacher took his own personal fitness regimes and driving abilities to the highest level while increasingly expecting both team and car to be molded around him (the one organizationally, the other physically). So it was well known that Schumacher immersed himself in relentless hours of testing to perfect his set up, often at the expense of his teammates in terms of their own car development and especially in terms of preferential strategies come race weekend. As a consequence, after the initial "teething" years of adapting Michael to the car and vice versa (and despite Schumacher missing much of the 1999 season with a broken leg), the Ferrari/Schumacher "machine" would dominate F1 between 2000 and 2004, when he won five of his championships. The nature of this dominance came close to being alienating for many F1 fans, however, given that Schumacher had no competition and no teams could match Ferrari, while his own teammate Rubens Barrichello was widely understood to have been contractually obliged to let Schumacher win (despite Barrichello's insistence in recent years that no such contract existed and that he was not a "number two" driver). The 2002 season exemplified this dominance. Michael Schumacher finished on the podium in every race (11 x 1st; 5 x 2nd; 1 x 3rd), having won the Drivers' Championship by round 11 of the season. With a total of 144 points for the season, his nearest "rival," Barrichello, finished a distant second with 77 points. The Ferrari/Schumacher machine obliterated the opposition in 2002. It is also significant, therefore, that the 2002 season was infamous for Ferrari stage-managing the Austrian Grand Prix result by having Barrichello, who led for the entire race, pulling over meters from the finish line to gift Schumacher the race victory.

This was one of the few occasions that I watched a televised Grand Prix with a large group of my friends in New Zealand. A group of approximately ten of us had gathered to watch the race live at midnight (given international time differences) as this was our final weekend together; several of our group being about to depart for an extended stay in Europe. The usual Ferrari procession was taking place at the front, so anything else of interest caught our attention (hence Villeneuve's charge and overtaking through the field that I reveled in as others reluctantly gave him credit). But things tended to get drawn back to Ferrari. Toward the end, when team orders were so blatantly applied and Barrichello pulled over to let Schumacher through, all of us in unison were decrying the manipulation, the deceit, the betrayal of "racing" by Ferrari. While one friend reeled off a litany of expletives around why F1 was not a sport, I, as the supposed F1 aficionado, could not disagree and could only suggest, rather weakly, that this was just one of the reasons I found Schumacher and Ferrari's overly blatant deployment of team order practices *so hard to stomach* (though otherwise intellectually understood). Even the two Schumacher fans among us looked sheepishly around and had little to say in defense of "Ferrari's" (i.e., team Schumacher's) actions. The television coverage of Schumacher's winning lap at Austria still had him giving the victor's raised arms from the cockpit and yet, becoming aware of the adverse crowd reaction—indeed the pervasive booing that grew as he exited the car—he adopted what can only be described as remorseful posturing, pushing Rubens on to the top of the podium and acting glum while accepting the winner's trophy (which he promptly handed to Rubens). Even his post-race reactions tried to deflect flak by identifying the action as a team call, a Ferrari decision which, of course, the literate F1 audience knew always involved a consultation with and mutually agreed favoritism toward Schumacher. The fact that Schumacher continued to be booed at the next two races, while Barrichello just overtook him as he slowed down to cross the line at Indianapolis late in the season (explanations ranging from a "payback" gift to miscalculating an attempted photo finish) did little to offset the feeling that something starkly impersonal about F1's workings had been revealed. My F1 fandom went through the doldrums of seeing Villeneuve languishing in the midfield in a car inferior to his talents, while having to stomach Schumacher's posturing at the front. I had enjoyed Schumacher's battles with Mika Hakkinen in 1998 when the former was the underdog but now, with the dominant package, the Ferrari machine was unassailable. Race victories were literally "no sweat" for Michael, while other top three finishers would look exhausted on the podium. Schumacher sprang from his car fresh and even jovial after his habitual Sunday afternoon cruise to collect the winner's trophy. He would then, in press conferences, have the audacity to "reveal" how difficult his victory was, to feign ignorance about how "boring" races had become for spectators and—especially—to remain nonplussed at any criticisms of manipulative team tactics.

DS

What becomes very clear from this autoethnographic moment in a fan's life is what briefly but revealingly crumbled in that moment—emotional dignity not just perhaps for the drivers being publicly manipulated by team orders but for the fans feeling betrayed, their passionate attachment, especially in front of each other, momentarily revealed as duped contributions to the workings of an impersonal machinery, where the vast sums of money involved were buying corporate success disguised as personal prowess. But what is particularly important about this is that Schumacher did not really lose his emotional dignity, because nothing easily identifiable as that in fact existed; indeed, he did exactly what was expected of him and clearly expected the same of the Ferrari management controlling the team orders. His subsequent enactment of an emotional micro-drama for fans merely tried to shift his behavior onto the terrain where the fans wanted to be, in order to "stomach" things. In fact, however, Schumacher had not betrayed something about F1 per se but revealed its inexorable logic as a high-tech site of massive corporate investments. By becoming near-perfect embodiments of that site's aims, the Ferrari/Schumacher machine had turned it inside out to reveal both the impersonality of its inner logic (the individual's subordination to the brand and the money) and the sham involved in the outward projection of personality as the defining ground of achievement.

Baudrillard, writing more generally and apparently without consideration of such details as team orders, nonetheless is able to note,

> There is no passion in this—except the passion for winning, of course, though that is not personal, but an operational passion. It shows up in the driver's brain the way the technical data show on the dashboard. It is in-built in the technical object itself, which is made to win, and which incorporates the driver's will as one of the technical elements required for victory. This seems inhuman, but to be honest about it, it is the mental logic of the race. (2002, 168)

So in fact it is the fan that F1 robs of otherwise implied emotional dignity in such moments, as the fan remains much more dependent on passion, not merely on calculated assessments of the technical objects involved, not merely on that kind of passionless mental logic. And so, perhaps, the fan's emotional dignity gets pushed down the grid, down the field of drivers, looking for the point where the "personality of things" becomes believable again. Enter a driver like Jacques Villeneuve. Villeneuve's seemingly reluctant commodification and resistance to corporate puppetry made him a good midfield focus for reinvested fan passion, after his rapidly achieved career peak in 1997, his subsequent remoteness from the winners' podium also opening up a space that seemed more free of the inexorable systemic logic getting more and more exposed at the front (which is not to say that his fans, or those of any other midfield runner did not want their driver to win of course). In fact, a glance through F1 websites, books, and magazines reveals two aspects of Villeneuve getting emphasized. The first, taking a career "profile" format, focuses on an early career rich with successes (often tying in connections to his famous racing father and Jacques' own Indy accomplishments in the United States), then attainment of the F1 championship before relative midfield obscurity in performance terms. The second, however, quite clearly embellishes Villeneuve's "personality," depicting him as free-spirited, his own man, standing apart, a rebel, eccentric, an individual, opinionated, and so on (the things that DS responded to, as charted in Chapter 4).

Of course, Villeneuve was always already a commodity given that the sponsorship-dependent corporate structure of Formula One sets that as the price of entry to the field. His style could be corporately appropriated and was even subject to imitation. His supposedly unfettered time with the BAR team could be seen as a matter of marketing convenience, allowing BAR to promote their "rebel" star driver in order to position their team's "personality" as aggressive upstarts un-cowed by the F1 establishment (and by criticism of tobacco industry sponsorship's deservedly non-PC credentials). While these kinds of detail are the trivia of F1 in one sense, in another they reveal the ways in which personality is constructed in the main body of the field despite the occasional exposure at the top of the utterly impersonal reality and always defining logic of F1's inner machinery. Indeed, one is tempted to wonder how wise it is for today's younger drivers to take the Ferrari/Schumacher risk, despite the extraordinary rewards, which is to say the risk of getting to and staying at the top by revealing too much of the passionless objectification involved, which can be more easily disguised farther down the field in the guise of marketable "personality," no matter how cleverly the latter is being produced and stage-managed. Indeed recent English F1 championship winner Lewis Hamilton—the sport's first black champion—has been criticized by previous F1 and IndyCar World Series champion and ex-Ferrari driver Nigel Mansell for being too "manufactured," an accusation that would barely have made sense in a pre-Schumacher era and one that undercuts the racially progressive connotations of Hamilton's achievement by suggesting that his "manufacture" was the price of success.

So the Ferrari/Schumacher machine of 2002 may have been our best opportunity ever to see behind the affective-representational constructions that disguise the inner logic of F1 as, in its own way, one pinnacle of publicly displayed man-machine interaction in the modern world. Reduced to a superefficient object in a system of high-tech objects, the man is required by this logic to perform as a corporate and technological marionette. The more successful he is in these terms the more stress gets put on the affective-representational construction of personality as the disguise worn by that reifying logic. We can generalize here too. The Ferrari/Schumacher machine of 2002 may have been one of our best opportunities ever to see behind the affective-representational constructions that, within contemporary technoculture, disguise the inner logic of the technologized lifeworld. At this level of generalization it suddenly becomes quite appropriate to consider Michael Schumacher and Optimus Prime side by side as features of a not uncontradictory contemporary social imagining of that lifeworld. Optimus Prime, as an imaginary artificial life-form, secures the affective-representational plane where the personality of things is held up as still believable (hinged around emotional dignity as a workably defining human characteristic in these complex times of less stable traditional values). Michael Schumacher, as human, ironically came to reveal (if only in brief moments when the veil tore because it was stretched so tight) the total absorption of the human into the machinic dimension, into a corporately sponsored object world dominated by an impersonal logic, where the "personality of things" is exposed as an ideological illusion. Regressing from this chilling moment of exposure to the boyhood fantasy of Optimus Prime is only to reflect the difficulty—perhaps the near impossibility—of living comfortably, once we have glimpsed it, with the impersonal world of purely operational "passion" or with its pure technologized logic of systemic performance-seeking intensity.

What "Jacques Villeneuve" names, then, is a site of emotional dignity that is typical of the many such places that men have gone to find some respite from that dilemma—the dilemma of whether to regress to the safety blanket of an Optimus Prime or to attempt the perhaps impossible recognition of a truth so difficult to live with. Very few, if any, readers of this book will have gone to the exact place —into Villeneuve fandom— but that is very much the point. Affect finds multitudinous places to settle within the nesting loops of contemporary culture. The regressive attachment to an Optimus Prime is somewhat different, reflecting not multitudinous dispersals of affect into those more varied places and affiliations but a collective convergence of a kind that becomes especially clear when we find media coverage of a member of Ohio's National Guard changing his name to Optimus Prime before shipping out to serve in Iraq: "I got a letter from a general at the Pentagon when the name change went through and he says it was great to have the employ of the commander of the Autobots in the National Guard." The soldier also revealed of his childhood attachment to the Transformers character, "My dad passed away the year before and I didn't have anybody really around, so I really latched onto him when I was a kid" (WKYC-TV Channel 3 news, Cleveland, Ohio, March 19, 2003). Prime serves doubly here, in this extreme but nonetheless rather revealing case, to secure a common affective-representational projection of imaginary coherence onto a complex contemporary reality and as a regressive personal site of affective palliation. Meanwhile, what a "Jacques Villeneuve" does (the quotes intended to de-realize him now in a way that Optimus Prime does not require) is to give one personality to the anonymous physical templates that get endlessly displayed in the male body imagery of *Men's Health*

Magazine: upper body images of glowingly healthy men looking confident, typically with the well-developed upper arms that, in the world of *Men's Health Magazine*, seem now to signify robust but nonthreatening masculinity and an appropriately groomed identity (Mikeala in the first *Transformers* film even offering the throwaway remark to Sam Witwicky that she likes this). Amidst the endlessly substitutable versions of this body image in the magazine pages it becomes possible to latch onto one specific manifestation and to invest one's interest affectively in a "Jacques Villeneuve" where the personality is less blandly replicable and the symbolic upper arm strength is in fact also literal, as it must be for a top racing driver, but additionally is the transmitter of "soul in the elbow," of grace in the machine. It helps enormously then that he is (perpetually, not just in a specific historical moment) "languishing" in the shadow of a Michael Schumacher (the specific word employed in the previous autoethnographic vignette) because that threatened enfeeblement becomes precisely the place to recognize emotional dignity being maintained and the place where the affective-representational illusion is still then also maintainable, that F1 is not in fact the very pinnacle of objectification, of the technologized and commercialized reification of the subject as a well-oiled component of the machine.

We could have looked, within motor racing, for evidence of this in fan attachments to a Juan Pablo Montoya (F1 and NASCAR), a Nicky Hayden (MotoGP motorcycle racing), a Dale Earnhardt Jr. (NASCAR), or any number of others (although neither the US National Association for Stock Car Auto Racing nor international Grand Prix motorcycle racing come close to pushing the technological limits the way F1 does) but the key point is that there is nothing particularly special about any such choice except that he would be special to some group of fans whose affective attachment happened, for largely arbitrary local or personal reasons, to settle there instead of somewhere else. So "Jacques Villeneuve" has been a subject here because he afforded an opportunity for fairly intensive autoethnographic scrutiny, thanks to the fandom of one of the coauthors, rather than merely reporting on the fandom of others. And we could have looked outside motorsport for similar examples, across other sports in the television environment, or outside sports to other places where fandom alights amidst technology or representations of technology (electronic dance music or electropop, cult science-fiction television, etc.). Again, though, a key point is not to privilege one such place over another or to find any one more supportive of generalizations than another but to insist that it is in the particularity of these attachments that any generalizable insight is to be found, so the overall movement of this book has been into and out of that particularity.

We need to remind ourselves, however, of the specific focus on technology here, especially the argued existence of an affective layer of fascinated attachment to technologies that carry the grace of humanlike vitality but an attachment that is almost immediately projected representationally into what we have persistently referred to as the personality of things. Shifting our point of view back from a Schumacher, an Optimus Prime, or a Jacques Villeneuve as various—and variously appropriated—locations for that projected "personality," where F1 and Transformers have been but sections isolated from the larger technologized lifeworld with its associated technoculture, and attending instead to the affective layer itself, is the interpretive move that the book has taken at various points but that now requires more focused attention at the finish.

To do this we need to introduce one further concept to the book's particular lexicon, that of rhythm and with it Henri Lefebvre's notion of rhythmanalysis (Lefebvre 2004): "We easily confuse *rhythm* with *movement* [*mouvement*], speed, a sequence of movements [*gestes*] or objects (machines, for example). Following this we tend to attribute to rhythms a **mechanical** overtone, brushing aside the **organic** aspect of rhythmed movements" (ibid., 5–6, emphases in original). Lefebvre's concept of rhythm is not reducible to (though it may be dependent upon) movement, speed, or objects and is not focused on the mechanical without some organic component, so it comes very close to being the one term we now need to pull together much of what has been argued here about "soul in the elbow" or "grace" in the machine, in the context of the always "mechanical overtone" of F1 or Transformers as our sampled materials from contemporary technoculture. That Lefebvre contrasts this way of thinking about rhythm with "representations that *conceal the production* of repetitive time and space" (ibid., 7, emphasis added) serves to further strengthen the connection we are making. We need to note that much of the autoethnographic material we have considered has displayed expressive subjective element frames, as we have identified them: language that indirectly suggested the presence of affect without "expressing" that affect. We can now suggest that the direct subjective frames, where they occurred, "expressed" not affect directly but arrested moments, in other words moments apprehensibly available to retelling in terms of arrested rhythm: being enchanted by a particular little toy, being left alone in a boyhood friend's room with his Transformers collection, having one's sporting passion arrested in a moment of indignity, recognizing that something is about to happen (the promise of transformation) . . . There is in all these moments a feeling of holding one's breath. But what may succeed these moments of arrest is the flooding back in of representations, in the case of Transformers never better exemplified than in the first Michael Bay film when the seductive moment we considered earlier (the first assembly of the group of machines around Sam and Mikeala) is immediately succeeded by a ramping up for the remainder of the film of sheer speed (in the end quite mind numbingly so). And much of F1 racing might seem to the uninitiated to be like this too—sheer monotonous speed rather than rhythm in the discriminating sense suggested by Levebvre, punctuated merely by pit stops, corners, and the occasional overtaking move that introduce only the crudest of rhythms in the sense of brief interruptions to the overall feeling of undifferentiated speed. So where is rhythm to be found in these instances? Surely, in watching the cinematic robot figure itself move *as if* inhabited by humanlike vitality and grace and in watching the racing car move *as if* inhabited by humanlike vitality and grace.

So the materializing of affect in the F1 car proffers levels of intensities that, in turn, are projected inwards via propulsion and rhythm, via fragility and potential destruction (grace reduced to carnage in the blink of an eye), and outwards onto its personalities. The notion of personalities in effect becomes twofold: first referring to the distinctions between machines via the mythic identities of teams (a Ferrari has a different personality from a Lotus); second of course reinvesting the man in the machine. This involves specific representations, such as characterizing the discernibly smooth, metronomic, and superefficient car control of a Schumacher or the ragged, hard charging, and risk-taking pursuits of a Villeneuve. But even the "showroom" display of an F1 machine at rest evokes the rhythms and promises the intensities on which this layering is premised. What audiences then actually witness, however, are the affectively charged moments when the machine embodies intensities that become lifelike, takes on vitality independently of the status-laden personality systems of either team or driver. In this respect, we see the symmetry of high-velocity cars in close formation pursuing one another (also morphing into animalistic form as the collective snake or hunting pack in unison around the circuit) with, on the one hand, the machine caressing and dancing over kerbing, slithering, and sliding in the wet or on rubber "marbles" shed by tires, and, on the other, a fascination in the man-machine at its performative limits, not knowing which component of the double will prevail (or on occasion fail).

There is an aura, a lure, a fascination which allows these intense moments, intense memories, and intense embodied inscriptions to be affectively "felt," which, in turn, we then complicate with representation and rationalization. It is too easy to individuate a key sporting moment—to inflect it as personality—and then to hold it up for objective measurement, to judge it, due to the sporting obsession with producing statistics, histories, and classifications via results and rankings and all the rest. But the moment is what it is—a fleeting affective fragment that transports intensities—it occurs as such, inscribing a memory, triggering a response (affective, embodied) while transcending the minutiae in order to fascinate, seduce, or move us in some manner.

The problem always with this way of writing is that representational thinking oscillates all the time around the affective stratum in which, finally, we are interested here. Movement, speed, and objects re-project themselves insistently as representations, which leaves only Lefebvre's *geste*. As his translators tell us, "The French word *geste* carries the fourfold meaning of 'gest', 'gesture', 'movement' and 'act'. It thus plays a crucial role in Lefebvre's attempt to translate the understanding of intentional human 'gestures' into a series of rhythms" (Lefebvre 2004, 104). Thus too, the staging of a gestural presence in the moving object carries the potential of a "time to act," as one of our autoethnographic subjects said of his boyhood fascination with Transformers. The car and the robot both twitching with vitality make this potential available to affective apprehension, which is to say they make it available to a fatal strategy that succeeds in turning away from the world of subjectivist representations in order to face the object world instead. In doing so, the personality of things dissolves to be replaced by a relation: the relation between the boy and the man connected by their apprehension of the same rhythm in things, their transportation from boy to man troubled only by a niggling worry about whether boy and man are one and the same (the philosophical Non-Identity Problem writing itself onto the everyday). And as for technology. . .

These machines that allow us to see affect do so in a way that "not only traverses the opposition of the organic and nonorganic; it also inserts the technical into felt vitality, the felt aliveness given in the preindividual bodily capacities to act, engage, and connect—to affect and be affected" (Clough 2007, 2) and, we would argue, it is this that gives form to the android *imaginaire*.

So we can see why the Transformers computer games (especially a flurry of 2007 releases) have not been very successful whereas F1 driving games tend to be more liked, for example, as judged by the online ratings aggregated by sites such as Metacritic. The Transformers games try to project these moments of felt vitality outwards into loud representations of penis-brained militarism, on the model of the films, whereas they should really be driving games, to be about automobility not the military. To "drive" a Transformer at speed in automobile mode and, with the flick of a game controller, to have it transform in one's hands into a machine with the grace of a Marty Kudelka should be rapturous, not a mere prelude to a fight. The obsessive attention to detailing that these games have (the F1 games reproducing tracks and cars in extraordinary detail, the Transformers games detailing robotic characters) tends to support representational elaborations, especially in the case of Transformers, when they could really be about the touch of grace in the machine.

Finally, we can see how the longitudinal lines of materialized motion intersect with the latitudinal lines of intensity in order to sustain the career of affect. Nigel Thrift says that "non-representational theory is resolutely anti-biographical" (2008, 7), which seems to undercut our autoethnographic interests here: but in fact we have been driving (auto) biography at increasing speed in order to discover, precisely, when it loses downforce.

Afterwords: Magnitude, Compression, Sharpness

Brecht had wet laundry put in the actress's laundry basket so that her hip would have the right movement, that of the alienated laundress. Well and good: but stupid too, no? For what weighs down the basket is not wet laundry but time, history, and how to represent such a weight as that?

—Roland Barthes 1977, 154, *emphasis in original*

The pedagogical scene (Vincent 1991, 6) remains deeply troubled by this dilemma, because in some way Brecht was right but Barthes' skepticism largely won the day. The basket full of wet laundry, its materiality weighing the hip of the woman on stage, does not easily get drawn into semiosis (which was Barthes' way of seeing it, his expectation) in such a manner as to express the larger weight. But if, instead of shifting our expectations outwards through (faltering) semiotic layers, we focus inwards, on the *movement* itself, what might we expect? That particular movement joins many others here—from a dancer and an ice skater lending grace with the help of motion capture technology to dancing machines in a television commercial, to free runners in a music video, fans in a mosh pit moving to extreme metal drumming, or any of the other instances we have touched on throughout the book. "Reducing" F1 and Transformers to moments and to this understanding of movement (though perhaps better as *geste*) has been part of our argument, while at the same time recognizing the inexorable reestablishment of representational thinking that remains inescapable, and where F1 and Transformers are so ineluctably *banal*. None of our examples has carried any "progressive" connotations as representations (where Brecht's basket was different, as that is precisely what was representationally aspired to in the end even if Barthes doubted that it could be achieved). Nor have we argued that movement/*geste* represents in some elemental way a "progressive" kernel on its own, much less some sort of playful politics. Instead the (nonrepresentational) argument has been that affect materializes in objects that have *geste* (movement, gesture, action). The affective aspect of Brecht's particular basket of wet laundry is very different from that of a lighter basket or no basket at all, from merely a verbal statement about alienation and time. And affect itself moves, we have suggested, not least through the stuff of media cultures (its nesting loops) searching for places to settle for a while, objects to attach itself to, often ignoring along its way generic and textual boundaries (the fetishized interests of production). John Urry has noted of automobility that it

> necessarily divides workplaces from the home producing lengthy commutes; it splits home and shopping and destroys local retailing outlets; it separates home and various kinds of leisure site; it splits up families which live in distant places; it necessitates leisure visits to sites lying on the road network; it entraps people in congestion, jams and temporal uncertainties. (2000, 59–60)

The *career of affect*, carried in these pages by wheeled vehicles at speed and that can change into something alien, is a matter of trajectories, of strategies, of intensities, of rhythm. This other automobility also divides, splits, "necessitates leisure visits" and entraps, but it is not so much retailing outlets, home, families, and traffic congestion that are reorganized in this way (though these all remain detectable as the indispensably present sites of everyday life) as the media landscape superimposed on them. Here parkour (*l'art du déplacement*) and the free runner become a much better metaphor for mobile affect than the cultural omnivore.

If affect can move at speed to take back in technological *re*production what technological production has taken away—a particular capacity for experience—then the "temporal uncertainties" (Urry) of this other kind of automobility are not the same as the somehow represented weight of time that Barthes could not see in Brecht's basket. Instead...

ASM: We need this space. We had it booked for this time.
Authors: OK. We're leaving now anyway. (*They exit as the actors come in*)

The scene is the Cook bar and café in the city of Hamilton, New Zealand. **DS** and **DF**, perched on wooden stools, have spread piles of photocopies, printouts and books across a large high wooden table by a window, a table that is also littered with many cups and bottles. **DF** has a laptop, with a winking blue wireless modem.

DF: (*lifting a menu off the table and turning it over*) There's a history of this place on the back. (*reading*) The Loyal Hamilton Lodge, Independent Order of Odd Fellows, Manchester Unity, was opened in Cook Street in Hamilton, New Zealand, on November 26, 1874. The Independent Order of Odd Fellows was founded on the North American continent in Baltimore, Maryland, on April 26, 1819 when four members of the Order from England instituted Washington Lodge No.1. That lodge received its charter from Manchester Unity of Odd Fellows in England. Independent lodges followed elsewhere. The building in Hamilton was known as the Odd Fellows Hall for many years. It was built by Mr. E. J. Pearson of mainly native kauri wood to the order of the Odd Fellows. Edward John Pearson had been a Militiaman in the Fourth Waikato Regiment, and was a carpenter by trade. Rheumatism made it difficult for him to carry on as a carpenter. During the depression of the 1870s Pearson took his family to the Thames Goldfields but returned 2 years later to Hamilton and filed for bankruptcy. At this time he started experimenting with soap, eventually patenting his own carbolic sand soap using the deposits of very fine pumice sand prevalent only on the banks of the Waikato River, mixed with caustic soda and Calverts carbolic acid. The building became the first factory in Hamilton. Mr. Pearson set up a sand soap manufactory in the hall, which he purchased in 1886. Today it is the Cook bar and café.

DS: So this was a soap factory. EJ sounds like a practical sort of guy. I wonder what he'd make of the work we're doing here? Actually, come to think of it, he wouldn't even recognize it as *work*. Do you know why they called themselves Odd Fellows?

DF: I think it meant they were "odd" in the sense of being non-guild craftsmen and tradesmen at a time when industrialization was eroding the influence of the old trades guilds, many of which were seen as resisting technological advances. So the Odd Fellows organized themselves as a more progressive fraternity. Masculinities have traveled some interesting roads to get here. They still exist. Wyatt Earp was an Odd Fellow. So was Charlie Chaplin.

The light fades on their table and comes up in the center of the space. The Borg Queen slowly descends from above.

ASM: Look, for this rehearsal we're going to keep using the animatronic even though her tail isn't working right. It should be flicking a lot more. The technician from Weta Workshop is coming up to fix it. But the digital projection system for her face is installed so we can get the idea. Let's take it from "An ambiguously gendered look . . ."

Borg Queen: An ambiguously gendered look directs itself at technology. I am intrigued by the android and he is intrigued by me. I want an orgiastic interpenetration of body and machine. What does *he* want?

The light comes up on the table again.

DF: Barry Buzan has recently written about Star Trek, arguing that it depicts a galactic "Westphalian international system," the 1648 Peace of Westphalia having enshrined what would become the Western world's vision of territoriality as the basis of coexisting states, where America as an inheritor of that vision has "fulfilled its liberal dream of remaking the whole world in its own image" (Buzan 2010, 176). He goes on to say,

> Federal America has become Federal Earth, which then becomes the United Federation of Planets. [. . .] Alien Others do not necessarily threaten the Federation Self, but help to define it through difference. On the whole, technology is good, and celebrated, and seen as the solution to most problems. (ibid.)

But a few years ago, Mark Bould, reviewing a selection of cultural studies type books about Star Trek, argued that science fiction (sf) at its best constitutes an always open-ended conversation about self and other and about technology that refuses to settle down into that kind of complacency and that Star Trek is, therefore, "incompetent as sf" (Bould 1999, 58). He suggested that "the remarkable thing about Star Trek is its withdrawal . . . from that conversation" and that it functions instead, like so many other media franchises, as "a concept exploitable in a host of media and commodity forms" (ibid.). The implication is that to do so Star Trek, along with other franchise formats like Transformers, has to collapse difference in the end into an ideologically determined unified vision:

> The Borg—powerful cyborged aliens with a hive mind who seek to assimilate every species they encounter—stand as a figure of everything that the Star Trek universe considers to be wrong . . . the Borg have subjected themselves . . . to the machine. [However] the Borg are not all that different from the Federation . . . like the Borg they claim to have no interest in power or politics while actively engaging in the politics of dominance by assimilation. (ibid., 59–60)

There is one *Star Trek: The Next Generation* story about the starship's black engineer, with prosthetic eyes, who befriends a Borg called Third of Five and renames him Hugh as part of giving him back a "personality." The engineer's own intimate reliance on technology is offered as grounds for empathy. But Mark Bould nails this when he notes "the horror of an Afro-Diasporic character so assimilated into Western culture that he is oblivious to what he is doing: that is, giving Third of Five a slave name" (ibid., 60).

Borg Queen: Technology is good.

A third pool of light comes up in the remaining area of the stage. A pale, gaunt man, shaven-headed, in white pajamas, is standing beside a fast-looking racing bicycle that leans against the wall. He holds a radio control unit with an aerial. He manipulates its levers. Accompanied by a mechanical buzz, a red toy Formula One racing car—a little Ferrari—comes in from back stage. He steers it under the suspended Borg Queen who looks down disdainfully at it as one might at some tiny irritating creature. He steers it round and round in a circle directly underneath her. Her exposed spine flicks like a tail as she watches it, round and round. Its mechanical buzzing sound gets louder. The little car goes faster and faster.

DS: So when does the Transformer arrive?
DF: You still haven't got it have you? This book is the Transformer. It always has been. That's what they do, they hide themselves in ordinary objects.

The light fades to black again on the table.

It was Saturday May 8, 1982. The Falklands War was underway between Britain and Argentina. The computer science department at Vanderbilt University in Tennessee had been hit by the so-called Unabomber just a few days earlier: Dr. Ted Kaczynski, child prodigy and academic, who had taken to a cabin in Montana without modern technology and lived as a recluse, before embarking on a campaign to mail-bomb universities and other targets in the hope of drawing attention to the ways in which modern technologies were, to his mind, eroding human freedom. His claims would later surface as his 35,000 word essay "Industrial Society and its Future," not long before his capture by the FBI. In

1982 I didn't know anything about this—just that a university department had been bombed—but somehow the later information, and that essay, have got retrospectively integrated into the memory. The background presence of the Falklands War on television that May was muted but irritating—the news was being carefully managed by the British government. I was living in an old four-room stone cottage in woodland on the edge of the Airthrey Estate near Stirling in Scotland, and trying to focus on finishing the writing of my doctoral thesis for the nearby university—it would be the first doctorate to be awarded by a Scottish university in the then new field of film studies. The coverage of the war had introduced a new word to my vocabulary that has stuck in my mind—the Exocet, a French-built long-range anti-ship missile that the Argentine military were using with considerable success against the British navy in the South Atlantic. There was much discussion of the Exocet's technology in the British media and the name entered the language almost overnight to refer to anything fast and deadly. On May 8, a British destroyer was still burning after being struck by an Exocet 4 days previously. It would sink 2 days later. Somehow all of this has intertwined in my memory of that day, which was in itself an unremarkable day until I slumped in front of my small portable television to watch the BBC's Nine O'Clock News, after struggling since early morning with my writing. My constant writing companion, an affectionate cat called Ebony, had settled on top of me and was purring contentedly. She would later be killed by a car.

I remember the newsreader, Sue Lawley. She had a bouffant hairstyle—the kind that must have needed spray to keep in place the mass of auburn hair framing her face. I don't know why I remember that or the fact that she was wearing a rib-knit orange cardigan over a blouse of the same color with a single button at the neck. The Nine O'Clock News studio had a large stylized "globe" logo on the panel behind her, sliced by horizontal lines with thin drop shadows. I was looking forward to television coverage of the Belgian F1 Grand Prix the next day—a break from writing—and started paying attention when she said "Formula One driver Gilles Villeneuve is critically ill in hospital..."

As she spoke, a tape of Villeneuve's accident was cut into her commentary on the words "he clipped the back" of another car. The trackside television camera was in position for that day's high-speed qualifying session that would determine grid positions for the Sunday race, which I had been looking forward to. It was following the other car as Villeneuve's red Ferrari came into the frame at the back, clipped the other car's rear and catapulted out of the frame again to the left. The television cameraman didn't have time to reframe and continued to follow the other car which slowed but was relatively undamaged. However the Ferrari somersaulted back across the frame, end over end, shattering as it did so. And if you happened to be looking at just that spot in the frame, Villeneuve's body, now without helmet, could be seen hurtling out of the car in mid-air—in fact at an astonishing height—and arcing over the track into a wire safety fence 20 yards away. Like an Exocet missile I involuntarily thought. He lay slumped against the bottom of the high fence as other cars slowed and debris settled everywhere. The cameraman searched the scene momentarily, zooming in on the Ferrari now cut in half, before "finding" Villeneuve's body again. It all must have taken about 6 seconds.

The Exocet missile, Gilles Villeneuve's accident, the bomb at a university, the later knowledge about the Unabomber. Somehow, that all becomes part of one "crash," one "text," which wasn't the way I was thinking about texts for my doctorate. Nor was I thinking about the screen that way. The cinematic frame, and theories about the organization of the look, had nothing to do with the randomness of that fatal fast-moving frame (Villeneuve would shortly be declared dead and taken off life support), or with the way that *happening* to see the body in the air amidst the hurtling debris and all the disorganized high-speed movement would organize a memory, along with that other apparently disconnected material, which etched itself, would draw in more information and persists so vividly to this day.

Exactly a quarter of a century later, on the other side of the world, with film, media and cultural studies well established in universities, I would meet a young doctoral student who was writing a thesis that was (in some way then still unclear) about Gilles Villeneuve's son Jacques, also an F1 driver.

DF

The light comes back up on the table. DS has gone. The gaunt man still stands mutely, radio control unit in hand. The toy car still circles, its noise slightly lessened. The Borg Queen, suspended in midair, still watches it warily.

DF: So he's gone. Another doctoral student. How many others have there been over the years? I've lost count. Maybe each peaks at these intensities if we're lucky, but the moment passes. Then their faces fade too, I forget to answer their occasional emails. What's this?

He picks up a DVD in its case, a yellow post-it note attached.

DF: (*reading*) To DF. I thought you might appreciate this.

He pulls off the post-it note and looks at the DVD case.

DF: George Kollias's Intense Metal Drumming. Three hours of footage with everything you need to know.

He takes out the DVD and slides it into his laptop. The sound of Kollias's drumming gradually rises as the lights all fade to black. The sound is almost deafening now, at a rapturous 280 beats per minute.

Glossary

Affect. A substrate of responses grounded in the body and on which feelings and emotion depend. Emotion can be thought of as narrativized affect, mediated by feelings.

Automobility. The automobile as android imaginare + materialization of affect + movement.

Body. "*A body is defined only by a longitude and a latitude*: in other words the sum total of the material elements belonging to it under given relations of movement and rest, speed and slowness (longitude); the sum total of the intensive affects it is capable of at a given power or degree of potential (latitude)" (Deleuze and Guattari 1987, 260, emphasis in original).

Fatal strategy. Derived from Baudrillard, the idea of subjects pushing to an extreme their subjection to any objective system, rather than rebelling against it, at which point an ironic reflexivity invested with intensity develops the potential to turn the system against itself. Contrasted with a banal strategy in which the subject feels erroneously that the object is always under their command, that they can "take it or leave it."

Field. A setting for subject positions, in this case also for structured mobility between positions.

Ideological interpellation. Derived from Althusser, the processes through which subjects are "hailed" or called into their social positions by the demands of various ideological apparatuses, such as schooling, law and the media. This is a tighter form of interpellation than object relational interpellation. There is a parallelism between the two forms of interpellation but potential for nonalignment.

Imaginaire. A specific form of social imagining, in this case characterized as android.

Intensity. The degree of potential that the body has for affective engagement with objects.

Machinic. Derived from Deleuze and Guattari, this is a concept of the social rather than just the technological. Historically, social machines have imposed containment and, later, ideological subjection on the person, while in the contemporary world a post-containment machine is developing that is highly technologized. Technology is part of but not synonymous with the machinic.

Materialization of affect. The appearance of affect in objects, for example, as a consequence of object relational interpellation, the cultural affordance of nesting loops and the engagement of the body in the machinic.

Nesting loop. Derived from the field of software programming, in the present context this is a more general concept intended to identify the ways in which intertextual material in the cultural field loops and folds across seemingly distinct texts, media, and locations, affording "nests" for affect to settle in.

Object relational interpellation. The processes through which subjects are affectively orientated toward their social positions through relationships with objects. This is a looser form of interpellation than ideological interpellation because of the potential for affective play. There is a parallelism between the two forms of interpellation but potential for nonalignment.

Organo-machinic. The organic or bodily components of the machinic.

Semiosis (drawn into). The sign processes through which meaning is produced by drawing unsemioticized material into the systems of signification and contexts of use where it obtains meanings.

Subject. A being with subjective consciousness but not necessarily a unitary identity, where identity is subject to social construction and interpellation (subject positioning). Here, the subject has a body within the machinic.

Techno-machinic. The technologized components of the machinic.

Bibliography

Allen, James. 2000. *Michael Schumacher: Driven to Extremes*. London: Bantam.

Althusser, Louis. 1977. *Lenin and Philosophy and Other Essays*. London: New Left Books.

Altieri, Charles. 2003. *The Particulars of Rapture: An Aesthetics of the Affects*. Ithaca, NY: Cornell University Press.

Archer, Margaret S. 2007. *Making Our Way through the World: Human Reflexivity and Social Mobility*. Cambridge: Cambridge University Press.

Armstrong, Lance, with Sally Jenkins. 2000. *It's Not about the Bike*. Crows Nest, NSW: Allen & Unwin.

Badcott, David. 2003. The basis and relevance of emotional dignity. *Medicine, Health Care and Philosophy* 6: 123–31.

Banks, John. 1998. Controlling gameplay. *M/C A Journal of Media and Culture* 1 (5) <www.uq.edu.au/mc/9812/game.php> (03.29.2010).

Barber, Kristen. 2008. The well-coiffed man: Class, race, and heterosexual masculinity in the hair salon. *Gender & Society* 22 (4): 455–76.

Barthes, Roland. 1977. *Roland Barthes by Roland Barthes*. New York: Hill and Wang.

Baudrillard, Jean. 1983a. *In the Shadow of Silent Majorities, or the End of the Social, and Other Essays*. New York: Semiotext(e).

Baudrillard, Jean. 1983b. *Simulations*. New York: Semiotext(e).

Baudrillard, Jean. 1984. Interview: Game with vestiges. *On the Beach* 5: 19–25.

Baudrillard, Jean. 1987. *Forget Foucault*. New York: Semiotext(e).

Baudrillard, Jean. 1988. *The Ecstasy of Communication*. New York: Semiotext(e).

Baudrillard, Jean. 1990a. *Fatal Strategies*. New York: Semiotext(e)/Pluto.

Baudrillard, Jean. 1990b. *Seduction*. New York: St. Martin's Press.

Baudrillard, Jean. 1994. *Simulacra and Simulation*. Ann Arbor, MI: University of Michigan Press.

Baudrillard, Jean. 1996. *The Perfect Crime*. London: Verso.

Baudrillard, Jean. 1998. *The Consumer Society: Myths and Structures*. London: Sage.

Baudrillard, Jean. 2002. *Screened Out*. London, New York: Verso.

Baudrillard, Jean. 2005. *The System of Objects*. New York: Verso.

Baudrillard, Jean. 2006. *Cool Memories V: 2000–2004*. New York: Polity.

Beck, Ulrich. 1992. *Risk Society: Towards a New Modernity*. London: Sage.

Bianco, Jamie 'Skye'. 2007. Techno-cinema: Image matters in the affective unfoldings of analog cinema and new media. In *The Affective Turn: Theorizing the Social*, ed. Patricia Ticineto Clough with Jean Halley, 47–76. Durham: Duke University Press.

Bignell, Jonathan. 2000. *Postmodern Media Culture*. Edinburgh: Edinburgh University Press.

Billig, Michael. 1995. *Banal Nationalism*. London: Sage.

Bishop, Matt. 2000. Hot property. *F1 Racing* Australian Edition, September, 42–47.

Bogue, Ronald. 1993. Gilles Deleuze: The aesthetics of force. *Journal of the British Society for Phenomenology* 24 (1): 56–65.

Bould, Mark. 1999. Whither our understanding of sf? *Public Understanding of Science* 8: 57–63.

Bourdieu, Pierre. 1977. *Outline of a Theory of Practice*. Cambridge: Cambridge University Press.

Bourdieu, Pierre. 1984. *Distinction: A Social Critique of the Judgement of Taste*. London: Routledge and Kegan Paul.

Bourdieu, Pierre. 1991. Sport and social class. In *Rethinking Popular Culture*, ed. Chandra Mukerji and Michael Schudson, 357–73. Berkeley, CA: University of California Press.

Bourdieu, Pierre. 1996. *The Rules of Art*. Cambridge: Polity.

Briggs, Matt. 2007. Teddy bears, television and play: Rethinking semiosis in children's media culture. *Social Semiotics* 17 (4): 503–24.

Bruce, Toni and Susan L. Greendorfer. 1994. Postmodern challenges: Recognising multiple standards for social science research. *Journal of Sport and Social Issues* 18 (3): 258–68.

Brumberg, Joan Jacobs. 1997. *The Body Project: An Intimate History of American Girls*. New York: Random House.

Buck-Morss, Susan. 1989. *The Dialectics of Seeing: Walter Banjamin and the Arcades Project*. Cambridge, MA: MIT Press.

Butryn, Ted M., and Matthew A. Masucci. 2003. It's not about the book. *Journal of Sport and Social Issues* 27 (2): 124 –44.

Buzan, Barry. 2010. America in space: The international relations of Star Trek and Battlestar Galactica. *Millennium: Journal of International Studies* 39 (1): 175–80.

Clarkson, Tom. 1999. Easy rider. *F1 Racing* Australian Edition, September, 76–84.

Clough, Patricia Ticineto. 2000. *Autoaffection: Unconscious Thought in the Age of Teletechnology*. Minneapolis, MN: University of Minnesota Press.

Clough, Patricia Ticineto, with Jean Halley, eds. 2007. *The Affective Turn: Theorizing the Social*. Durham: Duke University Press.

Connell, R. W. 1995. *Masculinities*. Cambridge: Polity.

Coriat, Benjamin. 1994. *Penser à L'Envers: Travail et Organisation dans L'Enterprise Japonaise*. Paris: Christian Bourgois.

Crawford, Garry. 2004. *Consuming Sport: Fans, Sport and Culture*. New York: Routledge.

Csikszentmihalyi, Mihaly. 1992. *Flow: The Psychology of Happiness*. London: Random Century.

Damasio, Antonio. 2004. *Looking for Spinoza: Joy, Sorrow and the Feeling Brain*. London: Vintage.

Davies, Bronwyn and Susanne Gannon, eds. 2006. *Doing Collective Biography: Investigating the Production of Subjectivity*. Maidenhead: Open University Press.

Deleuze, Gilles and Félix Guatarri. 1987. *A Thousand Plateaus: Capitalism and Schizophrenia*. Minneapolis, MN: University of Minnesota Press.

Denison, Jim. 1996. Sport narratives. *Qualitative Inquiry* 2 (3): 351–62.

Denzin, Norman K. 1997. *Interpretive Ethnography*. Thousand Oaks, CA: Sage.

Dyer, Richard. 1981. Entertainment and utopia. In *Genre: The musical*, ed. Rick Altman, 175–89. London: Routledge and Kegan Paul.

Dyson, Anne Haas. 2003. *The Brothers and Sisters Learn to Write: Popular Literacies in Childhood and School Cultures*. New York: Teachers College Press.

Eakin, Emily. 2003. I feel, therefore I am. *The New York Times*, April 19, sec. Arts.

Elder-Vass, Dave. 2007. Reconciling Archer and Bourdieu in an emergentist theory of action. *Sociological Theory* 25 (4): 325–46.

Ellis, Carolyn. 2004. *The Ethnographic I: A Methodological Novel about Autoethnography*. Walnut Creek, CA: AltaMira.

Ellis, Carolyn. 2007. Telling secrets, revealing lives: Relational ethics in research with intimate others. *Qualitative Inquiry* 13 (1): 3–29.

Ellis, Carolyn and Arthur Bochner. 2000. Autoethnography, personal narrative, reflexivity: Researcher as subject. In *Handbook of Qualitative Research*, ed. Norman K. Denzin and Yvonne S. Lincoln, 733–68. Thousand Oaks, CA: Sage.

Emmison, Michael. 2003. Social class and cultural mobility. *Journal of Sociology* 39 (3): 211–30.

Fairbairn, W. R. D. 1952. *Psychoanalytic Studies of the Personality*. London: Tavistock Publications.

Fleming, Dan. 1996. *Powerplay: Toys as Popular Culture*. Manchester: Manchester University Press.

Fleming, Dan. 2008. Managing monsters: Videogames and the "mediatization" of the toy. In *The International Handbook of Children, Media and Culture*, ed. Kirsten Drotner and Sonia Livingstone, 55–70. London: Sage.

Fleming, Dan. 2009. Cityscapes as play sites. In *Encyclopedia of Play in Today's Society*, ed. Rodney P. Carlisle, 139–40. Thousand Oaks, CA: Sage.

Flichy, Patrice. 2007. *Understanding Technological Innovation: A Socio-Technical Approach*. Cheltenham: Edward Elgar.

Frisby, David, and Mike Featherstone. 1997. *Simmel on Culture: Selected Writings*. London: Sage.

Frith, Simon 1996. *Performing Rites: Evaluating Popular Music*. Oxford: Oxford University Press.

Gannon, Susanne. 2006. The (im)possibilities of writing the self-writing: French poststructural theory and autoethnography. *Cultural Studies* ↔ *Critical Methodologies* 6 (4): 474–95.

Geraghty, Lincoln. 2008. Repackaging Generation One: Genre, fandom and The Transformers as adult/children's television. In *The Shifting Definitions of Genre*, ed. Lincoln Geraghty and Mark Jancovich, 181–200. Jefferson, NC: McFarland & Company.

Giulianotti, Richard. 2002. Supporters, followers, fans, and *flaneurs*. A taxonomy of spectator identities in football. *Journal of Sport and Social Issues* 26 (1): 25–46.

Grossberg, Lawrence. 1992a. Is there a fan in the house? The affective sensibility of fandom. In *The Adoring Audience: Fan Culture and Popular Media*, ed. Lisa Lewis, 50–65. New York: Routledge.

Grossberg, Lawrence. 1992b. *We Gotta Get Out of This Place: Popular Conservatism and Postmodern Culture*. New York, London: Routledge.

Gruneau, Richard and David Whitson. 1993. *Hockey Night in Canada*. Toronto: Garamond.

Gumbrecht, Hans Ulrich. 2006. *In Praise of Athletic Beauty*. Cambridge, MA: Belknap Press of Harvard University Press.

Gumbrecht, Hans Ulrich. 2009. "Lost in focused intensity": Spectator sports and strategies of re-enchantment. In *Theatralisierung der Gesellschaft*, ed. Herbert Willems, 439–46. Wiesbaden: V. S. Verlag für Sozialwissenschaften.

Habermas, Jürgen. 1996. Georg Simmel on philosophy and culture: Postscript to a collection of essays. *Critical Inquiry* 22 (3): 403–14.

Hansen, Mark. 2000. *Embodying Technesis: Technology Beyond Writing*. Ann Arbor, MI: University of Michigan Press.

Haraway, Donna Jeanne. 1991. A cyborg manifesto: Science, technology, and socialist-feminism in the late twentieth century. In *Simians, Cyborgs, and Women: The Reinvention of Nature*, 149–81. New York: Routledge.

Hardt, Michael. 1999. Affective labor. *Boundary 2* 26 (2): 89–100.

Hay, James, Lawrence Grossberg, and Ellen Wartella. 1996. Introduction. In *The Audience and Its Landscape*, ed. James Hay, Lawrence Grossberg, and Ellen Wartella, 1–5. Boulder, CO: Westview Press.

Hills, Matt. 2002. *Fan Cultures*. New York: Routledge.

Hills, Matt. 2005. *How to Do Things with Cultural Theory*. London: Hodder Arnold.

Holmes, Su and Sean Redmond, eds. 2006. *Framing Celebrity: New Directions in Celebrity Culture*. New York: Routledge.

Holt, Nicholas. L. 2001. Beyond technical reflection: Demonstrating the modification of teaching behaviors using three levels of reflection. *Avante* 7 (2): 66–76.

Horrell, Paul. 2010. Top Gear's schooldays. *Radio Times* 26 June-2 July: 12–17.

Humphreys, Michael. 2005. Getting personal: Reflexivity and autoethnographic vignettes. *Qualitative Inquiry* 11 (6): 840–60.

Jenkins, Henry. 1992. *Textual Poachers: Television Fans & Participatory Culture*. New York: Routledge.

Jewett, Laura M. 2008. *A Delicate Dance: Autoethnography, Curriculum, and the Semblance of Intimacy*. New York: Peter Lang.

Kapell, Matthew and John Shelton Lawrence. 2006. *Finding the Force of the Star Wars Franchise: Fans, Merchandise, & Critics*. New York: Peter Lang.

Karklins, Rasma and Roger Petersen. 1993. Decision calculus of protesters and regimes: Eastern Europe 1989. *The Journal of Politics* 55 (3): 588–614.

Kellner, Douglas. 1989. *Jean Baudrillard: From Marxism to Postmodernism and Beyond*. Stanford, CA: Stanford University Press.

Kelly, George. 1963. *A Theory of Personality: The Psychology of Personal Constructs*. New York: W. W. Norton.

Kress, Gunther R. and Theo Van Leeuwen. 2006. *Reading Images: The Grammar of Visual Design*. New York: Routledge.

Lambert, Joe. 2006. *Digital Storytelling: Capturing Lives, Creating Community.* Berkeley, CA: Digital Diner Press.

Lanier, Jaron. 2010. *You Are Not a Gadget.* London: Allen Lane.

Lash, Scott and Celia Lury. 2007. *Global Culture Industry.* Cambridge: Polity.

Lefebvre, Henri. 2004. *Rhythmanalysis: Space, Time and Everyday Life.* London: Continuum.

Lyon, David. 1994. *Postmodernity.* Buckingham: Open University Press.

Markula, Pirkko. 1998. Dancing within postmodernism. *Waikato Journal of Education* 4: 73–85.

Markula, Pirkko. 2003. Bodily dialogues: Writing the self. In *Moving Writing. Crafting Movement in Sport Research,* ed. Jim Denison and Pirkko Markula, 27–50. New York: Peter Lang.

McKee, Alan. 2007. The fans of cultural theory. In *Fandom: Identities and Communities in a Mediated World,* ed. Jonathan Gray, Cornel Sandvoss, and C. Lee Harrington, 88–97. New York: New York University Press.

Morley, David. 1992. *Television, Audiences, and Cultural Studies.* London: Routledge.

Morris, Meaghan. 1990. Banality in cultural studies. In *Logics of Television: Essays in Cultural Criticism,* ed. Patricia Mellencamp, 14–43. Bloomington, IN: Indiana University Press.

Mort, Frank. 1988. Boy's own? Masculinity, style and popular culture. In *Male Order: Unwrapping Masculinity,* ed. Rowena Chapman and Jonathan Rutherford, 193–224. London: Lawrence & Wishart.

Murphie, Andrew and John Potts. 2003. *Culture and Technology.* New York: Palgrave Macmillan.

O'Neill, Joseph. 2009. *Netherland.* London: Harper Perennial.

Parfit, Derek. 1984. *Reasons and Persons.* Oxford: Oxford University Press.

Pelias, Ronald. 2003. The academic tourist: An autoethnography. *Qualitative Inquiry* 9 (3): 369–73.

Peterson, Richard A. 1992. Understanding audience segmentation: From élite and mass to omnivore and univore. *Poetics* 21 (4): 243–58.

Pringle, Richard. 2001. Competing discourses: Narratives of a fragmented self, manliness and rugby union. *International Review for the Sociology of Sport* 36 (4): 425–39.

Pringle, Richard. 2003. "Doing the damage? An examination of masculinities and men's rugby experiences of pain, fear and pleasure." Unpublished doctoral thesis. Hamilton, NZ: University of Waikato.

Rail, Genevieve. 2002. Postmodernism and sport studies. In *Theory, Sport and Society,* ed. Joseph Maguire and Kevin Young, 179–207. Amsterdam: JAI.

Reed-Danahay, Deborah, ed. 1997. *Auto/Ethnography: Rewriting the Self and the Social.* Oxford: Berg.

Reynolds, Simon. 1998. *Energy Flash: A Journey through Rave Music and Dance Culture.* London: Picador.

Richardson, Laurel. 2000. Writing: A method of inquiry. In *Handbook of Qualitative Research,* ed. Norman K. Denzin and Yvonne S. Lincoln, 923–48. Thousand Oaks, CA: Sage.

Rinehart, Robert. E. 1998. *Players All: Performances in Contemporary Sport.* Bloomington, IN: Indiana University Press.

Rogers, Everett M. 1995. *Diffusion of Innovations*. 4th edn New York: Free Press.

Roth, W.-M., ed. 2005. *Auto/Biography and Auto/Ethnography: Praxis of Research Method*. Rotterdam: Sense Publishers.

Rutter, Carol Chillington. 2007. *Shakespeare and Child's Play: Performing Lost Boys on Stage and Screen*. New York: Routledge.

Ryan, Michael and Douglas Kellner. 1988. *Camera Politica: The Politics and Ideology of Contemporary Hollywood Film*. Bloomington, IN: Indiana University Press.

Sandvoss, Cornel. 2005. *Fans: The Mirror of Consumption*. Oxford: Polity.

Schirato, Tony. 2007. *Understanding Sports Culture*. London: Sage.

Schwartz, Theodore. 1978. Where is the culture? Personality as the distributive locus of culture. In *Making of Psychological Anthropology*, ed. George D. Spindler, 419–41. Berkeley, CA: University of California Press.

Shook, John R. and Liz Stillwagon Swan, eds. 2009. *Transformers and Philosophy*. Chicago, IL: Open Court.

Silverstone, Roger. 1996. From audiences to consumers: The household and the consumption of communication and information technologies. In *The Audience and Its Landscape*, ed. James Hay, Lawrence Grossberg, and Ellen Wartella, 281–96. Boulder, CO: Westview Press.

Simmel, Georg. 2004. *The Philosophy of Money*, ed. David Frisby. London: Routledge.

Souriau, Paul, and Manon Souriau. 1983. *The Aesthetics of Movement*. Amherst, MA: University of Massachusetts Press.

Sparkes, Andrew. 1995. Writing people: Reflections on the dual crises of representation and legitimation in qualitative inquiry. *Quest* 47 (2): 158–95.

Sparkes, Andrew. 1996. The fatal flaw: A narrative of the fragile body-self. *Qualitative Inquiry* 2 (4): 463–94.

Sparkes, Andrew. 2000. Autoethnography and narratives of self: Reflections on criteria in action. *Sociology of Sport Journal* 17 (1): 21–43.

Sparkes, Andrew. 2003. Bodies, identities, selves: Autoethnographic fragments and reflections. In *Moving Writing: Crafting Movement in Sport Research*, ed. Jim Denison and Pirkko Markula, 51–76. New York: Peter Lang.

Spry, Tami. 2001. Performed autoethnography: An embodied methodological praxis. *Qualitative Inquiry* 7 (6): 706–32.

Steiff, Josef. 2009. In the eye of the beholder. In *Transformers and Philosophy: More Than Meets the Eye*, ed. John R. Shook and Liz Stillwagon Swan, 55–64. Chicago, IL: Open Court.

Sturm, Damion. 2009. "Being Jacques Villeneuve: Formula One, *'agency'* and the fan." Unpublished doctoral thesis. Hamilton, NZ: University of Waikato.

Thrift, Nigel. 1997. The still point: Resistance, expressive embodiment and dance. In *Geographies of Resistance*, ed. Steve Pile and Michael Keith, 124–51. London: Routledge.

Thrift, Nigel. 2008. *Non-Representational Theory: Space, Politics, Affect*. New York: Routledge.

Tsang, Tosha. 2000. Let me tell you a story: A narrative exploration of identity in high-performance sport. *Sociology of Sport Journal* 17 (1): 44–59.

Tyler, Stephen A. 1986. Post-modern ethnography: From document of the occult to occult document. In *Writing Culture: The Poetics and Politics of Ethnography*, ed. James Clifford and George E. Marcus, 122–40. Berkeley, CA: University of California Press.

Urry, John. 2000. *Sociology beyond Societies: Mobilities for the Twenty-First Century.* New York: Routledge.

Vincent Michael. 1991. Author, authority and the pedagogical scene: Elvire Jouvet 40. *Journal of Dramatic Theory and Criticism* Fall: 5–13.

Wall, Sarah. 2006. An autoethnography on learning about autoethnography. *International Journal of Qualitative Methods* 5 (2): 1–12.

Wheaton, Belinda. 2000. "New lads?" Masculinities and the "new sport" participant. *Men and Masculinities* 2 (4): 434–56.

Wiebe, Janyce, Theresa Wilson and Claire Cardie. 2006. Annotating expressions of opinions and emotions in language. *Language Resources and Evaluation* 39 (2/3): 165–210.

Winnicott, Donald Woods. 1988. *Human Nature.* Abingdon: Taylor & Francis.

Zavalloni, Marisa. 1986. The affective-representational circuit as the foundation of identity. *New Ideas in Psychology* 4 (3): 333–49.

Index